Heroes
of Our Faith

Heroes of Our Faith

Inspiration and strength for daily living

Patrick Sookhdeo

Isaac Publishing

Published in the United States by
Isaac Publishing, 1934 Old Gallows Road, Suite 350, Vienna, VA 22182, USA

Copyright © Patrick Sookhdeo 2012, 2021
First edition 2012
Second edition 2021

Library of Congress Control Number: 2021936532

ISBN: 978-1-9524501-2-9

Book design by Lee Lewis Walsh, Words Plus Design

Printed in the United Kingdom

Contents

Foreword 1

1 January – 31 December 13

Select bibliography 373

Index of martyrs 381

Index of dates 386

Index of places 388

Index of Bible references 390

Index of quotations 395

Acknowledgments

I am very grateful to all those who have suggested stories or quotations, or helped in other ways with the compilation of this work. There are too many to name them all individually, but I would like to give special thanks to Judith Bishop, Steve Carter, William Evans, Andrew Fleet, Albrecht Hauser, Jennifer Ivers, Caroline Kerslake, Philippa King, Mark McNaughton, Patricia Ross and Lucy Walker.

Acknowledgment of Sources

The quotation from A W Tozer on page 350 is reprinted from *The Pursuit of God* by A W Tozer, copyright © 1948, 1982, 1993 by Zur Ltd. Used by permission of WingSpread Publishers, a division of Zur Ltd., 800.884.4571.

Front cover pictures: Top row from left: Stephen, Shamimu Muteteri Hassan, Hossein Soodmand, Edith Searell, Grand Duchess Elizabeth. Bottom row from left: Necati Aydin, Manche Masemola (photograph by Jean-Christophe Benoist); Esther John, David Abdulwahab Mohamed Ali, Dietrich Bonhoeffer (photograph by Bundesarchiv, Bild 183-R0211-316 / CC-BY-SA).

Back cover picture: Ignatius of Antioch.

Foreword

Jesus said to his disciples, "Whoever wants to be my disciple must deny themselves and take up their cross and follow me. For whoever wants to save their life will lose it, but whoever loses their life for me will find it." Matthew 16:24-25

During the Korean War (1950-1953), five hundred Christian ministers were captured by the Communists and shot. Pastor Yonggi Cho tells the story of one minister and his family who were put on trial in Inchon. At these "People's Trials", a chorus of voices would chant, "Yah, yah," agreeing with the prosecutors that the accused should be punished. In this particular case, a large hole was dug, into which the pastor, his wife and several of their children were placed. The pastor was then asked to admit his guilt and repent of having "misled" people for many years "with the superstition of the Bible". If he would not do so, the whole family would be buried alive.

His children cried out, "O Daddy, Daddy! Think of us, Daddy!" and the shaken father began to admit his guilt. But before he could finish his sentence, his wife nudged him, saying, "Daddy! Say NO!"

"Hush, children," she continued, "Tonight we are going to have supper with the King of kings and Lord of lords." She began to sing, "In the Sweet By and By", and her husband and children joined in. Meanwhile the soil was thrown back into the hole, and gradually the whole family was buried, each one continuing to sing until the soil had reached their neck, the children first. Many people watched this execution, and almost of all of them later became Christians.

On 27 July 2009, Nigerian pastor George Orjih, together with other Christians, awaited almost certain death at the hands of Islamist militants. Hoping that at least some of the group would survive to tell the tale, and with a true pastor's heart seeking to strengthen and encourage them all, he said, "Tell my brothers that I died well and am living with Christ. And if we all die, we know that we die for the Lord." Pastor George was beheaded, but some of his companions lived and were able to take his final message to his congregation.

The Korean family and Pastor George are heroes of our faith, who died because of their love for Christ. And Christ died because of His love for us. Jesus, the ideal martyr, came into the world to die. He died for a purpose, to bring in God's Kingdom, for our salvation from sin, for our liberation and deliverance. This giving of Himself was in fulfilment of the divine will. He chose to allow Himself to be martyred because it was the Father's will. The hour of His martyrdom was the hour of His glory (John 12:23-25). As many have pointed out, a crossless Saviour would be a crownless King; the crown blossoms on thorns. His life on earth and very existence cannot be dissociated from His death, and this death was born out of love. On the night before His martyrdom, Jesus told His disciples, "Greater love has no one than this: to lay down one's life for one's friends" (John 15:13).

Love is the essence of martyrdom, the driving force and supreme motive. Paul says that the love of Christ compels him (2 Corinthians 5:14). The love that gave itself willingly to death is the love that holds us and compels us to sacrifice our lives willingly for Christ, His people and His Kingdom.

He said: "For love, for love
I wear the vine and thorn."
He said: "For love, for love
My hands and feet were torn:
For love the wine-press Death I trod."
And I cried in pain: "O Lord my God."[1]

---

[1] Taylor, Mrs Rachel Annand, *Poems* (London, 1904), p. 52.

Although the disciples ran away and abandoned Him in the hour of His death (Mark 14:50), afterwards they embraced not only His life but also His death, striving to emulate both, to follow Him to the very end of life and then to die for Him.

Many other early Christians felt the same. Ignatius of Antioch, who was martyred around 107, begged his fellow Christians not to intervene to try to stop his impending execution at Rome.

I am writing to all the Churches and I enjoin all, that I am dying willingly for God's sake, if only you do not prevent it. I beg you, do not do me an untimely kindness. Allow me to be eaten by the beasts, which are my way of reaching to God.

Why did these first believers have such an intense longing and deep desire to die for Christ? The early Church saw martyrs as imitators of Jesus. Origen of Alexandria (185–254), author of *An Exhortation to Martyrdom*, wrote:

As we behold the martyrs coming forth from every Church to be brought before the tribunal, we see in each the Lord Himself condemned.

Tradition tells us that, before Peter was martyred, he had to watch his wife being executed under the Roman Emperor Nero. He called out to her by name, urging her, as she faced a cruel death, "Remember the Lord." The story is also told of Peter himself that he was persuaded to flee Rome to avoid persecution, and on his way, at night, he had a vision of Christ. William Watson's poem describes

A mournful Face – a Figure hurrying on –
Though haggard and dishevelled, frail and worn,
A King, of David's lineage, crowned with thorn.
"Lord, whither farest?" Peter, wondering, cried,
"To Rome," said Christ, "to be re-crucified."[2]

---

[2] *The Poems of William Watson* (New York and London, 1895).

Peter realised that it was through himself that Christ was to be crucified again. He turned round and went back to the Christians in Rome to explain, was arrested and crucified.

For 2,000 years martyrdom for Christ has been considered a glorious way of walking in the footsteps of our Saviour (John 12:25-26) and of entering triumphantly into eternal life. But now, in the 21st century, it is often misunderstood. Tragically, martyrdom has become linked in some people's minds with terrorist violence, where the giving of one's life involves the deliberate taking of others' lives. But even setting aside this aberration, the concept of martyrdom has become virtually irrelevant to many Christians in the safe and prosperous West, as it lies so far outside their experience. A materialistic worldview gives Christians such a love for this life that we cannot easily understand why anyone should embrace death. In a day of scientific materialism we can lose sight of the other world. When we make decisions, we may prioritise security, prudence, ease and comfort. Many Christians have lost a sense of faithfulness to Christ that includes, if necessary, giving up their life. Martyrdom constitutes the ultimate sacrifice. It is the highest form of renunciation, of that denying of oneself about which our Lord spoke in Matthew 16. Christian martyrs are truly heroes of our faith.

In other parts of the world, martyrdom is still viewed in the Biblical way, as a privilege and an honour. Many early theologians called it a "second baptism". "Baptism" was indeed a word that our Lord himself used, when He challenged James and John, who sought a place of high honour in His Kingdom, about whether they could share the suffering and death He was about to undergo. "Can you drink the cup I drink or be baptised with the baptism I am baptised with?" (Mark 10:38; see also John 18:11).

Egyptian Christian tradition tells the story of George, a convert from Islam many centuries ago. He longed to be baptised but could not find anyone with the courage to do it, as Christians feared retribution from angry Muslims. In the end George was stoned to death for leaving Islam, but, as he lay dying, he said that he was rejoicing because at last he was being baptised – in his own blood.

In Egypt, martyrdom is still considered one of the greatest blessings that can be bestowed on a Christian. It has been my privilege to know another Egyptian convert from Islam, who also felt that to suffer for Christ was an immense privilege. In the 1980s, while she was wrestling with the question of whether to follow her husband's recent example and leave Islam to follow Christ although persecution of the whole family would be likely, the Lord appeared to her and said, "I am the Lord Jesus Christ coming to bless you." He repeated this three times. She understood that this "blessing" meant martyrdom. But this promise did not discourage her; rather she embraced it willingly and made her decision. In tears she hurried to her husband and said, "I will become a Christian no matter what they do to us. Even if they kill us, they will only kill our bodies." The children also believed.

So what happened to this sister in Christ and her family? Did the Lord fulfil His promise that they would die for His Name? Space does not permit me to tell the whole story of the many things that various members of the family had to endure after they became Christians. But the worst was the slow martyrdom of their eight-year-old son, who was baptised with the name "Salib", meaning "cross". He was the most intelligent and winsome of the children, a great favourite with everyone who knew him. Therefore it was Salib whom the relatives targeted, as they tried to force the family back to Islam. His grandmother put a dose of powerful rat poison into the little boy's food and they waited for him to die. But he survived. He was, however, severely damaged, both physically and mentally, and unable to care for himself in any way. His growth was stunted and his disabilities never healed. His mother began to pray that the Lord would take him, so that his suffering would cease. But it was not until he was 24 that Salib finally died, having lived two-thirds of his short life with appalling disabilities. Truly he was a martyr, who died for the sake of Christ, albeit his martyrdom took 16 years to be accomplished.

This book is about our Christian brothers and sisters, like the Korean family, George Orjih, Ignatius, George the Egyptian convert from Islam and Salib, who have laid down their lives for their Lord and have received a heavenly crown. The rate of Christian martyrdom is increasing dramatically in many countries, where faith is central to life, even to the point of death.

For those living in great danger, where violence can be a constant threat, where faithfulness to Christ can mean sacrifice and death, a readiness for martyrdom often lies deep within their hearts, sustained by their great yearning and desire to be with Him. For them death is entrance to life.

In May 2011 a pastor's wife in Bauchi State, Nigeria, lay dying from gunshot and machete wounds inflicted by Muslim extremists who had already killed two of their children. She said to her husband, "Is this the end between us, so we shall not be together again?"

"Hold on to your faith in Jesus," replied Pastor James, "and we shall meet and never part again."

Then the pastor heard the cries of his 13-year-old daughter, who had suffered a severe machete cut to her abdomen. The militants had told her they would kill her and she should "see how your Jesus will save you". The girl had replied that Jesus had already saved her and that by killing her they would simply be enabling her to be with Him.

Pastor James and his daughter had a vision of glory: not one of physical reward, of earthly pleasures writ large, but rather of eternity in the presence of their Master whom they loved and of the whole angelic host. As God's Word tells us, those who have died for Him are clothed in white and anticipate vindication from God (Revelation 6:9-11). With all Christians who have come through the great tribulation, they will never again hunger or thirst or suffer, but the Lamb will lead them to springs of living water, and God will wipe away every tear from their eyes (Revelation 7:9-17).

Those who die for Christ are not, as the martyrs of some religions, actively seeking death. They give up their lives willingly but not wantonly. We should live with a Biblical attitude to the possibility of death. We must have the courage to look death in the face unflinchingly and meet it with hope, faith and confidence.

We cannot fear death, which, since Christ's death and resurrection, has lost its sting. But neither must we try to escape from serving Him on earth until He calls us Home. Theophane Venard, a French missionary who was beheaded in Vietnam in 1861 because he refused to deny Christ, wrote:

> I know the sorrow I will bring to my family. It has cost me tears of blood to take such a step and give those I love such pain. Who is there who cared for home and family more than I? All my earthly happiness was to be found there. But you, O God, who united us with such tender affection, weaned me from what I loved that I might serve you.

There are also many faithful Christians who are rightly hailed as martyrs although they were not killed specifically for refusing to deny Christ. These are the martyrs who have lost their lives while serving God in dangerous places. This does not mean soldiers who die on the battlefield; it means those who risk their lives to obey God's call, and meet their death because they continued faithfully to serve, not seeking to escape from disease, violent conflict, or other danger. There are also those who have died for standing up for their Christian principles, for example, Dietrich Bonhoeffer, who, together with others, resisted the Nazi regime in 1930s Germany, affirming that Jesus is Lord and signing the Barmen Declaration (1934). He died because he would not deny the supremacy of Christ over every regime and ideology. Another example, from the same context, is Casper Ten Boom and his daughter Betsie, Dutch Christians who were caught sheltering Jews in their home. They and Betsie's sister Corrie were sent to Nazi concentration camps, where Casper and Betsie died.

While not all are called or permitted to die for Christ, we must remember that He has called us all to deny ourselves and take up our cross each day (Matthew 16:24-25). This is a daily putting to death of the self, which all of us can and must seek. It is a living martyrdom. "I die daily," said the apostle Paul (1 Corinthians 15:31). And for some, who have been entrusted with a very heavy cross, it is perhaps more difficult to carry it year after year than it would be to die once. The tragedies of life can cause immense pain and hurt. In this book are wonderful examples of forgiveness in the face of hideous wrongs. The living martyrdom is to continue faithful and true, loving and forgiving, committed to our only Lord and Saviour, whose pathway we must walk despite every affliction.

One such living martyr was the Scotsman George Matheson (1842-1906), who very early in life began to lose his sight. The doctors declared his condition incurable, and his fiancée then broke off their engagement, saying she did not want to go through life with a blind man. In his twentieth year, while studying for the ministry, he became completely blind, but he continued with his studies and duly went into the ministry. He was cared for by his sister for the next two decades. When Matheson was 40, his sister married, and on the evening of her wedding, he wrote a poignant hymn, no doubt thinking of the loss of his fiancée, the loss of his sight, and now the loss of his sister and carer. He wrote of God's unchanging love for him and of giving back his life to the Lord:

O Love that wilt not let me go,
I rest my weary soul in thee;
I give thee back the life I owe,
That in thine ocean depths its flow
May richer, fuller be.

Later in life, Matheson, who never married, wrote of his experience as "an obstructed life, a circumscribed life … but a life of quenchless hopefulness, a life which has beaten persistently against the cage of circumstance, and which even at the time of abandoned work has said not 'Good night' but 'Good morning.'" These are the words and attitude of a living martyr.

But it is not for us to choose; we must accept with thankfulness and even joy whatever our Lord has appointed for us, knowing that He sees and understands our every struggle and every tear. Indeed we are surrounded by a cloud of witnesses, of fellow-believers already with the Lord, who watch compassionately and cheer us on (Hebrews 12:1).

Clement of Alexandria, who died in the year 215, wrote that:

If martyrdom consists in confessing God, then every person who conducts himself with purity in the knowledge of God and who obeys his commandments, is a martyr in his life and in his words: for in whatever way his soul is separated from his body, he will pour out his faith like blood, both during his life and at the moment of his death. This is what the Lord says in the Gospel: 'Whoever leaves his father, his mother, his brothers, his wife or his lands because of the Gospel and my name' such a man is blessed because he has realised in himself not only an ordinary martyrdom, but the true knowledge of martyrdom, in living and acting according to the rule of the Gospel, out of love for the Lord. For the true knowledge is to know the name and understand the Gospel.

The mark of a disciple of Jesus is bearing the cross (Matthew 16:24-25). In the early years of Christianity, while the scholars and theologians were developing the details of doctrine, this simple fact was already clear to all followers of Christ. They knew that self-denial and renunciation were the marks of a true Christian, and that these included a willingness to die for the Lord or for each other.

We must also remember the very significant truth that the Greek word *martyria* from which we get the word "martyr" is usually translated in the New Testament as "witness" or "testimony". This can be in the sense of eye-witness (Luke 24:48), of the act of making known the Gospel of Christ (Acts 23:11), or the Gospel itself (1 Corinthians 2:1). But it is also used very specially of the testimony of those who died for Christ (Revelation 6:9; 17:6; 20:4). We cannot all be martyrs, but we can all be witnesses. Whether we witness in our life or by our death, the important thing is that we are bearing witness to Christ.

Every Christian is called to be a living witness, a living martyr, and some are called to die for Christ as well. "Unless a grain of wheat falls to the ground and dies, it remains only a single seed. But if it dies, it produces many seeds." Dying to self is the process by which a Christian can live a fruitful life. And death itself can also, in the Lord's providence, produce much fruit. As Tertullian (c. 160-c. 225) observed about church growth, "The blood of the martyrs is the seed." Throughout the ages, it has been the blood of the martyrs that has often been the prelude to a great harvest of souls. Almost all of those who watched the Korean family being buried alive in Inchon later decided to follow their Saviour, and now there is a huge and vibrant Church in South Korea. Death is not to be feared, for it is often the means by which God brings His Church into being.

So, whether or not we shall in fact be numbered among the heroes of our faith by having the glorious privilege of dying for Christ, we must live day by day with an attitude of joyful renunciation, of gladly denying ourselves, and being ready for any sacrifice, even of our lives.

The English bishop William Walsham How, in his famous hymn, "For all the saints", first published in 1864, writes of living and dead believers together as one fellowship of God's people. In three verses not usually sung nowadays, he mentions specifically apostles, evangelists and then martyrs:

For Martyrs, who with rapture kindled eye,
Saw the bright crown descending from the sky,
And seeing, grasped it, Thee we glorify.
Alleluia, Alleluia!

He ends with a vision of the glorious day of Christ's return and the gathering of the faithful still on earth to join with those already in heaven:

But lo! there breaks a yet more glorious day;
The saints triumphant rise in bright array;
The King of glory passes on His way.
Alleluia, Alleluia!

From earth's wide bounds, from ocean's farthest coast,
Through gates of pearl streams in the countless host,
Singing to Father, Son and Holy Ghost:
Alleluia, Alleluia!

Patrick Sookhdeo
February 2012

*It is proper that the minds of Christians
should be familiar with thoughts of death.*

R L Dabney (1820-98)

Peace I leave with you; my peace I give you. I do not give to you as the world gives. Do not let your hearts be troubled and do not be afraid.
John 14:27

Egyptian Christians (2011)
Praying for Peace

On New Year's Day 2011, Egyptian Christians gathered at a church in Alexandria to pray for a happy and peaceful year ahead. The service had only just finished when their hopeful start to 2011 was violently shattered. A suicide bomber detonated explosives outside the church as worshippers were leaving; 21 Christians were killed. It was a scene of total carnage, with blood and bodies everywhere. As Christian mothers frantically searched for their children, Muslims were seen coming out of a nearby mosque chanting "Allahu Akbar", which means "god is great".

A senior Egyptian Church leader said, "Men, women, children and the elderly gathered together in prayer for a happy and peaceful new year. Instead, they became the innocent victims of a most horrific, callous and cowardly act of terror and violence."

The attack came two weeks after an Al-Qaeda front group, the Islamic State of Iraq, posted a statement on its website calling for militants to bomb Egyptian churches during Christmas celebrations.

O God, our refuge and strength, who art a very present help in time of trouble: have mercy upon thy Church in its hour of persecution from tyranny and oppression; save them from the dangers that beset them; and restore to them the blessings of freedom and peace; through Jesus Christ our Lord.

Let us rejoice and be glad and give him glory! For the wedding of the Lamb has come, and his bride has made herself ready. Fine linen, bright and clean, was given her to wear... Blessed are those who are invited to the wedding supper of the Lamb! Revelation 19:7-8a, 9b

Gadson and Rebeka Gachigi (1953)
"Now they are at the marriage supper of the Lamb!"

This young Christian couple lived in Njumbi, Kenya, at the time when the Mau Mau guerrillas were resisting British rule in the country. The Mau Mau hated the British and Christianity and wanted everyone to take a special oath of allegiance to them. Many Christians refused to do this because it meant swearing an ultimate allegiance other than to Christ, and also required grotesque actions, including digging up corpses and eating their putrefied flesh, to seal the pledge.

Gadson and Rebeka were kind to the Mau Mau but would not take their oath. Rebeka was a school teacher and Gadson was a carpenter and church leader. They had a one-year-old son, Timothy, and were expecting another child. One night in January 1953, Mau Mau fighters broke into their home while they were sleeping. They strangled the couple but left their child, before killing the sub-chief, his family and Gadson's Christian friend Nathaniel. Gadson's parents went to the home in the morning and found the baby screaming and Gadson and Rebeka dead.

Despite their shocking and untimely deaths, the funeral was not sombre but joyful. Preacher Heshbon Mwangi gave an uplifting sermon, saying that the "young couple were married here in this old church of Njumbi. Now they are at the marriage supper of the Lamb!"

Lord, we praise you; you are leading us to life's summit and giving us the exhilaration of victory over ourselves, over sin and death; victory for ourselves and all mankind.
Alan Gaunt (born 1935)

My soul thirsts for God, for the living God. When can I go and meet with God? Psalm 42:2

Rafah Toma Alkass Butras (2011)
Hostage Pursued

Just over two months after Rafah, an Iraqi Christian woman, had survived a deadly hostage siege on a church in Baghdad, she was killed in her bed by terrorists who broke into her home as she slept in the early hours of 3 January 2011. Rafah (44), who lived alone in central Baghdad, had refused to leave the Iraqi capital after the church massacre on 31 October 2010, despite the appeals of her elderly father. She was one of around 100 worshippers who were taken hostage by terrorists linked to Al-Qaeda during an evening service at the Baghdad church; over 50 people were killed in the ensuing siege. Rafah lost her 27-year-old cousin in the attack and had returned to the scene of his murder every other day to mourn. She said, "I am attached to this place... I feel like my soul is in this place with them."

Rafah's murder came amid a wave of attacks on Iraqi Christians in their homes and workplaces following the church siege.

Father, I see there is no escape from the groan that arises in our soul because of the suffering sin has brought into the universe. Help me enter into it and use it to whet my appetite for heaven. In Jesus' name. Amen.
Selwyn Hughes (1928-2006)

We preach Christ crucified: a stumbling block to Jews and foolishness to Gentiles. 1 Corinthians 1:23

Mukhtar Masih (2004)
A Bold Proclaimer

On an early January morning in 2004, Mukhtar, a pastor in Pakistan's Punjab province, was murdered on his way to catch a train. His life had been threatened several times previously because of his Bible readings that were broadcast on his church's loudspeaker every morning. This infuriated local Muslims, some of whom had been in a dispute with him over the matter.

Mukhtar, who had a wife and seven children, was shot once in the chest. None of his valuables was stolen, indicating that his murder was more akin to an execution than a robbery that had gone wrong.

If the devil were wise enough and would stand by in silence and let the gospel be preached, he would suffer less harm. For when there is no battle for the gospel it rusts and it finds no cause and no occasion to show its vigour and power. Therefore, nothing better can befall the gospel than that the world should fight it with force and cunning.
Martin Luther (1483-1546)

Onward, therefore, pilgrim brothers!
Onward, with the cross our aid!
Bear its shame and fight its battle
Till we rest beneath its shade.
Soon shall come the great awaking,
Soon the rending of the tomb,
Then the scattering of all shadows,
And the end of toil and gloom.
Bernhardt S. Ingemann (1789-1862)
Translated by Sabine Baring-Gould (1834-1924)

"My Father, if it is possible, may this cup be taken from me. Yet not as I will, but as you will." Matthew 26:39a

Nigerian Christians (2011-12)
"Religious Cleansing"

"I was leading the congregation in prayers. Our eyes were closed when some gunmen stormed the church and opened fire on the congregation."

Pastor Johnson Jauro's wife was killed, along with at least seven other Christians, during an attack on his church in Gombe, capital of Gombe State in Northern Nigeria. This violent incident, which happened on 5 January 2012, was one in a torrent of systematic attacks on Christians in the North by militant Islamist group Boko Haram at the end of 2011 and start of 2012. On Christmas Day, 25 December 2011, they conducted a coordinated series of bomb and gun attacks on churches and other targets that left more than 40 people dead. Among them were around 35 worshippers at a church in Madalla, near the capital Abuja; they were killed as explosives were hurled at the congregation as they left the service.

On New Year's Day (1 January 2012), Boko Haram, which wants to impose a version of sharia across Nigeria, gave Christians a three-day ultimatum to leave the North. As the deadline expired, attacks on Christians resumed. Ousman Adurkwa (65) and his son Moussa were shot dead in their home in Maiduguri, Borno State, on 4 January. Two days later, around 20 Christians were gunned down in Mubi, Adamawa State, as they gathered to mourn the death of another Christian who had been killed the night before. And on 11 January, four Christian men were killed in Potiskum town, Yobe State, as they were travelling southwards to join their families, who had already migrated to escape the violence. Church leaders, who held an emergency meeting about the attacks, said that the killings suggested "systematic ethnic and religious cleansing".

O Prince of Glory,
who dost bring Thy sons

to glory through the Cross,
Let us not shrink from suffering
Reproach or loss.
Amy Carmichael (1867-1951)

January 6

Do not be afraid of those who kill the body and after that can do no more.
But I will show you whom you should fear: Fear him who, after your
body has been killed, has authority to throw you into hell. Luke 12:4-5

Egyptian Christians (2010)
Triple Attack

Six Christians and a security guard were killed when three gunmen stormed a worship service at a church in the city of Nag Hammadi, Upper Egypt, on 6 January 2010, the eve of the Eastern Christmas Day, which is 7 January. This attack followed threats to the church minister, apparently because of his outspoken criticism of earlier violence against Christians in the neighbouring town of Farshout by a Muslim mob, and requests for compensation for those who had lost property and businesses there. During the violence on 21 November, ten pharmacies and 55 Christian-owned shops and businesses had been looted, vandalised and burnt; cars were attacked and Christian families thrown out of their homes, and at least seven Christians were injured.

Following the church shooting on 6 January, there were further assaults against the Christian community in the nearby town of Baghoura just two days later. A Muslim mob armed with swords and gas cylinders looted and torched homes, shops and cars belonging to local Christians. One woman died when her home was set alight.

In all time of our tribulation; in all time of our prosperity, in the hour of
death, and in the day of judgement, Good Lord, deliver us.
From the Litany, *Book of Common Prayer*

For the Spirit God gave us does not make us timid, but gives us power, love and self-discipline. 2 Timothy 1:7

Timothy (c. 97)
"My true son in the faith"

Timothy became the beloved disciple of Paul the apostle, and a companion to him on his missionary journeys. Acts 16:1-3 describes how they met when Paul was on a visit to Lystra. Paul wrote two letters to his "son in the faith" (2 Timothy 4:2), and it is clear from these that he gave Timothy oversight of the Christians around the city of Ephesus. In his first letter to Timothy, Paul urges him to "guard what has been entrusted to your care" (1 Timothy 6:20), not allowing anyone to look down on him because of his young age. The apostle called Timothy to "set an example for the believers in speech, in conduct, in love, faith and in purity... devote yourself to the public reading of Scripture, to preaching and to teaching" (1 Timothy 4:12-13).

However, from the first chapter of the second letter, it seems Timothy was struggling to be a robust leader, and Paul challenges his timidity, exhorting him to suffer for the Gospel's sake. This Timothy later had to do, for it is thought that he was stoned to death by a mob for opposing worship to the pagan goddess Diana.

God of our life, there are days when the burdens we carry chafe our shoulders and weigh us down; when the road seems dreary and endless, the skies grey and threatening; when our lives have no music in them, and our hearts are lonely, and our souls have lost their courage. Flood the path with light, run our eyes to where the skies are full of promise; tune our hearts to brave music; give us the sense of comradeship with heroes and saints of every age; and so quicken our spirits that we may be able to encourage the souls of all who journey with us on the road of life, to Your honour and glory.
Augustine of Hippo (354-430)

I pray that out of his glorious riches he may strengthen you with power through his Spirit in your inner being, so that Christ may dwell in your hearts through faith. And I pray that you, being rooted and established in love, may have power, together with all the Lord's holy people, to grasp how wide and long and high and deep is the love of Christ, and to know this love that surpasses knowledge – that you may be filled to the measure of all the fullness of God. Ephesians 3:16-19

Ugandan Christians (1997)
Targeted at an Open-air Prayer Meeting

Six Christians died in January 1997 when militants attacked a church in Kampala, the capital of Uganda. They were among 500 Christians who were taking part in an open-air prayer meeting in a suburb called Bwaise. Three of the victims died instantly, while the other three died in hospital. Around 40 other people were injured. The killers were unidentified, and no-one claimed responsibility, although the police suspected Islamic militants. Kampala newspapers reported that several preachers at the prayer meeting had criticised the Quran, which had angered Muslims. Traditionally Muslims and Christians in Uganda have lived together harmoniously.

Almighty God, our heavenly Father, have mercy upon the Muslims and all others who are strangers to thy redeeming love; and grant that thy Church may so powerfully exhibit to them the saving truth of the gospel that they may be brought to confess thy Son Jesus Christ as their Prophet, Priest and King, and to share with us the fellowship of the Spirit, to the glory of thy name; through the merits of the death and passion of the same thy Son, Jesus Christ our Lord.
Parish Prayers (no. 1370)

Jesus answered, "I am the way and the truth and the life. No one comes to the Father except through me." John 14:6

Columba (853)
Loyal to Christ

Spanish nun Columba was beheaded and her body was thrown into the river Guadalquivir after she said that Muhammad was a false prophet.

Columba became a nun as a young girl and had been living at a convent in Tabanos, Spain, when the community was forcibly disbanded by the invading Muslims from North Africa. She went before the Muslim magistrate in Cordoba and, after denouncing the founder of Islam and affirming her faith in Christ, was killed. The account of her death, which happened around 853, was related by Eulogius of Cordoba, who also suffered for his faith (see 11 March).

Lo, round the throne a glorious band,
The saints in countless myriads stand,
Of every tongue redeemed to God,
Arrayed in garments washed in blood.

Through tribulation great they came;
They bore the cross, despised the shame;
From all their labours now they rest,
In God's eternal glory blest.

So may we tread the sacred road
That saints and holy martyrs trod;
Wage to the end the glorious strife,
And win, like them, a crown of life.
Raymond Hill (1744-1833)

God is our refuge and strength, an ever-present help in trouble. There-fore we will not fear, though the earth give way and the mountains fall into the heart of the sea. Psalm 46:1-2

Jim Elliot, Peter Fleming, Ed McCully, Nate Saint and Roger Youderian (1956) No Fools

These five American missionaries and their families went to Ecuador in 1955 to reach an unevangelised native tribe known as the Aucas – a feared people who had previously killed several Shell oil company work-ers. When Jim had discussed with his wife the possibility of not returning alive, he had said, "If God wants it that way, darling, I am ready to die for the salvation of the Aucas."

Nate Saint was their skilled pilot, who had flown over Ecuadorian jungles on many occasions. His sister Rachel Saint had learnt the lan-guage of the Aucas while Jim, Nate and Ed planned an expedition into their territory. On 3 January 1956 they landed near to an Auca village, met for prayer and sang, "We rest on Thee, our Shield and our Defender" before going in.

Their first contact with the Aucas, which lasted a week, seemed very positive. However by end of the week Marj, Nate's wife, lost radio con-tact with the five. Four bodies were eventually picked up by the US Air Force; the fifth – Ed's body – was not recovered.

After the event an Auca girl, Dayuma, who had left her tribe to teach Rachel the tribal language, returned to her people. They were astonished, as they had thought that the missionaries had killed her. Instead she shared her new found faith, telling them that "just as you killed the for-eigners on the beach, Jesus was killed for you".

Many Aucas became Christians as a result of the missionaries' sacrifice – even the killers. Jim Elliot had famously said, "He is no fool who gives what he cannot keep to gain that which he cannot lose."

We rest on Thee, our Shield and our Defender,
We go not forth alone against the foe.

Strong in Thy Strength, safe in Thy keeping tender,
We rest on Thee, and in Thy name we go.

We go in faith, our own great weakness feeling,
And needing more each day Thy grace to know,
Yet from our hearts a song of triumph pealing,
We rest on Thee and in Thy name we go.

We rest on Thee, our Shield and our Defender,
Thine is the battle, Thine shall be the praise.
When passing through the gates of pearly splendour,
Victors, we rest with Thee through endless days.
Edith Gilling Cherry (1872-1897)

January 11

You shall have no foreign god among you; you shall not worship any god other than me. I am the LORD your God, who brought you out of Egypt. Open wide your mouth and I will fill it. Psalm 81:9-10

Concordius of Spoleto (c. 178)
"I am a Christian and confess Jesus Christ"

Early Roman Christians found themselves living in a hostile and pagan society that tested their faith to the utmost. As a sub-deacon in Umbria, Concordius was captured during the organised persecution under Emperor Marcus Aurelius. Taken in front of the governor Torquatus at Spoleto (in present-day Italy) he was pressured to renounce his faith. He replied, "I have already told you, I am a Christian and confess Jesus Christ". This led to a harsh beating and torture, yet still he remembered his Saviour by singing "Glory be to thee, Lord Jesus!"

After three days imprisonment, two soldiers brought a statue of the god Jupiter for Concordius to worship. Instead of doing this, the sub-deacon spat on the idol – an act that saw him beheaded immediately in his prison cell.

Oh! for a closer walk with God,
A calm and heavenly frame;
A light to shine upon the road
That leads me to the Lamb!

The dearest idol I have known,
Whate'er that idol be,
Help me to tear it from its throne
And worship only thee.

So shall my walk be close with God,
Calm and serene my frame;
So purer light shall mark the road
That leads me to the Lamb.
William Cowper (1731-1800)

January 12

For God's foolishness is wiser than human wisdom, and God's weakness is stronger than human strength. 1 Corinthians 1:25 (NRSV)

Sergei Bessareb (2004)
Church Founder

Sergei spent 18 years in prison for organised crime, but while behind bars, he met Christ. Upon his release he became an itinerant preacher until finally moving to Isfara in Tajikistan in 2003. Along with his wife Tamara, Sergei hoped to begin the first Christian church in the mosque-filled city. The couple's vision became reality and soon their house church grew until they were worshipping in a small building.

At 9 pm on Monday 12 January 2004, Sergei was alone at prayer in the church. As he knelt, in burst gunmen showering Sergei with Kalashnikov rounds. Hearing the shots, Tamara rushed in; her husband died moments later.

It is likely that Sergei's active evangelism and church planting were the motivation for his murder. Yet if the killers had intended to hinder the local church in Isfara, they were greatly disappointed. The event only served to motivate the Christians in the city to further Sergei's vision and enlarge the church, while throughout Tajikistan many prisoners who heard his story have committed their lives to Jesus.

Calamity clarifies and comfort confuses, persecution purifies and prosperity pollutes!
Kevin Turner

January 13

I have hidden your word in my heart that I might not sin against you.
Psalm 119:11

Gumesindus, Servusdei and Aurea (850-59)
Guilty of Preaching

Gumesindus, a parish priest, and Servusdei, a monk, were two of 48 Christians decapitated for their faith between 850 and 859 in the Spanish town of Cordoba, which was then part of al-Andalus (as the Iberian Peninsula was known by its Muslim rulers). Both were executed on 13 January 852 during the reign of Abd ar-Rahman II, Emir of Cordoba.

Most of the Christians who died in this series of killings were guilty of preaching openly outside churches. Some, however, were executed because they had converted from Islam. Aurea was one such victim, who was born of Muslim parents but became a Christian. She was brought before a judge by her relatives and forced to recant under duress. Yet despite this she continued to live as a Christian until her family finally ensured she was executed.

Let all the world in every corner sing,
"My God and King!"
The heavens are not too high,
His praise may thither fly:
The earth is not too low,
His praises there may grow,

The church with psalms must shout,
No door can keep them out:
But, above all, the heart
Must bear the longest part.
Let all the world in every corner sing,
"My God and King!"
George Herbert (1593-1633)

January 14

But whatever were gains to me I now consider loss for the sake of Christ. What is more, I consider everything a loss because of the surpassing worth of knowing Christ Jesus my Lord, for whose sake I have lost all things. I consider them garbage, that I may gain Christ and be found in him. Philippians 3:7-9a

Barbasymas (346)
Refused to Recant

Barbasymas, Bishop of Selucia and Ctesiphon (in present-day Iraq), was a man of great piety and honesty. He was arrested, along with 16 of his priests, during the brutal persecution under the Sassanid King Shapur II, and he was offered a cup filled with gold coins and a governorship if he would renounce his Christian faith. Their persecutors also tried to persuade them to participate in sun worship, by means of imprisonment, torture and deprivation of food and water. But neither bribery nor intimidation could shake them. Barbasymas told the king, "The more Christians you kill, the more their numbers will increase." Finally they were all beheaded.

O Lord Christ, who judgest the earth, and hast laid the sure foundation upon which thy Church has upraised its confession of faith: grant that we may not build our faith upon the sand, where storms may overthrow it; and establish us upon the rock which is steadfast in thee; to the glory of thy Name.
Mozarabic prayer

Rejoice in the Lord always. I will say it again: Rejoice! Philippians 4:4

John Hewitt (1942)
"Praise the Lord! Praise the Lord!"

John, an Irish Brethren missionary to Japan during World War II, was arrested for his Christian witness along with another Irish missionary, R G Wright, in October 1941. Japanese opinion of Christians and foreigners was very low, and the pair were subjected to five days of interrogation. They were grilled on *Ise Jingu* (a Japanese god), the "deity" of the Emperor, the Bible and the refusal of Christians to bow before Japanese shrines, before being released.

John was arrested again on 8 December 1941 and sent to Sugamo prison in eastern Tokyo. When he was first sent to the prison his health was very good, but he soon became seriously ill. He was then transferred to a mental asylum in Tokyo in mid-January 1942, where it is suspected that he was given experimental drugs.

Christians who asked about Hewitt's whereabouts were not given an answer. But some months later the authorities asked his Buddhist neighbour to make funeral arrangements for him. When two women missionaries heard about this, they went in search of John and found him in a pauper ward, lying on the floor and very malnourished, but calling out "Praise the Lord! Praise the Lord!" They stayed with him, but were helpless to save him from death. The women gained police permission for Hewitt to be given a Christian burial. John was one of many missionaries to be imprisoned by the Japanese during the war.

Father, make us more like Jesus. Help us to bear difficulty, pain, disappointment and sorrow, knowing that in your perfect working and design you can use such bitter experiences to shape our characters and make us more like our Lord. We look with hope for that day when we shall be wholly like Christ, because we shall see him as he is. Amen.
Ignatius of Antioch, before his martyrdom in 107

The hired hand, who is not the shepherd and does not own the sheep, sees the wolf coming and leaves the sheep and runs away—and the wolf snatches them and scatters them. The hired hand runs away because a hired hand does not care for the sheep. I am the good shepherd. I know my own and my own know me, just as the Father knows me and I know the Father. And I lay down my life for the sheep.
John 10:12-15 (NRSV)

Alphege (1012)
A Faithful Overseer

Alphege, Archbishop of Canterbury when the Vikings arrived in Britain in 1010, was a courageous defender of those under his care during the invaders' merciless regime of plunder and violence. On one occasion Alphege went to the Vikings and bought the freedom of several friends whom they had captured. He also sent food to others who were seized, and saw some of the attackers convert to Christianity.

This angered the invaders, who sought revenge. They attacked Alphege, and although many fled, the archbishop remained, since he would not abandon the people under his care. When the Vikings attacked the church, Alphege begged that the congregation might be spared and that they should kill only him. His plea was refused, and he was taken captive and forced to watch as his church burnt.

Alphege was then taken before a Danish chieftain in Greenwich for a hearing but, since he stood firm in his faith, was tortured. A Viking soldier, to whom Alphege had shown kindness, saw that he was suffering a lot of pain and was near to death, so mercifully killed him.

I am passing through the furnace, but blessed be my heavenly Shepherd, He is with me, and I shall not want. He has kept me in perfect peace and my soul rests and waits only upon Him. All I pray is that I may patiently await His good pleasure, whether it be for life or for death; that whether I live or die, it may be for His glory.
Allen Gardiner (1794-1851)

It is better to take refuge in the LORD than to trust in humans. It is bet-ter to take refuge in the LORD than to trust in princes. Psalm 118:8-9

Helmuth James Graf von Moltke (1945)
Only Obeying God's Orders

Helmuth lived during the Nazi period in Germany – a regime he opposed because of his Christian beliefs. He was from one of the aristo-cratic families of Imperial Germany and became an international lawyer. Helmuth was part of an anti-Nazi group and believed that Christianity was the only basis for a renewed Germany and Europe. While others who resisted Hitler used violence, Helmuth relied on the power of faith, intellect and morality, using his position as an officer in the German military intelligence service to spread word of the appalling atrocities the Nazis were committing.

In January 1944 he was arrested by the Gestapo, and put on trial a year later. He was condemned and executed, aged 37. Shortly before he was hanged in Plötzensee prison, Helmuth explained why his strictly moral and intellectual rebellion represented such a threat to Hitler: "What the Third Reich is so terrified of is ultimately a private individual [who has] discussed the practical, ethical demands of Christianity: for that alone we are condemned."

We pray to you, O Lord, who are the supreme Truth, and all truth is from you. We beseech you, O Lord, who are the highest Wisdom, and all the wise depend on you for their wisdom. You are the supreme joy, and all who are happy owe it to you. You are the light of minds, and all receive their understanding from you. We love you above all. We seek you, we follow you, and we are ready to serve you. We desire to dwell under your power for you are the King of all. Amen.
King Alfred the Great (849-99)

But I say to you, Love your enemies and pray for those who persecute you,
so that you may be children of your Father in heaven.
Matthew 5:44-45a (NRSV)

Manihera and Kereopa (1846)
Reaching Rivals

Manihera and Kereopa were part of a Maori tribe who, having received the Gospel from missionaries themselves, felt called to take the Good News to rival tribesmen.

Westerners had taken the message of Christianity to the Maoris of New Zealand in the early decades of the 19th century, and at Christmas 1846, a congregation of 2,000 gathered at Whanganui. The day after this, a missionary meeting was held at which Manihera and Kereopa of the tribe Ngatiruanui were sent out to teach the Gospel to their fellow Maoris. They chose first to go to Rangihaeata and then onto Tokanu, where a Maori warrior named Herekiekie lived. Despite the long-standing feud between Herekiekie's tribe and his own tribe, Manihera felt he was doing God's will by taking His message to this tribesman.

On their way to Tokanu, a group of 30 warriors lay in wait for them, and as the party of Christians approached, they were fired upon. Kereopa was shot dead on the spot. Manihera was wounded but then cut down by the warriors' hatchets.

A month later Manihera and Kereopa's pastor, Mr Taylor, went to the tribe that had killed them and negotiated a peace between the feuding tribes.

Let us help each other
by our prayers,
so that God and Christ
and the whole choir of angels, may come to our aid
in our time of suffering, when we shall need their
assistance the most.
Nemesian (died 257)

We fix our eyes not on what is seen, but on what is unseen, since what is seen is temporary, but what is unseen is eternal. 2 Corinthians 4:18

Haik Hovespian Mehr (1994)
"I am ready to die for the cause of the Church"

On 19 January 1994 Bishop Haik, who had spent much time making public the sufferings and persecutions of Christians in Iran, disappeared from a Tehran street. He loved the people of Iran, having dedicated his life to serving them, and especially spoke out for converts from Islam. For this reason he was targeted. Bishop Haik had campaigned for the release of an evangelist and convert from Islam, Mehdi Dibaj (see July 14), from prison, and he disappeared two days after Mehdi was finally freed.

Haik wrote, "I am ready to die for the cause of the Church so that others will be able to worship their Lord peacefully and without so much fear."

On 30 January his family was informed by the Iranian authorities of his death. He had been tortured and killed on 20 January, and although it remains unclear exactly who was responsible, the Iranian authorities refused to help his family discover the truth.

The servant of Christ must never be surprised if he has to drink of the same cup with his Lord.
J C Ryle (1816-1900)

Therefore put on the full armour of God, so that when the day of evil comes, you may be able to stand your ground, and after you have done everything, to stand. Ephesians 6:13

Roy Pontoh (1999)
"A soldier of God is ready to die for Christ"

Young Roy was 15 years old when he bravely lost his life for Christ in Indonesia. This country has been notorious for its anti-Christian violence fuelled by Islamist organisations. Roy lived in a particularly violent part of the Maluku Islands called Ambon, which has seen attacks on churches and the homes of Christians, and numerous killings.

On 20 January 1999 he was part of a 125-strong group of young people from the New Covenant Christian Church attending a Bible camp at Pattimura University. When the event had come to an end, many of the young people needed transport home. Pastor Meiky Sainyakit visited a local village to find a truck to hire, and upon leaving he and his party were attacked by a local mob. Pastor Sainyakit and his driver were killed.

A short time later the remaining youngsters were confronted by fighters from the Laskar Jihad terrorist organisation at the gates of the University. Armed with machetes, spears, knives and clubs the fighters began hunting down the defenceless young people, whose desperate attempts to hide were futile.

Roy was targeted by one of the attackers and, when asked who he was, the teenager answered, "a soldier of God". The attacker slashed Roy with a machete, almost severing his left arm. After being asked a second time Roy replied with the same answer. He received a blow to his right shoulder, leaving a big gash, and this time the attacker shouted, "What is God's soldier?"

"A soldier of God is ready to die for Christ" was Roy's final answer, at which the machete flew down upon him one last time. As he died he screamed, "Jesus!" Roy's body was later discovered by his family.

We pray thee, Lord, to guide and uphold thy Church with thy unfailing goodness; that in prosperity it lose not zeal, and in adversity have faith and patient endurance; through Jesus Christ our Lord.
Parish Prayers (no. 1310)

To the pure, all things are pure, but to those who are corrupted and do not believe, nothing is pure. Titus 1:15

Agnes (c. 305)
"Jesus Christ is my only spouse"

When Agnes, a 13-year-old Roman girl from a Christian family, was courted by the local governor's son, she replied, "Jesus Christ is my only spouse." Neither inducements nor imprisonment could convince her to renounce her faith or to worship in a pagan temple. Tradition says that as she went to be executed with a sword, her beautiful face was shining. She was buried in the cemetery on the Via Nomentana, where a church was built to honour her.

Lord Jesus, who didst enter into thy triumph by the hard and lonely way of the cross: May thy courage and steadfast loyalty, thy unswerving devotion to the Father's will, inspire and strengthen us to tread firmly and with joy the road which love bids us to take, even if it leads through suffering, misunderstanding and darkness. We ask it for thy sake, who for the joy that was set before thee endured the cross, despising the shame, O Lord, our strength and our Redeemer.
Parish Prayers (no. 245)

Brief life is here our portion, brief sorrow, short lived care;
The life that knows no ending, the tearless life, is there.
O happy retribution! Short toil, eternal rest;
For mortals and for sinners, a mansion with the blest.
Bernard of Morlaix (fl. 1146)
Translated by John Mason Neale (1818-1866)

Forgive as the Lord forgave you. Colossians 3:13b

Graham, Phillip and Timothy Staines (1999)
Father and Two Sons Burnt Alive

Graham Staines, from Australia, dedicated nearly 35 years of his life to serving the Lord in Orissa state, India, where he cared for leprosy victims and translated the Bible into the Ho tribal language. In January 1999, along with his two young sons Phillip (10) and Timothy (6), he took time out to travel to a Bible camp in the village of Monoharpur. Realising that accommodation was at a premium, they decided to sleep in their Jeep that night (22 January).

At this time Orissa state was experiencing much anti-Christian violence. One radical Hindu, Dara Singh, who had openly voiced his hatred of Christians, took a group to where the Staines were sleeping. Pouring petrol into the Jeep, they ignited it. Local villagers were woken by the sound of screaming, and they looked on as the Jeep was engulfed in flames, surrounded by a mob. Once the fire died down, the bodies of Graham, Phillip and Timothy were seen.

Despite the murder of her husband and their two sons by Hindu extremists, Gladys Staines and her daughter Esther remained in India to continue the family's work among the country's leprosy victims.

How was I able to forgive? The truth is that I myself am a sinner. I needed Jesus Christ to forgive me. Because I have forgiveness in my own life, it is possible for me to forgive others.
Gladys Staines (born 1951)

Whoever does not love does not know God, because God is love.
1 John 4:8

Vettius Epagathus (177)
"Comforter of the Christians"

During a violent outbreak of persecution against Christians in Gaul, one young man, Vettius Epagathus, stepped forward and asked to speak in defence of a group of Christians who had been abused and beaten by the angry mob and brought before the authorities. The governor rejected his request and merely asked, "Are you a Christian?" Vettius replied that he was, and was immediately put to death. Others were subsequently martyred also.

A contemporary letter, from the churches in Lyons and Vienne to their counterparts in Asia Minor, said about Vettius: "He was called the 'Comforter of the Christians' but he had the Comforter in himself, as evidenced in the love by which he laid down his own life for the defence of the brethren as a true disciple of Christ."

The same letter described the "intensity of the pressure here, the awful rage of the heathen against the saints, and the sufferings of the blessed martyrs" who "endured every punishment as they hurried to Christ, proving that the sufferings of this present time are not worthy to be compared with the glory that shall be revealed in us".

God is fire that warms and kindles the heart and inward parts. And so, if we feel in our hearts coldness, which is from the devil – for the devil is cold – then let us call upon the Lord and He will come and warm our hearts with perfect love not only for Him but for our neighbour as well.
Seraphim of Sarov (1759-1833)

Those who suffer according to God's will should commit themselves to their faithful Creator and continue to do good. 1 Peter 4:19

Irene Ferrel (1964)
Targeted by Rebels

Irene, an American missionary in the Congo, was among the many Christian and humanitarian workers who came under attack following the withdrawal of the Belgian colonial rulers in the early 1960s. They became the new target of the Marxist guerrillas who roamed the jungles, after the Belgians had been forced out by the Simba Uprising.

Irene, who had been in the Congo for ten years, served Christ at the Kwulu mission school, which was in a largely peaceful location. But on 24 January 1964, she and her companion Ruth Hege had to pack their bags for an evacuation. In fear and trepidation they made their way to a nearby clearing to await a helicopter. Minutes went by, turning into hours, and no helicopter arrived. Finally they gave up and turned in for the night. Awakened abruptly from their sleep they heard cries and shrieks coming towards their mission station.

Irene and Ruth could do nothing but attempt to escape the hostile rebels who descended upon them. They were dragged out, and Irene was shot by an arrow. Ruth fell, knocked unconscious by a blow, only to awaken and find the rebels gone and Irene dead. After peace returned to the Congo Ruth began again the work in Kwulu.

Eternal Lord God, you hold all souls in life: shed forth, we pray, upon your whole Church in paradise and on earth the bright beams of your light and heavenly comfort; and grant that we, following the good example of those who have loved and served you here and are now at rest, may at the last enter with them into the fullness of your eternal joy; through Jesus Christ our Lord. Amen.
The Alternative Service Book, 1980

I eagerly expect and hope that I will in no way be ashamed, but will have sufficient courage so that now as always Christ will be exalted in my body, whether by life or by death. For to me, to live is Christ and to die is gain. Philippians 1:20-21

Paul the Apostle (67)
"I have been exposed to death again and again"

Following his dramatic conversion on the road to Damascus, Paul went from chief persecutor of Christians to persecuted Christian leader. Defending his ministry in light of false apostles leading the church in Corinth astray, Paul writes in his second epistle to them:

I have worked much harder, been in prison more frequently, been flogged more severely, and been exposed to death again and again. Five times I received from the Jews the forty lashes minus one. Three times I was beaten with rods, once I was pelted with stones, three times I was shipwrecked, I spent a night and a day in the open sea, I have been constantly on the move. I have been in danger from rivers, in danger from bandits, in danger from my fellow Jews, in danger from Gentiles; in danger in the city, in danger in the country, in danger at sea; and in danger from false believers. I have laboured and toiled and have often gone without sleep; I have known hunger and thirst and have often gone without food; I have been cold and naked. Besides everything else, I face daily the pressure of my concern for all the churches. (2 Corinthians 11:23b-28)

The second half of the book of Acts focuses on Paul and his missionary journeys, which included Cyprus, Syria, Macedonia, Thessalonica, Athens, Corinth and Ephesus. It ends with the apostle going to face trial in Rome. Details of his life and ministry after this are unclear, although it is thought that he returned to Rome again at a later date and was martyred there in 67 AD. There is a strong tradition that he was executed on the Ostian Way by order of the Emperor Nero. Because he was a Roman citizen he was most likely to have been beheaded rather than crucified – a death reserved for non-Romans.

January 25 is the date that traditionally commemorates his conversion on the Damascus road, when, blinded by a light sent by God, he realised his need of Christ.

Praise for the light from heaven, praise for the voice of awe,
praise for the glorious vision the persecutor saw.
Thee, Lord, for his conversion, we glorify today;
so lighten all our darkness with thy true Spirit's ray.
Horatio Nelson (1823-1913)

January 26

May the God of hope fill you with all joy and peace as you trust in him,
so that you may overflow with hope by the power of the Holy Spirit.
Romans 15:13

Yona Kanamuzeyi (1964)
Praised God to the End

Pastor Yona chose to minister to his fellow Tutsis in a refugee camp after they had been made homeless by Rwanda's army, members of whom were from the rival Hutu tribal group.

One night in January 1964, a group of soldiers snatched him away, along with his friend Kayumba. They were taken to a military encampment, where Pastor Yona was singled out by the soldiers. He was marched away from Kayumba, but as he did so he sang hymns of worship to God. They took the pastor to a bridge, where he was executed by shooting and his body was thrown into the water below. Kayumba was released and was able to relate the account of Pastor Yona's brutal death.

Years later, St Paul's Cathedral in London honoured the witness and martyrdom of Pastor Yona by inscribing his name into the cathedral's book of modern martyrs.

The hymn for conquering martyrs raise,
The victor innocents we praise,
Whom in their woe earth cast away,

But Heav'n with joy received today;
Whose angels see the Father's face
World without end, and hymn His grace;
And while they chant unceasing lays,
The hymn for conquering martyrs raise.
The Venerable Bede (673-735)
Translated by John Mason Neale (1818-1866)

January 27

For the word of God is alive and active. Sharper than any double-edged sword, it penetrates even to dividing soul and spirit, joints and marrow; it judges the thoughts and attitudes of the heart. Hebrews 4:12

Lucian of Antioch (312)
Knowledgeable Defender

Thinker, scholar and founder of an important theological school at Antioch, Lucian was one of many who fell into the hands of the Roman authorities under Emperor Diocletian. This emperor, who was notorious in Church history as a persecutor of the faithful, had Lucian imprisoned for nine years. So memorable was the reign of terror inflicted on the Christians of the Roman Empire that the Coptic Church terms it the "Era of Martyrs".

Twice during this period Lucian was interrogated by those who wanted to see him deny his faith. Yet he stood firm, being able to defend himself using his masterful knowledge of Christianity. Since he refused to renounce his Saviour, he was put to death, either by starvation or the sword.

We may note in passing that He [Jesus] was never regarded as a mere moral teacher. He did not produce that effect on any of the people who actually met Him. He produced mainly three results: Hatred, Terror, Adoration. There was no trace of people expressing mild admiration.
C S Lewis (1898-1963), *God in the Dock*

I envied the arrogant when I saw the prosperity of the wicked... When I tried to understand all this, it troubled me deeply till I entered the sanctuary of God; then I understood their final destiny... you cast them down to ruin. Psalm 73:3, 16-18

Noor Alam (1998)
Undeterred by Threats

Noor Alam, the pastor of a church in the village of Sheikhupura, Pakistan, was murdered the month after his church building was burnt to the ground by a mob.

Pastor Noor had received death threats after openly declaring his decision to rebuild the destroyed church; he was warned that he had only a month to change his mind, but he refused to back down. Late at night on 28 January 1998, Pastor Noor was attacked at his home in front of his wife and daughter by three men who stabbed him four times before fleeing the scene. He died shortly afterwards in hospital and was buried the following day.

The congregation had bought the land to build the church nearly three years previously, and had begun building work the following year despite threats. The mob attacked the building just as it was ready to be roofed in December 1997. The assailants reportedly said that they had held off to the last moment to discourage the Christians and cause the greatest waste of their money. Members of 25 Christian families from the village received death threats following the destruction of their church and the murder of their pastor.

O most glorious and exalted Lord,
you are glorified in the heights above by ministers of fire and spirit in
*   most holy fashion,*
yet in your love
you wished to be glorified by mankind on earth as well, so that you
*   might exalt our mortal race*
and make us like supernal beings and brothers in your dominion.
Free us, Lord, in your compassion

from whatever cares hinder the worship of you,
and teach us to seek the kingdom and its righteousness
in accordance with your holy commandments that bring life;
and may we become worthy of that kingdom
along with all the saints who have done your will,
and may we sing your praises.
Maronite Shehimto, from the *Syrian Orthodox Daily Office Book*

January 29

We make it our goal to please him, whether we are at home in the body or away from it. 2 Corinthians 5:9

Severino Bagtasos (1996)
"I am ready to die for Jesus"

Severino was shot dead by an Islamic extremist during a Sunday morning service at the church where he was a pastor in January 1996. His fiancée Joy witnessed the death of her beloved husband-to-be; they had planned to marry in May 1997 and were looking forward to serving God together.

Severino, a 30-year-old Filipino, had courageously shared the Gospel with the local Muslim community in the town of Alat on Jolo Island in the Philippines. These efforts had brought death threats before the shooting, and were most likely the motive for his murder. Severino had once said, "If I am killed so be it. I am ready to die for Jesus. But I would prefer to die in church, doing the Lord's work."

In spite of her pain, Joy dedicated her life to reaching out with the Gospel to Tausug and Sama Muslims in the Philippines. She said, "I learned to accept whatever circumstances come my way and look at them as God's instruments in moulding me and in making me a better person. Through [Severino's] life I learned commitment to the ministry and to prayer. Through his death, I learned to always be prepared to face the Author and Finisher of my faith. Through this tragedy, I learned to live each day as though it were my last."

Almighty God, who in thy wisdom hast so ordered our earthly life that we needs must walk by faith and not by sight; grant us such faith in thee that, amidst all things that pass our understanding, we may believe in thy fatherly care, and ever be strengthened by the assurance that underneath are the everlasting arms; through Jesus Christ our Lord.

January 30

And he will be called Wonderful Counsellor, Mighty God, Everlasting Father, Prince of Peace. Of the greatness of his government and peace there will be no end. Isaiah 9:6b-7a

Antonius Hambroeck (1661)
Mediator Murdered

Antonius was a pastor in Delft, Holland, in the 17th century, who was sent to take the Gospel to Formosa (now called Taiwan). There he was killed while trying to mediate between warring military leaders. He had firstly gone to the church in Batavia (Jakarta), Indonesia, which asked him to preach Christ in Formosa. He joined an established team of indigenous Christians and, in 1657, set up a teachers' college there. He also translated the Gospels of Matthew and John into the local language.

Sadly, Antonius' mission to Formosa was brought to an untimely and brutal end as a result of the war between the Dutch and the Chinese. As a community figure, he tried to mediate between the rival military leaders. This led to his and his family's capture and subsequent decapitation.

When I survey the wondrous cross,
On which the Prince of Glory died,
My richest gain I count but loss,
And pour contempt on all my pride.

Were the whole realm of nature mine,
That were an offering far too small;
Love so amazing, so divine,
Demands my soul, my life, my all.
Isaac Watts (1674-1748)

Consider it pure joy, my brothers and sisters, whenever you face trials of many kinds, because you know that the testing of your faith produces perseverance. Let perseverance finish its work so that you may be mature and complete, not lacking anything. James 1:2-4

James the Just (c. 62)
Epistle Author

James was called the brother of Jesus because Joseph was his father. He was known as "the Just" because of his exceptional virtue and wisdom, and he was chosen to oversee the Church in Jerusalem. James was a devoted man of prayer, whose "knees became hard like a camel's from his continual kneeling in worship of God and in prayer for the people", according to early Church writer Hegessipus. The New Testament letter of James, which emphasizes the importance of faith showing itself in action, is attributed to him.

In this period there was fierce hostility from the Jewish leaders towards the new Christian faith. As a result of James' ministry, many Jews had become Christians, much to the vexation of the scribes and Pharisees. They called upon James to deny publicly that Jesus was the Christ at a celebration of the Passover, but instead he courageously affirmed Jesus' identity. Outraged by his testimony, the Jews began to stone James, who like his Saviour, prayed that God would forgive his assailants. A fatal blow to the head was delivered by the club of a laundryman.

All shall be Amen and Alleluia.
We shall rest and we shall see,
We shall see and we shall know,
We shall know, and we shall love,
We shall love and we shall praise.
Behold our end which is no end.
Augustine of Hippo (354-430)

In all their distress he too was distressed. Isaiah 63:8

Anastasios (1655)
Renounced Forced Conversion

Anastasios, an artist in the city of Naupoin, Greece, was forcibly circumcised by a group of Muslims while suffering ill health. This procedure was seen as conversion to Islam by the Muslims, and upon recovery Anastasios decided to correct the situation as best he could. Openly declaring his Christianity, he was met with hostility and anger. Anastasios was now considered by the Muslims as an apostate, and apostosy is punishable by death under sharia. He was swiftly arrested but refused to recant his Christian faith. Anastasios was taken into the street, set upon by a group of frenzied attackers and hacked to pieces by their knives on 1 February 1655.

With a weak faith and a fearful heart, many a sinner stands before the Lord. It is not the strength of our faith, but the perfection of Christ's sacrifice that saves! No feebleness of faith, nor dimness of eye, no trembling of hand can change the efficacy of Christ's blood. The strength of our faith can add nothing to it, nor can the weakness of our faith take anything from Him. Faith (weak or strong) still reads the promise, "the blood of Jesus Christ His Son cleanses us from all sin" (1 John 1:7b). If at times my eye is so dim that I cannot read these words, through blinding tears or bewildering trials, faith rests itself on the certain knowledge of the fact that the promise is there, and the blood of Christ remains in all its power and suitableness upon the altar, unchanged and unaffected.
Horatius Bonar (1808-1889)

"Truly I tell you," Jesus replied, "no one who has left home or brothers or sisters or mother or father or children or fields for me and the gospel will fail to receive a hundred times as much in this present age: homes, brothers, sisters, mothers, children and fields — along with persecutions — and in the age to come eternal life". Mark 10:29-30

Esther John (1960)
"This girl was in love only with your Christ"

Esther John, whose decision to leave the Muslim religion of her birth greatly angered her family, was almost certainly murdered by one of her own brothers.

She was born in India, where she attended a Christian school as a teenager and was struck by the life and love of her Christian teacher. She studied the Bible at this school and one day encountered the grace of the Lord Jesus Christ while studying Isaiah 53. Esther, who changed her name from Qamar Zia, said, "I began to realise that Jesus is alive forever. Thus God put faith in my heart and I believed in Jesus as my Saviour and the forgiver of my sins. Only he could save me from everlasting death. Only then did I realise how great a sinner I was, whereas before I thought that my good life could save me."

In 1955, several years after converting to Christianity, Esther - whose family had moved to Pakistan shortly after it was formed in 1947 - fled her home and went into hiding to avoid being forced to marry a Muslim man by her parents. Esther first went to live at an orphanage in Karachi, where she helped care for the children and studied the Bible with one of the staff. After her brother tracked her down, she moved several hundred miles north to Sahiwal in the Punjab. Over the next few years she lived in various places, completing her studies at the United Bible Training Centre in Gujranwala in April 1959.

On 2 February 1960 she was battered to death, aged 30, whilst she slept in a missionaries' home near Chichawatni; her skull was crushed. Esther was most likely killed by one of her own brothers seeking to expunge the perceived shame she had brought upon her family by converting to Christianity. When the police were making their investigations, they considered the possibility that she may have been murdered by a disappointed lover and went through her books and papers. When they had completed their search, they said, "We have found no clue. This girl was in love only with your Christ."

Almighty and everlasting God, who enkindles the flame of your love in the hearts of the saints, grant to our minds the same faith and power of love; that as we rejoice in their triumphs, we may profit by their examples; through Jesus Christ our Lord. Amen.
Gothic Missal

February 3

Bless those you persecute you; bless and do not curse. Romans 12:14

Martyrs of Japan (1597)
"I do gladly pardon . . . all who have brought about my death"

Paul Miki, a Japanese priest, was among 26 Christians who were tortured then crucified on a hill overlooking the city of Nagasaki by the ruling shogun in February 1597. Japan was persecuting many Christians in this period, fearing a European conquest of the country. On this occasion the shogun was furious at the arrival of new missionaries.

Six of those killed were non-Japanese missionaries. The remainder were Japanese Christians, three of whom were boys. As Paul Miki was being executed he shouted, "My religion teaches me to pardon my enemies and all who have offended me. I do gladly pardon the emperor and all who have brought about my death, and I beg them to seek Christian baptism." He looked at the other Christians who were hanging on crosses, all of whom had joy on their faces, and encouraged them. Some of them looked serene, and some urged the bystanders to lead worthy Christian lives.

God of righteousness and mercy,
Who grafted your holy martyrs of Japan

on to the Tree of Life,
Grant us courage to honour their example,
That when we are called to bear you witness,
We may not be ashamed of your gospel,
Nor fail in the assurance of your promises;
through Jesus Christ our Lord.
For All the Saints (Canada)

February 4

They will be my treasured possession… And you will again see the distinction between the righteous and the wicked, between those who serve God and those who do not. Malachi 3:17b, 18

Tarachus, Probus and Andronicus (c. 304)
Faith Examined

When these three Christians were taken prisoner and brought before Maximus, the Roman governor of Cilicia, for interrogation, they did not shrink from defending their faith.

Tarachus was first to be questioned, and, asked whether he would sacrifice to the gods, he replied that the emperors were deceived in their worship of idols. Probus was next. He was asked if he would renounce his faith, answering that having formerly been rich he saw no benefit in giving up Christ. Andronicus was the last to stand before Maximus. He too would not worship idols and instead chose to suffer for his Saviour. The three Christians then underwent two more examinations, accompanied by tortures, before being sentenced to death by wild beasts. This was a customary Roman death for criminals, which Emperor Diocletian used on many Christians. When thrown to the animals, Tarachus, Probus and Andronicus remained unharmed, so they were put to death by the sword.

To learn strong faith is to endure great trials. I have learned my faith by standing firm amid severe testings.
George Muller (1805-98)

For I am already being poured out like a drink offering, and the time for my departure is near. I have fought the good fight, I have finished the race, I have kept the faith. Now there is in store for me the crown of righteousness, which the Lord, the righteous Judge, will award to me on that day – and not only to me, but also to all who have longed for his appearing. 2 Timothy 4:6-8

Raymond Lull (c. 1315)
Martyred for Muslims

After he was converted Raymond had three aims: to write books that would persuade unbelievers of the truth of the Gospel; to found schools for training missionaries; and thirdly, to give his life, in martyrdom if necessary, in the service of Christ as a witness to Muslims. He embarked on what would become an extraordinary missionary journey, which was ended by the fulfilment of his third goal at the age of 82.

He sailed from his birthplace of Majorca to Tunis, North Africa, where he met groups of learned Muslims. Raymond sought to convince them about Christianity with arguments he had been developing over the years – for which he was condemned to death by the local ruler. But the decree was changed to banishment, and Raymond went to Naples. In 1307 he journeyed to North Africa again, this time to Bugia, in modern-day Algeria, where a Muslim reformer had been influencing the Muslims towards fanaticism. Lull preached openly in the market place. The crowd was angered, and a local magistrate had to intervene to save Raymond's life. He was put in prison and then deported.

Undeterred, he sailed for North Africa again in 1314 at the age of 82. After giving letters of commendation from King James of Aragon to the ruler of Tunis, Raymond was allowed to be involved in preaching tours and debates with some Muslim leaders. He went again to Bugia and preached in the market place. He was stoned by an angry mob and probably died on board the ship that had tried to rescue him.

It is interesting to note that many Kabyle Berbers in Algeria have become Christians in the 20th century, often through receiving revelations of Jesus Christ at the place where Raymond was martyred.

O Lord, convert the world – and begin with me.
Chinese student's prayer

February 6

Now a slave has no permanent place in the family, but a son belongs to it forever. So if the Son sets you free, you will be free indeed.
John 8:35-36

John Smith (1824)
Stood up for Slaves

John, from Northamptonshire, England, had been evangelising both freemen and slaves on a plantation in Demerara, Guyana, for over six years when a slave revolt broke out in August 1823. John was falsely accused of inciting and aiding the rebellion, because of his well-known love for the slaves he worked with, many of whom attended his chapel. The plantation owners also hated his staunch abolitionist stance. John was arrested and tried, and, finding him guilty, the judge sentenced him to death. Amazingly the conviction was remitted, but sadly John died in prison on 6 February 1824, before his release.

The attention his death received in the House of Commons in London was an important factor leading to the abolition of slavery throughout the British Empire in 1833. His slave congregation named him the "Demerara martyr".

If Christians followed the teachings of a benign dead man, their lives would display an innocuous piety. But when Christians stand up for righteousness and justice, they evidence the power of the living God.
Charles Colson (1931-2012)

God chose the foolish things of the world to shame the wise; God chose the weak things of the world to shame the strong. God chose the lowly things of this world and the despised things – and the things that are not – to nullify the things that are, so that no one may boast before him.
1 Corinthians 1:27-28

Sabas the Goth (372)
"Insignificant" Martyr?

Sabas served as a reader at a church in Targoviste in northern Romania where, in 372, the Gothic ruler of the area decided to persecute his Christian subjects. Sabas was arrested but then released, since he was regarded as a person of little significance "who can do us neither good nor harm".

He was arrested again and beaten, but when he was given a chance to escape he did not take it. He spoke defiantly against his captors and the commander, who ordered him to be drowned. Sabas was tied to a pole and held down in the river Buzau until he died. A letter written soon after his death, describing what happened, said, "This death by wood and water was an exact symbol of man's salvation".

The supreme test of service is this: For whom am I doing this? Much that we call service to Christ is not such at all... If we are doing this for Christ, we shall not care for human reward or even recognition. Our work must again be tested by three propositions: Is it work from God, as given us to do from Him; for God, as finding in Him its secret of power; and with God, as only a part of His work in which we engage as co-workers with Him.
Arthur Tappan Pierson (1837-1911)

May the groans of the prisoners come before you; with your strong arm preserve those condemned to die. Psalm 79:11

Eritrean Prisoners (2007, 2010)
Endless Cruelty

Thousands of Christians, including most leaders of unregistered churches, are imprisoned in Eritrea's notoriously cruel detention system. They have to endure atrocious conditions, and some of them die in custody. Christians who fall ill can be denied medical treatment unless they renounce their faith. This is what happened to Magos Solomon Semere in 2007: he died because he would not save himself by denying Christ. During Magos' detention he had endured torture, and his fiancée was forbidden to see him.

Senait Habta, a 28-year-old university student, similarly became another Christian martyr of the Eritrean prison system. She was held for two years in a metal shipping container, which was sweltering hot during the day and bitterly cold at night. Senait became seriously ill and was reportedly offered medical care and freedom if she would deny Christ. But she refused, and she eventually died on 23 April 2010. She had been arrested with 15 other students simply for attending a Bible study group. Eritrea is one of the world's worst persecutors of Christians. The government sees them as a threat to national unity because they give their ultimate allegiance to God and not to the state.

No one, who is fit to live need fear to die. Poor, timorous, faithless souls that we are! How we shall smile at our vain alarms, when the worst has happened! To us here, death is the worst terrible word we know. But when we have tasted its reality, it will mean to us birth, deliverance, a new creation of ourselves. It will be what health is to the sick man. It will be what home is to the exile. It will be what the loved one given back is to the bereaved. As we draw near to it, a great solemn gladness should fill our hearts. It is God's great morning lightening up the sky.
George Spring Merriam (1843-1914)

Now for a little while you may have had to suffer grief in all kinds of trials. These have come so that the proven genuineness of your faith – of greater worth than gold, which perishes even though refined by fire – may result in praise, glory and honour when Jesus Christ is revealed.
1 Peter 1:6-7

Apollonia (249)
Her Faith Survived Flames

During a riot against Christians in the city of Alexandria, Egypt, a mob killed several of them, including this aged deaconess. Apollonia sustained a heavy beating to her face, which knocked out her teeth. Under the threat of death she was asked to leave her faith, but instead of denying her Lord Jesus she chose the flames of the fire that had been lit by the mob.

These third-century rioters looted, pillaged and killed Christians. Such an incident would not be unheard of in today's Egypt, where there are still mobs attacking the Christian minority, despite the 1800 years since Apollonia's time.

Pardon me, O my God, That I, dust, ashes approach Thee,
Yet that which caused my tears to flow Was the remembrance of suff'ring;
The cruel death of Thy martyrs, Defenceless lambs, altogether,
Innocent, led to the water and fire, To the sword and beast's devouring;
There to suffer and there to die For Thy name's sake most holy;
There to suffer and there to die, For Thy name's sake, O my God!

Patiently bear, I besought them, Without gainsaying or flinching;
Suffer the sentence of death urging them At the place of execution,
Scaffold and stake, saying to them, Fight valiantly, sisters, brethren,
The crown awaits you – and died thus with them, So great my love
bound up with them,
There to suffer and there to die For Thy name's sake most holy;
There to suffer and there to die, For Thy name's sake, O my God!
Anabaptist Martyrs' Hymn

He will wipe every tear from their eyes. There will be no more death or mourning or crying or pain, for the old order of things has passed away.
Revelation 21:4

Indonesian Christians (2001)
Thousands Killed

A Christian on Ambon Island, Indonesia, was shot in the neck and killed on 10 February 2001 as he was going to pick fruit. Six days later, another Christian was also shot and killed in a similar incident. Their only "wrong" was their faith in the Lord Jesus Christ.

Over 9,000 Indonesians are believed to have died in anti-Christian violence in the province of Maluku, of which Ambon is the capital, between January 1999 and February 2001. The terrorist group Laskar Jihad was responsible for most of the deaths that occurred. Their intention was to end the Christian presence in that part of Indonesia, primarily by genocidal killing and forced eviction. This campaign of terror left people uprooted, homeless and lonely with as many as half a million refugees created.

Oh Maluku
A thousand islands

Tragedy from Ambon town
All the way to Halmahera
Blood stained tears
Oh, Lord help us.

Burned from Tolebo town
All the way to Morotai
Clothed in smoke and fire
Oh Lord help us.

Oh, Oh Lord reveal Your power
To us the children of the Lord
In our refugee camps.

Oh, Oh Lord reveal Your love
To us the children of the Lord
In our grief and sorrow.
Rony Sapulete, "Maluku Tragedy"

February 11

For it has been granted to you on behalf of Christ not only to believe in him, but also to suffer for him. Philippians 1:29

George (1515)
"I am ready to die"

George, a young goldsmith in Serbia at the time of the Ottoman Empire, was burnt alive on this date in 1515. He was a handsome man whose faithful Christianity had come to the attention of some local Muslims. In a bid to convert George, they sent a *mufti* (an Islamic religious law expert) to talk with him about faith. Ably defending Christianity in a discussion with the *mufti*, George provoked the anger of those who wished to see him convert to Islam, and he was summoned by the local *qadi* (magistrate). This time he was offered great wealth if he would deny Christ. But yet again George defended his faith, and that night he was imprisoned to await a public hearing the next day.

"For the truth about Christ, I proclaim it, and I am ready to die for it," exclaimed George under examination from the *qadi* and in front of a hostile crowd. Answering him the *qadi* replied, "Because you do not want to deny Christ, you are worthy of death." George was burnt alive.

O love that wilt not let me go,
I rest my weary soul in thee:
I give thee back the life I owe,
That in thine ocean depths its flow
May richer, fuller be.

O cross that liftest up my head,
I dare not ask to fly from thee:

I lay in dust life's glory dead,
And from the ground there blossoms red
Life that shall endless be.
George Matheson (1842-1906)

---

*They will treat you this way because of my name, for they do not know
the one who sent me.* John 15:21

Twelve Egyptian Martyrs (1997)
Massacred at Worship

Twelve Egyptian Christians were killed in a horrific massacre as they
listened to a sermon in Mari Guirguis Church in the Abu Qurqas area
of al-Minya province, Egypt, on 12 February 1997. The gunmen respon-
sible, allegedly members of an extremist group, stormed the church fir-
ing bullets into the helpless congregation. A joint funeral was held the
following day for all the victims, which was opposed by the Egyptian
security forces, who wanted the families to have separate funerals. One
father refused to accept condolences saying, "My son died as a martyr. No
condolences are needed for martyrdom."

> *We offer you simple praise, Lord Jesus, for, unworthy as we are,*
> *You have defended us from the errors of the pagans, and in your mercy,*
> *You have allowed us to come to this time of suffering for the*
>   *honour of your name.*
> *As you have permitted us to share in the glory of your saints,*
> *We offer you glory and praise and we commend to your keeping our*
>   *lives and our souls.*
Lucian of Antioch (martyred 312) (see January 27)

Your throne, O God, will last for ever and ever; a scepter of justice will be the scepter of your kingdom. Psalm 45:6

Early Christians (64-67)
Persecution under Nero

Nero was the first that persecuted this doctrine... We glory in having such a man the leader in our punishment. For whoever knows him can understand that nothing was condemned by Nero unless it was something of great excellence. Tertullian (c. 160-c. 225)

The first period of Christian persecution began under the reign of the Roman Emperor Nero. In AD 64 the city of Rome was set on fire, and it was widely suspected that the emperor had ordered this himself. But Nero laid this crime upon the Christians as a pretext to persecute them. A great number were charged, not with arson but with ill-will towards humankind in general, and their deaths were turned into a form of entertainment. Some Christians were sewed up in the skins of wild beasts and then ravaged by dogs, while others were fixed to crosses and set on fire in his garden.

It was during Nero's reign that the apostle Paul was beheaded in Rome and the apostle Peter crucified. Among other martyrs of this period were Barsabas, who is deemed one of the 70 sent out by Jesus (Luke 10:1), Ananias, Bishop of Damascus, and Trophimus, a Gentile converted to Christianity by Paul.

Despite his brutal efforts, Nero was unable to quash this new and spreading faith, which only gained momentum in the face of persecution. Christians enjoyed a period of peace under Nero's successor, Vespasian, but subsequent emperors were severe persecutors of Christians and created countless martyrs. This caused the Gospel to spread beyond the boundaries of the Roman Empire as Christians were forced to flee, taking the message of Christ with them "to the ends of the earth" (Acts 1:8b).

From Pharaoh to Nero there have been many persecutors.
Let us stand brave when facing our Nebuchadnezzars.

Our blood may be spilled like the many martyrs,
But oh may we have the faith of our fathers.
Carlisle Clarke (2007)

The Lord appeared to us in the past, saying: "I have loved you with an
everlasting love; I have drawn you with unfailing kindness."
Jeremiah 31:3

Valentine (c. 269)
Wrongly Remembered for Romance

Valentine's day has become the celebration of romance and love, and
the memory of the man as a martyr has been forgotten. Valentine's life
in fact seems to have had no connection with the romantic notions with
which he is now associated, these being a later popular custom that over-
shadowed the real man. His death was part of the widespread persecution
of Christians under the Roman Emperor Claudius II. Valentine, a priest,
was arrested and sent by the emperor to the prefect of Rome, where he
refused to renounce his faith. He was consequently beaten with clubs and
afterwards beheaded near Rome in c. 269.

Batter my heart, three-person'd God; for you
As yet but knock; breathe, shine, and seek to mend;
That I may rise, and stand, o'erthrow me, and bend
Your force, to break, blow, burn, and make me new.
I, like an usurp'd town, to another due,
Labour to admit you, but O, to no end.
Reason, your viceroy in me, me should defend,
But is captived, and proves weak or untrue.
Yet dearly I love you, and would be loved fain,
But am betroth'd unto your enemy;
Divorce me, untie, or break that knot again,
Take me to you, imprison me, for I,
Except you enthrall me, never shall be free,
Nor ever chaste, except you ravish me.
John Donne (1572- 1631)

And you will be hated by all because of my name. But the one who endures to the end will be saved. Matthew 10:22 (NRSV)

Mosul Christians (2010)
Eight Killed in Ten Days

Eight Christians were killed within the space of ten days in the northern Iraqi city of Mosul in February 2010. The first, Rayan Salem Elias, was killed outside his home on the 14th by armed assailants, and the next day a Christian greengrocer, Fatukhi Munir, was gunned down in his shop in a drive-by shooting. On the 16th two Christian students, Zia Toma (21) and Ramsin Shmael (22), were on their way to the local university when gunmen opened fire on them. Zia was killed and Ramsin wounded. They had already been displaced from their homes in Baghdad by the instability there.

Another student, Wissam George (20), went missing on the 17th on his way to the institute where he was studying to be a teacher. His body was found in the street that afternoon, riddled with bullets. Sabah Yacob Dahan was found murdered on the 19th, having been abducted from his shop five days earlier. And on the 24th Aiechoa Metoka and two of his sons, Mukhlos and Basem, were killed in their home by three gunmen. They were the father and brothers of a prominent Christian leader, who had himself been kidnapped (and later released) two years previously.

These murders were part of a series of anti-Christian incidents in Mosul around this time; seven bomb attacks on Christian targets left many injured and property damaged. As a result of this outbreak of violence, hundreds of Christian families fled the city. They joined the hundreds of thousands of Iraqi Christians who have been driven out of their homes by anti-Christian hostility since the Gulf War of 1990-91.

In truth, without affliction there is no life.
Isaac of Syria (7th century)

*He died for all, that those who live should no longer live for themselves
but for him who died for them and was raised again.*
2 Corinthians 5:15

Janani Luwum (1977)
Tackled a Tyrant

Janani Luwum was the Anglican Archbishop of Uganda when, in
1971, Colonel Idi Amin overthrew the elected government and went on
to commit many atrocities in the country. Luwum was a gentle, cheerful
man who initially did not want to protest against the injustices of the
regime. But by late 1976 he felt he could no longer keep silent about the
perpetration of violence and terrorism.

Luwum started to canvass other bishops, hoping to make a united
protest to Amin. The dictator reacted by having the homes of Luwum
and the bishops ransacked. Undeterred, they sent a formal protest to
Amin on 12 February 1977, explaining that they had a duty to bear wit-
ness against injustice. On 16 February, Luwum and the bishops were
summoned to a meeting with Amin and were taken to a field outside
the Kampala Conference Centre, where the dictator's guards harassed
them. Luwum was singled out and accused of being involved in a plot to
overthrow the regime.

After a short time, the bishops were released, but Luwum was
detained. At 6.30 pm Radio Uganda announced that Luwum and two
others had been arrested, prompting the bishops and Luwum's wife to
attempt to make contact with the archbishop. At 9 pm it was announced
that he had died of internal injuries, the result of an accident. Inquiries
later gave a different story: Luwum had been shot many times. His body
was never released to his family, although it was buried in Acholi, the
village where he had grown up.

*O Lord Jesus Christ, give us a measure of Thy Spirit that we may be ena-
bled to obey Thy teaching to pacify anger, to take part in pity, to moderate
desire, to increase love, to put away sorrow, to cast away vain-glory,*

not to be vindictive, not to fear death, ever trusting our spirit to immortal God, who with Thee and the Holy Spirit liveth and reigneth world without end.

Apollonius (martyred c. 185) (see April 21)

Why, you do not even know what will happen tomorrow. What is your life? You are a mist that appears for a little while and then vanishes.
James 4:14

Ziwar Muhammad Isma'il (2003)
Killed at Work

When Christian taxi driver Ziwar Muhammad Isma'il, a convert from Islam, took a call for a fare on 17 February 2003, he could never have guessed it would be his last. Unlike many Christian converts in Iraq, Ziwar was quite open about his new faith and as a result was threatened by his relatives and others. He was arrested twice, though not charged, and also received death threats.

Ziwar worked in Zakho, in the autonomous region of Iraqi Kurdistan. Taking a call for a taxi was an everyday occurrence for him, but on this day in 2003 he was shot early in the morning at a taxi rank. His assailant approached Ziwar and challenged him to leave his new faith. At Ziwar's refusal, the gunman shot him 28 times with an automatic rifle, shouting, "Allahu Akbar" ("god is great").

Other taxi drivers gave chase, caught the killer and handed him over to the police. The murderer claimed that Muhammad, the founder of Islam, appeared to him in a dream and told him to kill Ziwar. The taxi driver left a widow and five children.

I thank you Lord Jesus Christ for your goodness in accepting me, an offering by fire for your Name's sake; for you offered yourself upon the cross as a sacrifice for the sins of all the world. I offer myself in death to you who lives and reigns with the Father and the Holy Spirit, ages without end. Amen.

Afra of Augsburg (martyred c. 304)

Since therefore Christ suffered in the flesh, arm yourselves also with the same intention (for whoever has suffered in the flesh has finished with sin), so as to live for the rest of your earthly life no longer by human desires but by the will of God. 1 Peter 4:1-2 (NRSV)

Neil Edirisinghe (2008)
Persecution in Sri Lanka

Neil was a pastor in Sri Lanka who was murdered amid a spate of violence against Christians in the country. He was killed by gunmen outside his house in Ampara on 17 February 2008. The attackers also shot and wounded his wife, who was holding their young son at the time.

On the same day a mob of about 50 people, armed with rods, gathered on the road leading to a church in Mathugama, Kaluthara District, and put up anti-Christian posters during the Sunday service. As the worshippers left the building, the mob hurled verbal abuse and threats at them and barred their way, pushing and pulling them. One man and a ten-year-old child were assaulted, and two women were manhandled and pulled by their hair.

The harassment continued the following Sunday when a crowd armed with various tools – on the pretext of cutting grass on the roadside – waited for members of the congregation to arrive for the service. They threatened the Christians and blocked them from attending. Then on 2 March ten Bible school students were attacked on their way to their college in Lunuwila, Putlam District, by a group of about ten masked men on motorcycles. The men beat the students with fists and sticks. More men in a van joined them, and one of the students was pulled into the van and beaten and kicked severely. The attackers left the injured students on the road and disappeared. Nine students required hospital treatment.

O Christ, give us patience and faith and hope as we kneel at the foot of thy Cross, and hold fast to it. Teach us by thy Cross that however ill the world may go, the Father so loved us that he spared not thee.
Charles Kingsley (1819-75)

*In God, whose word I praise, in the LORD, whose word I praise, in God
I trust; I am not afraid. What can a mere mortal do to me?*
Psalm 56: 10-11 (NRSV)

Rafaralahy (1838)
Betrayed by an Infiltrator

Rafaralahy was an active Christian during the reign of Queen Rana-
valona I on the island of Madagascar when the monarch pronounced,
in 1835, that no Malagasy should profess Christianity, a religion seen
as subversive. This began a period of persecution against the Christians.

Rafaralahy was troubled over whether to comply with the queen's
edict, but finally decided to continue in his Christian activities of pray-
ing, talking about Jesus and caring for others. Yet not all remained faithful
to Christ, and Rafaralahy was tricked by one man, Rafiakarana, who
claimed that he was still a Christian. Once he had gained the trust of
Rafaralahy he was able to discover the whereabouts and activities of the
Christian community. Motivated by the fact that he owed Rafaralahy
money and by his fear of the authorities, Rafiakarana informed on him.
Rafaralahy was immediately seized and then tortured in an attempt to
get him to reveal the names of fellow Christians. But he stood firm and
on 19 February 1838 was taken to a place called Ambohipotsy, where he
was speared to death.

*God, who foresaw your tribulation, has specially armed you to go through
it, not without pain but without stain.*
C S Lewis (1898-1963), *The Problem of Pain*

I am the resurrection and the life. The one who believes in me will live, even though they die. John 11:25

Sadoth (345)
"We shall not die but live eternally"

Sadoth, bishop of Seleucia and Ctesiphon in Persia, had a vision while on retreat with some of his clergy that indicated he would soon die a martyr's death. His predecessor, Simeon Barsabba'e, had been martyred under King Shapur II. The diocese was the most important in the Persian kingdom and also the one that suffered most from persecution.

An edict was published declaring it a capital offence to confess Christ, and when King Shapur II came to Seleucia, Bishop Sadoth and 128 others were thrown in prison, where they suffered for five months. The Persian officers exhorted them to join their religion: "Adore the sun and obey the king if you would save your lives."

Sadoth answered on behalf of the rest of them that they would only serve God, who created the sun. When the officers told them to obey the orders or suffer death, the Christians replied, "We shall not die but live eternally with God and His Son, Jesus Christ."

The king passed the death sentence on them all. Sadoth was separated from them and beheaded in the province of the Huzites.

Increase our faith, O merciful Father, that we do not swerve at any time from thy heavenly words, but augment in us hope and love, with a careful keeping of all thy commandments, that no hardness of heart, no hypocrisy, no concupiscence of the eye, no enticement of the world, do draw us away from thy obedience. Amen.
John Knox (c. 1515-72)

Though my father and mother forsake me, the Lord will receive me.
Psalm 27:10

Manche Masemola (1928)
Martyred by her Mother

When Manche found Christ through the work of foreign missionaries in the Transvaal (modern-day South Africa), her parents were greatly angered at her embracing what they saw as a deviant religion that might steal their young daughter away. They began to beat her, insisting she stop attending the local mission in their home town of Marishane, Sekhukhuneland.

Concluding that their daughter was bewitched by the Christians, her parents sought the advice of a *sangoma* (spirit-priest). He prescribed a traditional medicine, and her parents beat Manche until she drank it. But this did not stop her attending church and praying. Incensed, they took Manche, who was around 15 years old at the time, to a secluded place, where they beat her to death. Her mother denied killing the teenager and for almost four decades continued to denounce Christians. But in 1969 she was baptised a Christian and changed her name to Magdalene.

He who loveth God with all his heart feareth not death, nor punishment, nor judgment, nor hell, because perfect love giveth sure access to God. But he who still delighteth in sin, no marvel if he is afraid of death and judgment.
Thomas à Kempis (c. 1380-1471)

Only, live your life in a manner worthy of the gospel of Christ, so that, whether I come and see you or am absent and hear about you, I will know that you are standing firm in one spirit, striving side by side with one mind for the faith of the gospel, and are in no way intimidated by your opponents. For them this is evidence of their destruction, but of your salvation. And this is God's doing. Philippians 1:27-28 (NRSV)

Naimat Ahmer (1992)
A Fanatic Strikes

Naimat was a Christian teacher in Pakistan whose Muslim colleagues wanted him dismissed. They asked him what he thought of Muhammad, and he replied that as a Christian he believed that Jesus was the only way to God and to salvation. The teachers then claimed that he had insulted Muhammad, an offence that carried a mandatory death sentence under an amendment to Pakistan's controversial "blasphemy laws" in 1991. Naimat left the school temporarily, but a relative of one of his former colleagues, Farooq Ahmed, sought him out and murdered him with a butcher's knife. Ahmed said he took the law into his own hands since he considered the authorities did not respond to the claims of blasphemy against Naimat.

Many Christians accused of blasphemy in Pakistan have been killed by Muslim vigilantes intent on defending the honour of their prophet. The blasphemy laws are often used to settle personal scores, with Christians and other non-Muslims particularly vulnerable to malicious, false accusations. Naimat was 45 when he was martyred, leaving a wife and five children.

Eternal Light, shine into our hearts,
Eternal Goodness, deliver us from evil,
Eternal Power, be our support,
Eternal Wisdom, scatter the darkness of our ignorance,
Eternal Pity, have mercy on us;
That with all our heart and mind and strength

We may seek thy face and be brought by
Your infinite mercy to your holy presence;
Through Jesus Christ our Lord.
Alcuin (735-804)

February 23

To the angel of the church in Smyrna write.... Do not be afraid of what
you are about to suffer. I tell you, the devil will put some of you in prison
to test you, and you will suffer persecution for ten days. Be faithful, even
to the point of death, and I will give you life as your victor's crown.
Revelation 2:8a, 10

Polycarp (c. 155-56)
"How can I blaspheme against my King and Saviour?"

Polycarp was a disciple of the apostle John, and became bishop to
the Christians in Smyrna, a city on the western coast of Asia Minor
(modern-day Turkey), whose persecution was prophesied in the Bible
(Revelation 2:8-11).

He was betrayed at the end of his life and given into the hands of the
Roman authorities, who were in that period of history extremely hostile
to Christians. Polycarp was brought before the Roman proconsul, who
asked him to renounce his faith. He replied, "For 86 years I have been
His servant and He has done me no wrong. How can I blaspheme against
my King and Saviour?"

He was bound, stabbed with a sword and burnt at the stake. Poly-
carp's martyrdom was the first to be regularly commemorated by the
early Church.

Let us therefore become imitators of His endurance; and if we should
suffer for His name's sake, let us glorify Him. For He gave this example
to us in His own person, and we believed this.
Polycarp (martyred c. 155-56)

We know love by this, that he laid down his life for us—and we ought to lay down our lives for one another. 1 John 3:16 (NRSV)

The Forty Martyrs (320)
Frozen to Death

In the year 320, when the emperor Licinius announced that Christians in the East should give up their faith or die, 40 Christian soldiers of different nationalities stationed in Sebaste (Sivas), Lesser Armenia, refused to renounce Christ.

They were left naked on the ice of a frozen pond whilst baths of hot water were stood on the banks as a temptation to recant their faith. Most died on the first day. The youngest of them, Melito, who survived till the second day, was encouraged by his widowed mother. Only one of the soldiers could not undergo the torture, but one of the guards, who had been converted to Christianity by a dream of angels and by the heroism of those who were being tortured, took his place.

> *Flung to the heedless winds,*
> *Or on the waters cast,*
> *The martyrs' ashes, watched,*
> *Shall gathered be at last;*
> *And from that scattered dust,*
> *Around us and abroad,*
> *Shall spring a plenteous seed*
> *Of witnesses for God.*
>
> *The Father hath received*
> *Their latest living breath;*
> *And vain is Satan's boast*
> *Of victory in their death;*
> *Still, still, though dead, they speak,*
> *And, trumpet-tongued, proclaim*
> *To many a wakening land*
> *The one availing name.*

Martin Luther (1483-1546)
Translated by John A. Messenger (fl. 1843)

I can do all this through him who gives me strength. Philippians 4:13

Jane Stevens (1900)
Commitment to China

In 1900, 188 foreign missionaries and around 32,000 Chinese Christians were massacred in China during the Boxer Rebellion. The mobs of Boxers would scream *Sha kuei-tzu* ("kill the devils") as they attacked Christians. All foreigners and Christians, both those from overseas and Chinese converts, came under frequent attack by the Boxers, whose aim was to rid China of all foreign influence.

Among the martyrs were Jane Stevens, who, along with her colleagues Dr and Mrs William Millar Wilson and Mildred Clarke, was killed in a massacre at T'ai-yüan-fu, Shan-si, in 1900. They had taken refuge in the premises of the Baptist Missionary Society. The city gates were closed so that neither foreigners nor Chinese Christians could escape.

Jane, a nurse, had left England for China in 1885. She spent much of her time in T'ai-yüan-fu, where, as well as assisting in medical work, she received numerous women visitors, visited Chinese homes and taught school children. Jane struggled with her health, and during a furlough period back in England a friend had asked if she did not think a position in her home country would be easier for her. Jane replied with a look of peace and joy on her face, "I don't feel I have yet finished the work God has for me in China. I must go back. Perhaps – who knows? I may be among those who will be allowed to give their lives for the people."

> *Ah, well we know*
> *What faith and reason say, that love and power,*
> *Alike unfailing, bless us every hour:*
> *That, that is best*
> *Which God deems so;*
> *That all is good which cometh of His will;*
> *Yet "why, oh, why?" our hearts are asking still,*
> *Nor will they rest.*
> *We can but wait;*

Life's mystery deepens with the rolling years,
Life's history, hardly read through blinding tears,
Seems dark and vain;
Yet not cold Fate,
But a kind Father's hand controls our way,
And when that hand has wiped the tears away
All shall be plain.
Marshall Broomhall (1866-1937) of China Inland Mission

February 26

He called the crowd with his disciples, and said to them, 'If any want to become my followers, let them deny themselves and take up their cross and follow me. Mark 8:34 (NRSV)

Nestor (c. 251)
"With Him shall I be for evermore"

While dying by crucifixion for his faith, Nestor, bishop of Magydus in the area of Pamphylia and Phrygia, exhorted the Christians who looked on to remain firm in their faith.

Nestor was a godly man, respected by believers and pagans alike. He had realised his life was in danger, but his only concern was the church under his care. He was arrested during the reign of the Roman Emperor Decius, and a magistrate tried unsuccessfully to persuade him to renounce his faith. He was then taken to the governor, Polio, but despite threats of torture he remained firm.

Even while being tortured, Nestor still was able to give thanks to God. When asked again whether he would renounce his faith, he said, "With my Christ, I have ever been; with Him, am I now; and with Him shall I be for evermore."

We cannot learn fear of God and the basic principles of godliness, unless we are pierced by the sword of the Spirit and destroyed. It is as if God were saying that to rank among his sons our ordinary nature must be wiped out.
John Calvin (1509-64)

All these people were still living by faith when they died. They did not receive the things promised; they only saw them and welcomed them from a distance, admitting that they were foreigners and strangers on earth... they were longing for a better country – a heavenly one. Therefore God is not ashamed to be called their God, for he has prepared a city for them. Hebrews 11:13,16

Nigerian Christians (2002, 2004)
History Repeating Itself

Christians were killed at the hands of Muslim extremists in attacks on 27 February in both 2002 and 2004. The first incident happened in the town of Ilorin, Kwara state, Nigeria, where Christians were targeted after Muslims who were celebrating Eid became violent. Three Christians were murdered in the ensuing clashes.

On the same date two years later, Yelwa Muslims brought along visiting militiamen to attack the village of Ngwazam. This incident also saw three Christians martyred.

Violence against Christians in some parts of Nigeria is quite frequent, and often appears to be planned rather than spontaneous. The result is an ever-growing list of martyrs from the country, which is divided between a predominantly Muslim North and a mainly Christian South with a Middle Belt where numbers of Muslims and Christians are roughly equal.

Alleluia! Sing to Jesus! His the sceptre, His the throne.
Alleluia! His the triumph, His the victory alone.
Hark! The songs of peaceful Zion thunder like a mighty flood.
Jesus out of every nation has redeemed us by His blood.
William C Dix (1837-98)

For our light and momentary troubles are achieving for us an eternal glory that far outweighs them all. 2 Corinthians 4:17

Moises Alean Lopez (1994)
Caught up in Conflict

Moises, a 32-year-old pastor and father of two, was caught up in the conflict between the Colombian government, left-wing insurgents and right-wing paramilitaries. The country has been in this state of civil war since the 1960s, and Moises was forced on numerous occasions to entertain groups of leftist guerrillas at his small farm in the Uraba region, which was also the site of his church. In February 1994 right-wing paramilitary troops came to Moises' farm and accused him of using his religion to help support their enemy. They would not listen to Moises' explanations, shot him dead and wounded his wife.

May my work be faithful;
May my work be honest;
May my work be blessed;
May my work bless others;
May my work bless you.
May the wealth and work of the world be
Available to all for the exploitation of none.
Celtic Prayer

Be strong and courageous. Do not be afraid; do not be discouraged, for the Lord your God will be with you wherever you go. Joshua 1:9b

Agape, Chionia and Irene (304)
Sisters Slain

These martyrs were three sisters who were put in prison in Thessalonica, Greece, before being burnt to death. Initially they wanted to remain quiet about their Christian faith and chose to live in a lonely place. When they were discovered and seized, their fear gave way to boldness, and they prayed to God for strength for the trial they would undergo.

Agape was brought before the governor Dulcatius, who questioned her. She said she could not obey any laws that required the worship of idols, and Chionia replied in the same way. Since the governor could not persuade them to renounce their faith, he condemned them to death, and the two sisters were taken out and burnt. Irene, who was only 18, was forced to watch in the hope that she would give in. But the teenager refused and remained firm in her faith. She was then dragged through the streets and also burnt to death.

All the great temptations appear first in the region of the mind and can be fought and conquered there. We have been given the power to close the door of the mind. We can lose this power through disuse or increase it by use, by the daily discipline of the inner man in things which seem small and by reliance upon the word of the Spirit of truth. It is God that worketh in you, both to will and to do of His good pleasure. It is as though He said, "Learn to live in your will, not in your feelings".
Amy Carmichael (1867-1951)

March 1

Lord, there is no one like you to help the powerless against the mighty.
2 Chronicles 14: 11b

Tula Mosesa (2008)
Church Massacre

Tula, a 45-year-old father of four, was beheaded when Islamic militants attacked three churches in a strongly Muslim part of Ethiopia in early March 2008. They entered the churches in the village of Nenasebo, Bale, during Sunday worship and locked the doors behind them. Shouting "Allahu Akbar" ("god is great"), they started indiscriminately attacking men, women and children in the congregations with machetes. Tula was killed and 17 people were injured, some losing hands or arms.

A Christian minister who visited victims of the attacks said Ethiopia was being targeted by Muslim fanatics, who were "declaring underground war to clear Christianity from the land by sword". He said they aimed to Islamise Christian-majority Ethiopia and so gain control of the entire Horn of Africa.

Give us the wings of faith to rise
within the veil, and see
the saints above, how great their joys,
how bright their glories be.

Our glorious Leader claims our praise
for his own pattern given;
while the long cloud of witnesses
show the same path to heaven.
Isaac Watts (1674 – 1748)

March 2

Fight the good fight of the faith. Take hold of the eternal life to which you were called when you made your good confession in the presence of many witnesses. 1 Timothy 6:12

Shahbaz Bhatti (2011)
A Voice for the Voiceless

"As a Christian, I believe Jesus is my strength. He has given me a power and wisdom and motivation to serve suffering humanity. I follow the principles of my conscience, and I am ready to die and sacrifice my life for the principles I believe." These were the courageous words of Shahbaz Bhatti, Pakistan's Minister for Minority Affairs and its only Christian government minister at the time, just a month before he was martyred on 2 March 2011. He had received death threats because of his tireless campaigning against Pakistan's notorious "blasphemy laws" and for his support of Christian mother-of-five Aasia Bibi, who was accused and convicted under one of these laws and sentenced to death in November 2010.

Shahbaz used his high position to speak out on behalf of his persecuted Christian brothers and sisters in Pakistan, against whom the blasphemy laws are often used. He knew that his days might be numbered, but he had dedicated himself to serve Christ and His people, whatever the cost. Shahbaz had said, "I want that my life, my character, my actions speak for me and indicate that I am following Jesus Christ. Because of this desire, I will consider myself even to be more fortunate if – in this effort and struggle to help the needy, the poor, to help the persecuted and victimised Christians of Pakistan – Jesus Christ will accept the sacrifice of my life. I want to live for Christ and I want to die for Him."

Shahbaz's voice was silenced when Pakistani Taliban gunmen opened fire on his car as he left his mother's home to travel to work on 2 March 2011. But the legacy of his life is an enduring inspiration to other Pakistani Christians, including members of his own family, who are following in his footsteps.

Goodness is stronger than evil;
Love is stronger than hate;
Light is stronger than darkness;
Life is stronger than death;
Victory is ours through Him who loves us.
Archbishop Desmond Tutu (born 1931)

March 3

Come, you who are blessed by my Father; take your inheritance, the kingdom prepared for you since the creation of the world. Matthew 25:34b

Marinus (c. 262)
A Soldier's Stand

Marinus was a distinguished soldier of the Roman Empire, stationed at Caesarea in Palestine. He was about to be promoted to the post of centurion when he was denounced as a Christian by a jealous rival who wanted to receive the coveted appointment. The magistrate interrogated him and demanded he sacrifice to the gods to demonstrate his allegiance to the emperor. Marinus refused and was given three hours to decide whom he was going to serve. He was counselled by Bishop Theotecnus of Caesarea, who asked him whether he preferred his sword or the Gospel. Marinus did not hesitate in his response – the Gospel. He returned to the magistrate and reaffirmed his faith in Christ, for which he was executed.

O Heavenly Father, who hast called us by thy grace to be a colony of heaven here on earth: Deepen within us, we beseech thee, a sense of our citizenship with the saints in glory; and grant that through all the days of our pilgrimage in this world we may humbly walk with thee in the way of holiness, and faithfully care for the needs of others, till we come to thy everlasting kingdom; through the mercy of thy Son Jesus Christ our Lord.
Frank Colquhoun (1909-1997)

Who would true valour see,
Let him come hither;
One here will constant be,
Come wind, come weather
There's no discouragement
Shall make him once relent
His first avowed intent
To be a pilgrim.
John Bunyan (1628-1688), *The Pilgrim's Progress*

March 4

I have learned to be content whatever the circumstances.
Philippians 4:11b

Leonides (202)
Lost Everything

Leonides, a distinguished and respected philosopher in Alexandria, Egypt, was imprisoned and had all his property confiscated when it was discovered that he was a Christian. He was later beheaded in the persecution under the Roman emperor Septimius Severus. One of his sons, Origen, went on to become a leading theologian in the 3rd-century Egyptian church. It is said that Origen's mother hid her son's clothes to prevent him from joining his father in martyrdom.

Teach me, Lord Jesus, to live simply and love purely, like a child, and to know that You are unchanged in Your attitudes and actions toward me. Give me not to be hungering for the strange, rare and peculiar when the common, ordinary, and regular – rightly taken – will suffice to feed and satisfy the soul. Bring struggle when I need it; take away ease at Your pleasure.
Jim Elliot (1927-1956) (see January 10)

Jerusalem the golden, with milk and honey blest,
Beneath thy contemplation sink heart and voice oppressed.
I know not, O I know not, what joys await us there,
What radiancy of glory, what bliss beyond compare.
Bernard of Morlaix (fl. 1146)
Translated by John Mason Neale (1818-1866)

March 5

Yes, my soul, find rest in God; my hope comes from him. Truly he is my rock and my salvation; he is my fortress, I will not be shaken.
Psalm 62:5-6

Teuku Masrul (c. 2008)
Killed for Preaching

Teuku Masrul, an Indonesian evangelist, was attacked and killed in Banjarmasin, Kalimantan. A Bible was placed on his face by his attackers, suggesting that he was killed for preaching the Gospel.

His father, Zainuddien, a convert from Islam, had been in prison and faced many threats to his life because of his ministry to Muslims. When Teuku was killed, Zainuddien was left alone, his wife and two daughters having already died. In March 2008 Zainuddien survived an attempt to poison him. As he began to vomit blood, his Christian friends prayed, and he survived. The poisoner was so amazed at seeing prayers answered that he confessed to what he had done.

Jesus feels for thee; Jesus consoles thee; Jesus will help thee. No monarch in his impregnable fortress is more secure than the cony in his rocky burrow. The master of ten thousand chariots is not one whit better protected than the little dweller in the mountain's cleft. In Jesus the weak are strong, and the defenceless safe; they could not be more strong if they were giants, or more safe if they were in heaven. Faith gives to men on earth the protection of the God of heaven. More they cannot need, and need not wish. The conies cannot build a castle, but they avail themselves of what is there already: I cannot make myself a refuge, but Jesus has provided it, His Father has given it, His Spirit has revealed it, and lo, again tonight I enter it, and am safe from every foe.
C H Spurgeon (1834-92)

March 6

We have our hope set on the living God, who is the Saviour of all people, especially of those who believe. 1 Timothy 4:10 (NRSV)

Filipino Christians (2003)
Targeted by Islamists

In March 2003, six Christians were shot dead by rebels from the Moro Islamic Liberation Front (MILF), an Islamic separatist group on the island of Mindanao in the Philippines. Over 100 MILF rebels were stopping vehicles, one of which was a bus carrying nine men from a Christian community, along a major road. Those who could not speak the local Muslim dialect were shot, while those who could were spared.

The 12,500 strong MILF were actively targeting Filipino Christians. In another clearly anti-Christian attack that month, a bomb exploded near a cathedral in Cotabato. Amazingly no one was injured.

O Almighty Father, fountain of light and salvation, we adore thine infinite goodness in sending thy only begotten Son into the world that,

believing in him, we may not perish but have everlasting life; and we pray thee that, through the grace of his first advent to save the world, we may be ready to meet him at his second advent to judge the world; through the same Thy Son Jesus Christ our Lord.
W Walsham How (1823-97)

March 7

So in Christ Jesus you are all children of God through faith, for all of you who were baptised into Christ have clothed yourselves with Christ. There is neither Jew nor Gentile, neither slave nor free, nor is there male and female, for you are all one in Christ Jesus. Galatians 3:26-28

Perpetua and Felicitas (203)
"Stand fast in the faith and love one another"

Perpetua, a well-educated woman, was arrested with Felicitas, a slave, after they both converted to Christianity, an act banned in Carthage (in present-day Tunisia) by the Roman emperor Septimus. They were baptised before being imprisoned. Felicitas was pregnant and Perpetua, who was still nursing her baby son, was granted special permission for him to stay with her in prison. Perpetua's father begged her to renounce her new faith, and pleaded with the judge, who also tried to persuade her to change her mind, but she held firm. The two women, along with three others, were sentenced to be thrown to wild beasts in the circus. Felicitas gave birth to a healthy baby girl two days before the execution, and her daughter was adopted by a Christian woman from Carthage.

The prisoners were paraded before a jeering crowd, but they were unperturbed, laughing at the mockers for being so foolish as to deny that Jesus was the Son of God. Their jailers stripped them and tried to dress them up as pagan gods before throwing them to the animals, but they resisted. Perpetua and Felicitas were stunned and gored by a mad bull and were then killed with a sword. Perpetua's final words were, "Stand fast in the faith and love one another."

O Lord Jesus
Stretch forth your wounded hands in blessing over your people,
To heal and restore,
And to draw them to yourself and to one another in love.
Prayer from the Middle East

March 8

You endured in a great conflict full of suffering... You need to persevere so that when you have done the will of God, you will receive what he has promised. Hebrews 10:32b, 36

Archbishop Paulos Faraj Rahho (2008)
Endured Harassment

It seems that Iraqi Archbishop Paulos Faraj Rahho was prepared for martyrdom. Before his death he had said, "We Christians of Mesopotamia are used to religious persecution and pressures by those in power. After Constantine, persecution ended only for Western Christians whereas in the East threats continued. Even today we continue to be a Church of martyrs."

He was kidnapped in February 2008 by armed gunmen who ambushed his car just after he had led a church service in Mosul. Rahho's driver and two companions were killed during the abduction. He was put in the boot, where he managed to pull out his mobile phone and call his church, instructing them not to pay any ransom demands. Rahho's body was found in a shallow grave the following month.

The kidnapping and murder of Iraqi Christians and Church leaders became a regular occurrence in the years following the fall of Saddam Hussein in 2003; Islamist extremists did not hide the fact that they were trying to "cleanse" the country of any trace of Christianity by violence, threats and intimidation.

Rahho had been outspoken about the persecution of Iraqi Christians, and in 2006 he raised concerns about the inclusion of some aspects of sharia in the new Iraqi constitution. The Archbishop had endured harassment and threats; on one occasion he was accosted by gunmen in the street, but he walked on, daring them to shoot him, and in 2004 he was forced to watch as his official residence was set ablaze.

Rahho served the Christian community in Mosul for the majority of his life. He opened an orphanage for children with disabilities and became archbishop in 2001. Rahho was described as a warm, humble and compassionate man who courageously defended his flock. He died aged 65.

May Jesus Christ, the king of glory, help us to make the right use of all the myrrh [suffering] that God sends, and to offer to him the true incense of our hearts; for his Name's sake. Amen.
Johann Tauler (1300-1361)

March 9

Let us hold unswervingly to the hope we profess, for he who promised is faithful. Hebrews 10:23

Mehr Khan (1915)
Killed and Son Kidnapped

Mehr was in charge of a small Christian mission hospital in Thal (now part of Pakistan) near the border with Afghanistan when he was murdered by raiders who also kidnapped his young son. The hospital served the needs of the tribal people as well as Afghan patients who came from across the border in search of healing. Mehr was killed in March 1915, and his five-year-old son was carried off by the raiding party. Outwardly it appeared he had been attacked by the clan of a former watchman, whom he had had to dismiss for irregularities. However, when the raiders attacked they told Mehr that his life would be saved if he would say the Islamic creed. He refused to do this, and he died professing faith in Jesus Christ.

Because of pressure from the authorities, a tribal council (*jirga*) convicted the outlaws for this crime and enforced the release of the kidnapped son. The culprits were handed over to the British authorities and sent as prisoners to the Andaman Islands. The clan also had to pay some compensation to Mehr Khan's heirs.

God you are with me and you can help me;
You were with me when I was taken, and you are with me now.
You strengthen me.

The God I serve is everywhere - in heaven and earth and the sea,
But he is above them all, for all live in him:
All were created by him, and by him only do they remain.

I will worship only the true God; you will I carry in my heart
No one on earth shall be able to separate me from you.
Quirinus of Siscia (martyred c. 308)

March 10

The salvation of the righteous comes from the Lord; he is their stronghold in time of trouble. Psalm 37:39

K'pa Lot (2010)
Beaten to Death

Vietnamese Christian K'pa Lot died on 11 March 2010 after nearly three years in prison. He had been jailed on 20 May 2007 because of his public support for religious liberty in the country, where Christians face many restrictions. Lot, a married father of two, was held in isolation and suffered daily beatings. He was taken to hospital two days before he died, apparently from internal bleeding caused by the violence. His grieving family could barely recognise him because he was so swollen and bruised. They were not allowed to take his body home for a proper burial.

Christians in Vietnam, particularly those associated with unregistered house churches, face severe persecution and restrictions on their activities. The most heavily affected are from the minority-ethnic Degar community, who live in the central highlands of Vietnam. At around the time of Lot's death, at least 300 Degar Christians were in prison for their faith.

Oh! That I might repose on Thee!
Oh! that Thou wouldest enter into my heart and inebriate it, that I may forget my ills, and embrace Thee, my sole good!

What art Thou to me? In Thy pity, teach me to utter it.

Or what am I to Thee that Thou demandest my love, and if I give it not,
   art wroth with me, and threatenest me with grievous woes?

Is it then a slight woe to love Thee not?

Oh! For Thy mercies' sake, tell me, O Lord my God, what Thou art unto
   me.

Say unto my soul, I am thy salvation.

So speak, that I may hear.

Behold, Lord my heart is before Thee;

open Thou the ears thereof, and say unto my soul, I am thy salvation.

After this voice let me haste, and take hold on Thee.

Hide not Thy face from me.

Let me die – lest I die – only let me see Thy face.

Augustine of Hippo (354-430)

March 11

*I appeal to you therefore, brothers and sisters, by the mercies of God,
to present your bodies as a living sacrifice, holy and acceptable to God,
which is your spiritual worship.* Romans 12:1 (NRSV)

Eulogius of Cordoba (859)
Encouraged Persecuted Christians

In 850 the North African Muslims who occupied Cordoba in Spain
began to persecute Christians. Eulogius, a well-educated priest, was
arrested, and from prison wrote a letter of encouragement to other Chris-
tians who were also behind bars. He was released and in the next seven
years wrote a record of Christians who suffered, called "Memorandum
of the Saints". There had been a lot of anti-Muslim agitation, and the
Church council at Cordoba warned Christians against behaviour that
was provocative.

Eulogius was named Archbishop of Toledo but was never consecrated; he
was arrested again for sheltering Leocritia, a convert from Islam. When he
was brought before the magistrate he refused to renounce his faith and was

beheaded on 11 March in 859, four days before Leocritia (see 15 March). They were buried in the cathedral of Oviedo.

Lord God, graciously comfort and care for all who are imprisoned, hungry, thirsty, naked and miserable; also all widows, orphans, sick and sorrowing. In brief, give us our daily bread, so that Christ may abide in us and we in him forever, and that with him we may worthily bear the name of Christian.
Martin Luther (1483-1546)

March 12

I know that my redeemer lives, and that in the end he will stand on the earth. And after my skin has been destroyed, yet in my flesh I will see God. Job 19:25-26

Alexander Puasa and his Daughter (2002) Kidnapped and Killed

Alexander, 46, was killed along with his 15-year-old daughter in Jakarta, Indonesia, during a period of serious violence in the country. Both father and daughter disappeared in March 2002, most likely kidnapped by Islamic extremists. Their bodies were recovered several days after they were taken. One reason put forward for their deaths was that extremists wanted to derail the peace negotiations between Muslims and Christians that sought to end the communal violence.

Our life is seed, sown in the earth to rise again in the world to come,
Where we will be renewed by Christ in immortal life.
I did not frame this body, nor will I destroy it;
God you gave me life, you will also restore it.
Jonas of Beth-Iasa (martyred c. 327)

I truly understand that God shows no partiality, but in every nation anyone who fears him and does what is right is acceptable to him.
Acts 10:34b-35 (NRSV)

Elder Pak Kwanjoon (1945)
A Bold Activist

Born in Korea in 1875, Pak Kwanjoon studied Buddhism until he became a Christian in 1905. In 1923 he founded a church and became burdened with the desire to speak out against the Japanese religion of Shintoism. The police became aware of this, and detectives started to follow him. Eventually he chose to go to Japan and protest to the Imperial *Diet* (national legislature) of Japan, along with his son and Miss Ahn Eesok.

In Japan they visited prominent church leaders and spoke about how Christians suffered in Korea, which was then under Japanese control. They entered the *Diet* on 21 March 1939 with appeal leaflets hidden in their clothing. Four hundred members were assembled for the *Diet* and were discussing the religious law when the three Christians, who were sitting in the gallery, threw their leaflets down. The leaflets entreated the Japanese government to stop enforcing shrine worship, to make Christianity the religion of Japan and to stop persecuting Christians. The three Christians were jailed for three months and sent back to Korea. Constantly under police surveillance, Elder Pak was urged by his son to flee to Manchuria, but he replied, "I'm working for the Korean church and must stay."

In 1941 he was put in prison for opposing the law for the control of religions. He died in the Pyenyang penitentiary on 13 March 1945, aged 70.

We must, furthermore, protest the notion of manifest destiny that permits our nation to do anything it chooses. For if we insist on walking down this road, then at some point - as God is God, the God in whose eyes there is real good and real evil - we who have trampled so completely on all of God's amazing gifts to this country are going to wake up and find that

He cares very much what we do. We must not suppose that we are playing only intellectual and political games. If God exists, and if He judges good and evil, then we must realize that those who trample on His great gifts will one day know His judgment. The scriptures bear solemn witness to this. Our nation is not immune.
Francis Schaeffer (1912-1984), *Who is for Peace?*

March 14

We live by faith, not by sight. 2 Corinthians 5:7

Larry and Jean Elliot (2004)
"Absent from the body, present with the Lord"

After only 23 days in Iraq, Larry and Jean, veteran missionaries who felt called to serve God in this war-torn country, were killed in a drive-by shooting. This was a dangerous time for Christians in Iraq, who were frequently targeted by militants who associated them with the US-led Western forces.

The Elliots went to Iraq after 25 years' service in poverty-stricken Honduras, where many local pastors had been nurtured by Larry's mentoring. When friends and family voiced their concerns about the couple getting killed in Iraq, Larry would thoughtfully answer – in the words of Paul the apostle – "Absent from the body, present with the Lord" (2 Corinthians 5:8).

Larry and Jean, along with fellow Christian workers, David and Carrie McDonnall and Karen Watson, were attacked in March 2004. They had been searching for sites for a water purification project near the city of Mosul, and as they sat together in their car, a group of gunmen drove by and fired at them with AK-41 rifles. Only Carrie walked away alive.

The Lord rewards faithfulness above fruitfulness, which puts us all on the same footing, whether famous for our effectiveness or unknown in our faithfulness.
John Piper

God has said, "Never will I leave you; never will I forsake you."
Hebrews 13:5b

Leocritia (859)
Brave Convert

Conversion to Christianity was punishable by death in Spain during the period of Islamic rule. Despite this, Leocritia secretly converted to Christianity. Her parents, who were wealthy Muslims, were strongly against this, and, as their opposition intensified, Leocritia fled the family home. A kind priest, Eulogius (see March 11), gave her shelter, for which he was put on trial. When questioned, he explained that it was his Christian duty to help the destitute, and that if the judge were impoverished, he would do the same for him. Leocritia was beheaded on 15 March 859, four days after the execution of Eulogius.

O God, I am Mustafah, the tailor, and I work at the shop of Muhammad Ali. The whole day long I sit and pull the needle and thread through the cloth. I am attached to you and I follow you. When the thread tries to slip away from the needle it becomes tangled up and must be cut so that it can be put back in the right place. O God, help me to follow you wherever you may lead me. For I am really only Mustafah, the tailor and I work at the shop of Muhammad Ali on the great square.
Prayer of a Muslim Convert

Rejoice that your names are written in heaven. Luke 10:20b

Madobe Abdi (2010)
Hit-listed by Militants

Madobe, a Christian convert from Islam, was the leader of an underground church in the village of Mahaday, near Jowhar, in the strongly

Islamic nation of Somalia. His name was on a list of people suspected of being Christians who were sought by Islamist militant group al-Shabaab. Madobe managed to evade a kidnapping attempt by al-Shabaab on 2 March 2010, but he did not escape their clutches for long. Less than two weeks later, on 15 March, he was shot dead. The militants are reported to have said that his body must not be buried but instead "left to the dogs" as a warning to other Christians in Somalia. Speaking days after the murder, al-Shabaab's Sheikh Ali Hussein said, "We aim to get rid of the barbaric and non-Islamic culture in the country."

There are very few Christians in Somalia, where converts from Islam live in great peril. Many have been murdered by Somali Muslim radicals.

Blessed are you Lord, and may your Son's name be blessed forevermore,
I can see what those who persecute me cannot;
On the other side of this river there is a multitude
Waiting to received my soul and carry it to glory.
Sabas the Goth (martyred c. 372)

March 17

I looked, and there before me was a great multitude that no one could count, from every nation, tribe, people and language, standing before the throne and before the Lamb. They were wearing white robes and were holding palm branches in their hands. And they cried out in a loud voice: "Salvation belongs to our God, who sits on the throne, and to the Lamb."
Revelation 7:9-10

Christians in Pakistan (2002)
International Church Bombed

A grenade attack upon the Protestant International Church in Islamabad on 17 March 2002 killed four Christians. The church was mainly attended by foreign diplomats and their families, and most consider this to have been an anti-Western as well as anti-Christian attack. However, quite a number of Pakistani, Iranian and Afghan Christians also regularly worshipped at the church, some of them from amongst the most influential sections of Pakistani Christian society.

Four of the people killed in the blasts were: Anwar Baizar, an Afghan Christian; Rabia Edward, a Pakistani woman; and Barbara Green and Kristen Wormsley, an American mother and daughter. The fifth victim was believed to be a Pakistani man, and there is speculation that he was in fact the bomber, who may have deliberately killed himself as part of a planned suicide attack. Seven others were injured.

O Lord, in your great mercy, keep us from forgetting what you have suffered for us in body and soul. May we never be drawn by the cares of this life from Jesus our Friend and Saviour, but daily may we live nearer his cross.
Captain Hedley Vicars (1826-55)

March 18

You, however, know all about my teaching, my way of life, my purpose, faith, patience, love, endurance, persecutions, suffering – what kinds of things happened to me ... the persecutions I endured.
2 Timothy 3:10-11

Alexander (251)
Worn out by Suffering

Alexander, bishop of Cappadocia (in modern-day Turkey), was imprisoned from 204 to 211 for his faith. Upon his release he went on a pilgrimage to Jerusalem, where the aged bishop, Narcissus, pressured him to stay and become his assistant and designated successor. Alexander, who developed a famous theological library in Jerusalem, was tortured during the persecution by Roman emperor Decius but came out alive. Tradition says that he was eventually thrown to wild beasts, but that they refused to maul him and instead licked his feet and footprints in the sand. Worn out by his sufferings, he died in jail in the Roman city of Caesarea, on the Mediterranean coast of modern-day Israel, in 251.

Lord and Master of our Lives,
Take from us the spirit
of laziness, half-heartedness,

selfish ambition and idle talk.
Give us rather the spirit
of integrity, purity of heart,
humility, faithfulness and love.
Lord and King,
help us to see our own errors,
and not to judge our neighbours;
for your mercy's sake.
Syrian Orthodox Liturgy

March 19

For, as I have often told you before and now tell you again even with tears, many live as enemies of the cross of Christ. Philippians 3:18

Lutheran Pastors (1918-19)
Persecuted by Bolsheviks

After the Russian Revolution of 1917, the Church in Bolshevik Russia suffered greatly. In the spring of 1917 the nations on the western border of Russia began to declare their independence. Finland led the way, but the Baltic states such as Latvia found breaking away too difficult, as they had been the scene of many Bolshevik battlefields.

Under Bolshevik control an organised persecution of the Lutheran church began. During 1918 and 1919 eight Lutheran pastors were martyred in the city of Riga, capital of Latvia. Twenty-three more were killed in the countryside. Fortunately for the Church, the situation stabilised in May 1919 after the rebels and German volunteer forces drove out the Bolsheviks.

Who are these of dazzling brightness,
clothed in God's own righteousness?
These, whose robes of purest whiteness,
shall their lustre still possess,
still untouched by time's rude hand?
Whence came all this glorious band?

These are they who have contended
for their Saviour's honour long,
wrestling on till life was ended,
following not the sinful throng;
these who well the fight sustained,
triumph through the Lamb have gained.
Heinrich Theobald Schenk (1656-1727)
Translated by Frances Elizabeth Cox (1812-1897)

March 20

Those the LORD has rescued will return. They will enter Zion with singing; everlasting joy will crown their heads. Gladness and joy will overtake them, and sorrow and sighing will flee away. Isaiah 51:11

Minka Hanskamp and Margaret Morgan (1975) Held Hostage

Minka and Margaret nursed leprosy patients in southern Thailand at a time when Muslim liberation militias were fighting against government troops to try and gain independence for predominantly Muslim provinces. The seasoned missionaries, from Holland and Wales respectively, were unexpectedly abducted by Islamic extremists on their way to a clinic in Pujud town on 20 April 1974. Shortly after, their mission agency got news that a ransom demand was being made on the women's lives. Negotiations were tried, but failed. Soon the abductors were demanding that the US withdraw support from Israel; the gang issued a statement saying that the women would not be released unless the "Christian world stop any support to Israel against the Palestinian people." Within a few months, letters from the two women stopped coming.

In March 1975 an informer came forward to say that both women had been shot. He reported that as they were about to die they had asked, "Give us a little time to read and pray."

Proof of this story came later that month when the skeletons of Minka and Margaret were found in the jungle. To the astonishment of the Christians attending their funeral, an unexpected number of people asked to know more about the Christianity of the women.

A seed of rice, one grain, cannot become a lot
Unless it is planted in the ground and there disintegrates.

Then only can it sprout and bring forth many grains,
We men are like that, too, We men are like that too.

The one who clings to life, who counts his own life dear,
Cannot receive new life from God, He always stays alone.

But he who will not love or count his own life dear.
That man will get new life from God and live for evermore.
Malay Christian song from south Thailand

March 21

You are the light of the world. A town built on a hill cannot be hidden.
Matthew 5:14

Liibaan Ibraahim Xasan (1994)
A Distinctive Life

Liibaan was a Somali Christian who was ambushed by two Muslim extremists when walking to work in Mogadishu on 21 March 1994. He was shot at close range and died within minutes. He is thought to have been targeted because of his widely-known Christian activities in the strongly Islamic city. The year before his death, Islamic radicals had criticised him in newspaper articles.

When Liibaan first received a New Testament after his conversion from Islam, he said it was the most precious gift he had ever been given. His wife too became a Christian and was baptised. At the hospital where he worked as a nurse, staff noticed a difference in the way he treated the wounded by not discriminating against anyone because of tribe or clan. He was completely open about his faith, witnessing boldly to Christ, and was involved in the conversion of other Somali Muslims to Christianity. His home had become a place for Christian meetings and pastoring other Christians in the city. Liibaan was just 25 years old when he died.

I care not where I go, or how I live, or what I endure so that I may save souls. When I sleep I dream of them; when I awake they are first in my thoughts… no amount of scholastic attainment, of able and profound exposition of brilliant and stirring eloquence can atone for the absence of a deep impassioned sympathetic love for human souls.
David Brainerd (1718-47)

March 22

The blameless spend their days under the LORD's care, and their inheritance will endure forever. Psalm 37:18

Maximilian (c. 295)
God's Soldier

The son of a North African veteran of the Roman army, the youthful Maximilian was brought before a court to be enrolled as a soldier but refused on account of his Christian faith. Maximilian told the proconsul Dio, "My army is the army of God, and I cannot fight for this world."

The proconsul said that there were other Christians serving in the army. Maximilian replied, "That is their business. I am a Christian too, and I cannot serve." His father was asked to correct his son but he answered, "He knows what he believed, and he won't change his mind."

When Maximilian was threatened with death if he did not renounce his faith, he replied, "I shall not die. When I leave this earth I shall live with Christ my Lord."

He was sentenced to death, said farewell to his family and friends, and was beheaded, aged 21, around the year 295.

Faith is rest, not toil. It is the giving up all the former weary efforts to do or feel something good, in order to induce God to love and pardon; and the calm reception of the truth so long rejected, that God is not waiting

for any such inducements, but loves and pardons of His own goodwill, and is showing that goodwill to any sinner who will come to Him on such a footing, casting away his own poor performances or goodnesses, and relying implicitly upon the free love of Him who so loved the world that He gave His only-begotten Son.
Horatius Bonar (1808-89)

March 23

Whoever has ears, let them hear. Matthew 11:15

Zia Nodrad (1988)
"I have counted the cost and am ready to die for Christ"

Zia Nodrad was a remarkable Afghan Christian who first encountered Jesus by listening to Radio Voice of the Gospel in order to improve his English. He was blind and a highly gifted linguist, fluent in several languages including English, Russian and German. He knew the Quran by heart and even won a gold medal from Saudi Arabia at a Quran recitation contest, when the Communist government sent him to represent Afghanistan.

When Zia first disclosed his interest in the Christian faith it was pointed out to him that this could mean death under sharia. But he replied, "I have counted the cost and am ready to die for Christ, since Christ has already died for me on the Cross."

He immersed himself deeply in the Word of God and was involved in translating the Bible into his mother tongue, Dari. He was an able leader of other believers (who could not publicly proclaim themselves Christians), encouraging them in their faith and understanding of the Gospel. In 1985 he fled Afghanistan to Pakistan, where he was a pillar and strength to the small Afghan Christian community in exile. In 1988 he was invited by the *mujahidin* of the Islamist group Hezb-e Islami to discuss ways to help disabled people in the refugee camps. But this was a trap, and he was shot dead by them on 23 March. It was reported that he was cruelly tortured and even had his tongue cut out before he was killed - because he remained faithful to Christ.

Let Him lead the blindfold onward,
Love needs not to know;
Children whom the Father leadeth,
Ask not where to go.
Thou the path be all unknown,
Over moors and mountains lone.
Gerhard Teerstegen (1697-1769)

March 24

Speak up for those who cannot speak for themselves, for the rights of all who are destitute. Speak up and judge fairly; defend the rights of the poor and needy. Proverbs 31:8-9

Oscar Romero (1980)
"I don't believe in death without resurrection"

Oscar's life was threatened many times because he spoke out against the injustices perpetrated by the regime of his birthplace, El Salvador in Central America. The country was governed by a small elite who ruled through money and violence. Oscar was a man of prayer who was troubled by the violence of the regime and also by the Marxist beliefs of the Salvadorian resistance movement. For a long while he did not make any protest, but within a year of becoming archbishop of San Salvador he underwent a transformation. He started to speak out against the regime's injustices and gave support to the resistance, much to the government's displeasure. Two months before he died he wrote in a Mexican newspaper:

> "My life has been threatened many times. I have to confess that, as a Christian, I don't believe in death without resurrection. If they kill me, I will rise again in the Salvadorian people... As a Shepherd I am obliged by Divine Law to give my life for those I love, for the entire Salvadorian people, including those who threaten to assassinate me. If they should go so far as to carry out their threats, I want you to know that I now offer my blood to God for justice and the resurrection of El Salvador..."

On 24 March 1980, just as he finished preaching, a shot rang out. He fell and died on the spot.

You don't have a soul. You are a soul. You have a body.
C S Lewis (1898-1963), *Mere Christianity*

Place me like a seal over your heart, like a seal on your arm; for love is as strong as death, its jealousy unyielding as the grave. It burns like blazing fire, like a mighty flame. Song of Solomon 8:6

Concordia (c.64)
Apostle's Wife

Concordia was the wife of the apostle Peter, and she accompanied him on his missionary travels. Her mother had been miraculously healed by Jesus: "He touched her hand and the fever left her, and she got up and began to wait on him." (Matthew 8:15)

Concordia was martyred before Peter during the persecution under Emperor Nero in Rome and, according to tradition, he saw her being taken away to be killed. The early Christian writer Clement of Alexandra related that Peter was "delighted" because "she had been called and was going home". He called out to her "in a consolatory and encouraging voice," exhorting her to "remember the Lord".

Peter was also martyred under Nero, having been arrested and imprisoned with the apostle Paul. He was severely flogged before being crucified with his head downwards (see June 29).

O Truth who art Eternity! And Love who art Truth! And Eternity who art Love! Thou art my God, to Thee do I sigh night and day. Thee when I first knew, Thou liftedst me up, that I might see there was what I might see, and that I was not yet such as to see. And Thou didst beat back the weakness of my sight, streaming forth Thy beams of light upon me most strongly, and I trembled with love and awe.
Augustine of Hippo (354-430)

I tell you, whoever publicly acknowledges me before others, the Son of Man will also acknowledge before the angels of God. Luke 12:8

George (1437)
Defending Jesus

George, a 30-year-old Bulgarian, served in the army of the Ottoman Turks at the time when they had established themselves in Europe. One day he overheard some soldiers making fun of Jesus Christ. Jumping to the defence of his Saviour, he found himself suddenly under attack from the men. He was tied up, brought before a governor and twice asked to retract his words. But when he refused to stop witnessing for Christ, he was beaten again and imprisoned. The next day he was brought before the religious leaders of the area, who, encouraged by an angry mob, sentenced him to death by fire. George was burned to death on 26 March 1437 for defending his Lord.

Almighty God, our Heavenly Father, Whose mercies are new unto us every morning, and Who, though we have in no wise deserved Thy goodness, dost abundantly provide for all our wants of body and soul: Give us, we pray Thee, Thy Holy Spirit, that we may heartily acknowledge Thy merciful goodness and serve Thee in willing obedience; through Jesus Christ, Thy Son, our Lord. Amen.
The Common Service Book of the Lutheran Church, 1917

I pray to you, LORD, in the time of your favour; in your great love, O God, answer me with your sure salvation. Rescue me from the mire, do not let me sink; deliver me from those who hate me, from the deep waters.
Psalm 69:13-14

Irshad Masih (2005)
In the Firing Line

Irshad was killed as he tried to protect some children who were playing in the churchyard when four militants opened fire after an Easter Sunday morning service on 27 March 2005. Seven other Christians were injured in the attack outside Victory Church in the village of Khamba, Punjab, Pakistan.

It was just after 10.30 am and the congregation was coming out of the building when, suddenly, members of a local clan opened fire in a sustained attack that lasted half an hour. As men rushed to save the playing children, 22-year-old Irshad was shot through the head and killed outright. Others who sustained injuries were Arshad Masih, Imran Masih, Ismaeel Masih, Jamil Masih, Naeem Masih, Niamat Masih and Pervez Masih. Though all sharing a very common surname for Pakistani Christians they are not directly related to one another.

The attackers all belonged to a local Muslim clan known as the Dogars, who were trying to claim land that had been allocated to the Christian community. They had previously demolished some Christian graves with a tractor, insisting that the Christians relinquish the graveyard and adjoining church property.

O God and Father of all, whom the whole heavens adore: let the whole earth also worship you, all kingdoms obey you, all tongues confess and bless you, and the sons of men love you and serve you in peace; through Jesus Christ our Lord.
Eric Milner-White (1884-1963), quoted in Philip Law,
Seasons of Devotion

You intended to harm me, but God intended it for good to accomplish what is now being done, the saving of many lives. Genesis 50:20

Sudanese Christians (1983-2005)
Civil War

During the Second Sudanese Civil War of 1983-2005, the strongly Muslim North fought to impose a version of sharia on the non-Muslim, mainly Christian South. The South had been granted autonomy in a peace treaty that ended the First Sudanese Civil War of 1955-72, but violence broke out again in 1983 when Northern rule was re-introduced in the South.

Over two million people, many of whom were Southern Christians, were killed in the fighting, died of disease or starved to death. Christians were frequently harassed by the regime; pastors were arrested, homes and church buildings were demolished, and there were credible reports of massacres, kidnappings and forced labour. Children were abducted and either conscripted to the army or subjected to an Islamisation process by Islamic education groups. At least five million people were displaced by the violence.

But the influx of displaced Southerners into the North led to the establishing of many active churches in areas with previously unreached peoples. The North's campaign to Islamise the South failed; in fact the Church in the South grew massively during the conflict, especially among the Dinka and Nuer peoples.

A Comprehensive Peace Agreement was signed in 2005; one of the provisions of this stated that sharia would have no jurisdiction over non-Muslims anywhere in the country. In 2011 a referendum was held in which the South voted overwhelmingly to secede from the North. South Sudan thus became an independent nation, heralding a new dawn of peace for the long-suffering people. But the prospects for Christians in the North were ominous as President Omar Hassan al-Bashir declared plans to adopt an entirely Islamic constitution and strengthen sharia there, making the North an official "Muslim state".

We are exhausted with living
the days of Cain,
the tower of Babel
and the oppression
and attempted extermination
of the sons of Jacob.

Come to update us, Lord,
to your civilisation of love,
of justice and peace,
of grace and mutual forgiveness,
of solidarity and reconciliation.

May this Jubilee of your Birth
bring you to life in our country
and into the life of each one of us.
It is from the depth of misery
that we cry out to you.
Bring hope into this misery.
Be our Saviour, be our Brother,
Be in all things.
Thank you, Lord Jesus.
Amen.
From "A Prayer for the Year 2000", Gabriel Zubeir Wako,
Archbishop of Khartoum, Sudan (born 1941)

March 29

If you suffer for doing good and you endure it, this is commendable before
God. To this you are called, because Christ suffered for you, leaving you
an example, that you should follow in his steps. 1 Peter 2:20b-21

Jonah and Berikjesu (327)
Horrific Deaths in Persia

After they were arrested for encouraging Christians who were in
prison, Jonah was dismembered, scalded and crushed to death in a press,

and Berikjesu, after having long splinters driven into his flesh, was killed by having burning pitch poured down his throat. Each had been tortured and told that the other had renounced his faith, but they would not yield.

Also known as Jonas and Barichisius, they died in the persecution of the Sassanid Persian king Shapur II.

The God and Father of our Lord Jesus Christ open all our eyes, that we may see that blessed hope to which we are called; that we may altogether glorify the only true God and Jesus Christ; whom he has sent down to us from heaven; to whom with the Father and the Holy Spirit be rendered all honour and glory to all eternity.
Bishop John Jewel (1522-71)

March 30

All have sinned and fall short of the glory of God, and all are justified freely by his grace through the redemption that came by Christ Jesus.
Romans 3:23-24

Lai Manping (1993)
Beaten by Church Members

In March 1993, eight Public Security Bureau (PSB) officers broke up a meeting of a house church (unregistered church) in Taoyuan, Shaanxi Province, China, and beat church members with truncheons and electric batons. The officers singled out five of the congregation who had travelled from another area in order to attend the meeting. They then forced the 26 remaining church members to beat the five visiting Christians. The next day the officers wanted to take the quintet to the regional PSB centre but the men and women had been beaten so violently that the regional command would not accept them. One of the men, Lai Manping, was in a very bad condition. The authorities released him eight days after the beating, but he died the following day as a result of his injuries.

*They tell me I must bruise
 The rose's leaf,*

Ere I can keep and use
  Its fragrance brief.

They tell me I must break
  The skylark's heart,
Ere her cage song will make
  The silence start.

They tell me love must bleed,
  And friendship weep,
Ere in my deepest need
  I touch that deep.

Must it always be so
  With precious things?
Must they be bruised and go
  With beaten wings?

Ah, yes! by crushing days,
  By caging nights, by scar
Of thorn and stony ways,
  These blessings are!
Annie Johnson Flint (1866-1932) from *Streams in the Desert*

March 31

On my account you will be brought before governors and kings as witnesses to them and to the Gentiles. But when they arrest you, do not worry about what to say or how to say it. At that time you will be given what to say, for it will not be you speaking, but the Spirit of your Father speaking through you. Matthew 10:18-20

Acacius (3rd century)
A Witty Witness

Acacius was a third-century priest who provided support to the Christian community in Antioch during persecution under the Roman emperor

Decius. Acacius encouraged Christians to pray for the emperor, but he would not participate in emperor worship. He was arrested, tried and sentenced to death, although the priest's wit and wisdom at his trial reportedly made the emperor smile when he read a transcript of the proceedings. Acacius' faithful witness so impressed the governor, Maximus, that he became a Christian, for which he also was killed.

Lord teach me your wisdom
Let all my members truly belong to you
In this time of sacrifice.
You alone are the true God, for you alone
I will suffer and die.
To die for you is to live.
Arcadius of Caesarea (fl. 300)

April 1

Very truly, I tell you, servants are not greater than their master, nor are messengers greater than the one who sent them. John 13:16 (NRSV)

Chhirc Taing and Minh Tinh Voan (1975) Death Foretold

During a Cambodian Evangelical church's celebration of communion at Chhirc's home one Good Friday, one member uttered some prophetic words: "I believe that for some of us there will be death." They were reading from John 13 and Chhirc, following Jesus' example at the Last Supper, was washing the feet of all the others in attendance.

A few years later, in April 1975 – shortly after the fall of Phnom Penh to the Communist organisation the Khmer Rouge – Chhirc and another Christian, Minh Tinh Voan, were walking along a road in the town of Neak Long. Everyone with them was fearful, but the two men comforted and encouraged them all and gave out Christian literature. They were spotted by soldiers and suddenly surrounded. The soldiers tied their hands behind their backs, and clubbed them to death with a hoe.

I have no home but the world,
no bed but the ground
no food but what Providence sends me
from day to day,
and no other object but to do your will
and suffer,
if need be, for the glory of Jesus Christ
and for the eternal happiness
of those who believe in his name.
Francis de Capillas (martyred 1648)

April 2

Anyone who resolves to do the will of God will know whether the teach-ing is from God or whether I am speaking on my own. John 7:17

Pierre Chanel (1841)
Lasting Legacy

Frenchman Pierre went to the Pacific in 1836 and was killed on Futuna Island three years after his arrival, becoming the first martyr of Oceania. He had gone there with two others, and they were initially well received. But when the local ruler Niuliki's son became a Christian and was baptised, the chief became angry with Pierre. Furthermore, the missionary's good standing and evident popularity scared Niuliki. Soon after the baptism, Pierre was clubbed to death in April 1841 by Niuliki's warriors. Within five months of his death the entire island had become Christian.

All our difficulties are only platforms for the manifestation of His grace,
power and love.
Hudson Taylor (1832-1905)

For all the saints, who from their labours rest,
Who Thee by faith before the world confessed,
Thy name, O Jesus, be forever blest:
Alleluia! Alleluia!

Thou wast their rock, their fortress, and their might,
Thou Lord, their captain in the well-fought fight;
Thou, in the darkness drear, their one true light:
Alleluia! Alleluia!
W Walsham How (1823-1897)

April 3

What, then, shall we say in response to these things? If God is for us, who can be against us? Romans 8:31

Irfan Masih (2009)
Just a Boy

When Taliban militants launched an offensive against a Christian community in Taiser Town, near Karachi, Pakistan, in April 2009, an 11-year-old boy called Irfan Masih was shot in the head. He died five days later, leaving his family devastated.

The violence started after the Taliban defaced the Christians' homes and churches with graffiti slogans such as "Long Live Taliban" and "Be prepared to pay *jizya* (Islamic tax on non-Muslims) or embrace Islam". The residents cleaned off the graffiti and staged a peaceful demonstration in the hope of attracting local government attention to their need for protection. During the demonstration, the Taliban attacked. Homes, shops and Bibles were set on fire, several women were sexually assaulted, and dozens of people were beaten with clubs, whips and iron rods. Three people were seriously injured.

The attack happened at a time of intense violence between the Pakistani military and the Taliban, who were fighting to establish a form of sharia across the country.

There let the way appear, steps unto Heav'n;
All that Thou sendest me, in mercy giv'n;
Angels to beckon me nearer, my God, to Thee.
Nearer, my God, to Thee, nearer to Thee!

There in my Father's home, safe and at rest,
There in my Saviour's love, perfectly blest;
Age after age to be nearer, my God, to Thee.
Nearer, my God, to Thee, nearer to Thee!
Sarah F Adams (1805-1848)

April 4

Hope that is seen is no hope at all. Who hopes for what they already have? But if we hope for what we do not yet have, we wait for it patiently. Romans 8:24b-25

Xaaji Maxamed Xuseen (1996)
The Last Christian?

Xaaji was kidnapped from his home in Mogadishu, Somalia, on 3 April 1996, and his body was discovered the next day in an abandoned building. Islamic extremists claimed responsibility for his death. They said that they believed he was the last Christian in the Somali capital and so they would then turn their attention to Christians in Nairobi, Kenya.

Xaaji had become a Christian in the 1980s while he was studying in Canada. He was a university professor who worked for UNESCO. As an active Christian in the community he had received death threats and had seen his friend Liibaan Ibraahim Xasan killed two years earlier (see March 21), but still continued to witness. He left a wife and six children.

O God, whose loving kindness is infinite, mercifully hear our prayers; and grant that as in this life we are united in the mystical body of thy Church, and in death are laid in holy ground with the sure hope of resurrection; so at the last day we may rise to the life immortal, and be numbered with thy saints in glory everlasting; through Jesus Christ our Lord. Parish Prayers (no. 288)

Whoever serves me must follow me; and where I am my servant also will be. My Father will honour the one who serves me. John 12:26

Iraqi Church Leaders (2007-08) Top Targets

Church leaders in Iraq have been frequently targeted by Islamic militants who are intent on "cleansing" the country of all Christians. Such attacks send a message to the entire Christian community that they are all in danger because of their faith.

On 3 June 2007, a church minister and three deacons were shot dead as they drove away from their church in Mosul, northern Iraq, after the evening service. They were about a hundred metres from the church when a group of gunmen opened fire. Another Iraqi church leader, Yousif Adil Abbodi, was assassinated in a drive-by shooting on 5 April 2008. The 47-year-old church leader had previously received several death threats. He was shot dead just after he left his home in Baghdad.

Lead, kindly Light, amid th'encircling gloom, lead Thou me on!
The night is dark, and I am far from home; lead Thou me on!
Keep Thou my feet; I do not ask to see
The distant scene; one step enough for me.

So long Thy power hath blest me, sure it still will lead me on.
O'er moor and fen, o'er crag and torrent, till the night is gone,
And with the morn those angel faces smile, which I
Have loved long since, and lost awhile!

Meantime, along the narrow rugged path, Thyself hast trod,
Lead, Savior, lead me home in childlike faith, home to my God.
To rest forever after earthly strife
In the calm light of everlasting life.
John Henry Newman (1801-1890)

I am the vine; you are the branches. If you remain in me and I in you, you will bear much fruit; apart from me you can do nothing. John 15:5

Reuben Gitau (1954)
"Never Leave Jesus"

When the Mau Mau guerrillas emerged in Kenya, Reuben and his wife refused to take the tribe's oath of allegiance, and, in 1953, their house in Kagumwini was burnt down. Reuben, a school teacher and evangelist, and his family went to live with the Rev. Heshbon Gawai and his family. One Friday in April 1954 Reuben went to teach in the local school, and his wife went to meet him in the afternoon. At about 4pm a Mau Mau came and struck Reuben, who said, "Do what you must – I am ready to go to heaven."

Other soldiers appeared and Reuben said to his wife, "Go home to the children. Train them well, and never leave Jesus!" The Mau Mau shot him, cut him with knives and left his body. Christians from his church came and buried Reuben; his wife and children were taken to live in Weithaga, where the church was able to look after them.

It pleases the Father that all fullness should be in Christ; therefore there is nothing but emptiness anywhere else.
W Gadsby (1773-1844)

The light shines in the darkness, and the darkness has not overcome it. John 1:5

Shamoun Babar and Daniel Emanuel (2005)
Shot and Dumped

Pastor Babar and the driver of his car, Daniel, were kidnapped on 5 April 2005 by extremists in Peshawar, Khyber Pakhtunkhwa, Pakistan's most strictly Islamic region. Two days later their bodies were found dumped on a road near Mulazai village in Nasirbagh. The evidence of the recovered corpses of the two men, who were both in their 30s, showed they had been badly tortured and shot several times.

Pastor Babar was committed to his church work and organised many activities for his congregation and the local community, despite threats. He was also a well-known evangelist in Peshawar. His life was targeted because of his love and enthusiasm for Christ and the Gospel.

Light dispelled by darkest night,
Yet God remains,
Seen by the eye of faith …
His purposes are good
And in time the clouds will lift,
The darkness be dispelled,
And He in glorious light
Will turn night into day.
Patrick Sookhdeo (born 1947), *With the Eye of Faith*

April 8

Get Mark and bring him with you, because he is helpful.
2 Timothy 4:11

Mark the Evangelist (c. 68)
Gospel Writer

Mark is traditionally thought to have been converted to Christianity by Peter and became a close follower of the apostle. The first we hear of him in the Bible is when he fled from danger and persecution, leaving his garment behind, on that terrible night when Jesus was arrested (Mark 14:51-52). The author of the Gospel of Mark wrote his account of Jesus' life based on the teachings and recollections of Peter. It came about because those who heard Peter's message wanted a written summary, so they asked Mark, who had followed Peter for years, to write it all down.

Early Church Bishop Papias of Hierapolis wrote this about Mark:

Mark became Peter's interpreter and wrote down accurately, but not in order, all that he remembered of the things said and done by the

Lord... He had one overriding purpose: to omit nothing that he had heard and to make no false statements in his account.

The Mark mentioned in Peter's first letter is understood to be the Gospel writer; Peter refers to Mark here as "my son", indicating the closeness of their bond. Mark accompanied Paul and Barnabas on their first missionary journey but turned back at Perga (Acts 12:3). He then went with Barnabas to preach the Gospel in Cyprus (Acts 15:37-39).

Mark is thought to have been the first person sent to Egypt to preach the Gospel and the first to found churches in Alexandria, where there were a great number of converts. According to the Church in Egypt, he was martyred here in the year 68 when Easter Day coincided with a big pagan religious celebration. A pagan mob broke into the church where he was leading a communion service, tied him with rope and dragged him through the streets. By the end of the day, he was badly wounded but still alive, so the next day they dragged him over rocks and rougher ground until he was dead.

For him, O Lord, we praise Thee,
The weak by grace made strong,
Whose labours and whose Gospel
Enrich our triumph song.
May we in all our weakness
Find strength from Thee supplied,
And all, as fruitful branches,
In Thee, the Vine, abide.
Horatio Nelson (1823-1913)

April 9

But God will never forget the needy; the hope of the afflicted will never perish. Psalm 9:18

Dietrich Bonhoeffer (1945)
Anti-Nazi Resistance

Dietrich was a German Lutheran pastor and theologian who stood against Nazi tyranny during World War Two. He was one of the first

German Protestants to recognise the dangers of Nazism, and he believed that it was his Christian responsibility to challenge its evils. Dietrich knew that the cost would be great, but he did not shrink back, warning in a sermon in Berlin in 1932, "We must not be surprised if also for our Church there will be times again when the blood of martyrs will be called for."

After Hitler came to power in 1933, Dietrich helped to organise the Pastors' Emergency League, which developed into the Confessing Church of anti-Nazi German Protestants. He went on to found a clandestine seminary to train pastors for the anti-Nazi cause. As war became increasingly inevitable, friends arranged a lecture tour for Dietrich in America, hoping that he would stay there where he would be safe. But after just six weeks he decided to return to Germany. He became a member of the German resistance movement, convinced that this was the only way he could help save his country from Hitler.

In early 1943 Dietrich got engaged to Maria von Wedemeyer, but just three months later their plans were hijacked when he was arrested. Dietrich was placed in various prisons and concentration camps over a two-year period.

On 9 April 1945 he was hanged in Flossenburg concentration camp by the personal order of Heinrich Himmler, commander of the Nazi SS. As Dietrich was being led out to his death he said, "This is the end, for me the beginning of life."

In me there is darkness,
But with thee there is light,
I am lonely, but thou leavest me not.
I am feeble in heart, but thou leavest me not.
I am restless, but with thee there is peace.
In me there is bitterness, but with thee there is patience;
Thy ways are past understanding, but
Thou knowest the way for me.
Dietrich Bonhoeffer (1906-45)

May I never boast except in the cross of our Lord Jesus Christ, through which the world has been crucified to me, and I to the world.
Galatians 6:14

James Chalmers (1901)
Daring Missionary

James came from Scotland, and those who knew him always thought that he would become a missionary. So indeed he did. Although he was not well-educated he began to study other languages, including Rarotongan, the language of the Cook Islands in the Pacific. It was to these islands that he sailed with his wife, arriving in 1867.

For 34 daring years he worked with the indigenous tribes of the Pacific, visiting isolated places to spread the Gospel. In April 1901, on a final trip to the region of Goaribari Island, New Guinea, his ship was boarded by the Niue tribe. The following morning they invited his party ashore and into a long building. There the whole group was massacred and then eaten by the Niue.

Glory be to God in the highest, the Creator, and Lord of heaven and earth, the Preserver of all things, the Father of mercies, who so loves mankind as to send His only begotten Son into the world, to redeem us from sin and misery, and to obtain for us everlasting life. Accept, O gracious God, our praise and our thanksgivings for your infinite mercies towards us. And teach us, O Lord, to love you more and serve you better; through Jesus Christ our Lord. Amen.
John Hamilton (1512-71)

What does the LORD your God ask of you but to fear the LORD your God, to walk in obedience to him, to love him, to serve the LORD your God with all your heart and with all your soul? Deuteronomy 10:12

Antipas (c. 92)
"My faithful witness"

Antipas was a disciple of the apostle John. During the reign of the Roman Emperor Domitian he was roasted to death in a bronze bull at Pergamum (in modern-day Turkey), where he was a leader of the church.

John mentions Antipas in Revelation 2:13, in the letter to the Church in Pergamum: "...even in the days of Antipas, my faithful witness, who was put to death in your city."

"Not called!" did you say? "Not heard the call," I think you should say. Put your ear down to the Bible, and hear Him bid you go and pull sinners out of the fire of sin. Put your ear down to the burdened, agonised heart of humanity, and listen to its pitiful wail for help. Go stand by the gates of hell, and hear the damned entreat you to go to their father's house and bid their brothers and sisters, and servants and masters not to come there. And then look Christ in the face, whose mercy you have professed to obey, and tell him whether you will join heart and soul and body and circumstances in the march to publish his mercy to the world.
William Booth (1829-1912)

Glory to thee, O God, for all thy saints in light,
Who nobly strove and conquered in the well fought fight,
Their praises sing who life outpoured
By fire and sword for Christ their king.

Thanks be to thee, O Lord, for saints thy Spirit stirred
In humble paths to live the life and speak thy word.
Unnumbered they, whose candles shine
To lead our footsteps after thine.
Howard Charles Adie Gaunt (1902-1983)

Though an army besiege me, my heart will not fear; though war break out against me, even then will I be confident. Psalm 27:3

Noshi Girgis (2006)
Church Raids

Noshi Girgis, a 63-year-old Egyptian Christian, was killed in co-ordinated attacks by Islamists on three churches in Alexandria on 14 April 2006, the last day of Lent. Knife-wielding Islamic militants stormed three church buildings in separate neighbourhoods, shouting, "There is no god but Allah" and "Allah is the greatest" before stabbing worshippers at Lent services. At least 12 people were wounded, three of whom sustained serious injuries. During Noshi's funeral, radical Muslims hurled stones at the mourners.

As often happens in cases of anti-Christian violence in Egypt, the authorities failed to pursue justice for the victims. On this occasion, despite the fact that the three attacks were carried out almost simultaneously in different parts of the city, the interior ministry claimed that only one man was responsible. Mahmoud Salah-Eddin Abdel-Raziq was said to be "psychologically disturbed" and was later committed to a mental hospital after a medical evaluation and without trial.

If martyrdom consists in confessing God, then every person who conducts himself with purity in the knowledge of God and who obeys his commandments, is a martyr in his life and in his words: for in whatever way his soul is separated from his body, he will pour out his faith like blood, both during his life and at the moment of his death.
Clement of Alexandria (died 215)

Blessed is the one who perseveres under trial because, having stood the test, that person will receive the crown of life that the Lord has promised to those who love him. James 1:12

Choo Ki-Chul (1944)
"I've gone the road I'm supposed to go"

Choo Ki-Chul, a church pastor in Pyongyang, Korea, was strongly opposed to shrine worship, which was a big issue in the Japanese-controlled country. From a non-Christian family, Ki-Chul had chosen to follow Christ after studying at the Christian Ohsan Academy and hearing the teaching of Kim Ikdoo.

He expressed his views about shrine worship with restraint. The authorities did not imprison him at first, since the Japanese constitution guaranteed freedom of religion, but in August 1939 he was arrested after preaching boldly that shrines were idolatrous. His children and elderly mother cried greatly, but his wife remained firm. She prayed that the Lord would help him to "be strong and of good courage to the end, and be offered up as a sacrifice on the altar of the Korean Church".

Ki-Chul was tortured and beaten several times, remaining in prison for six years. Although his wife was ill, she visited him the day before he died. On his deathbed he said to his wife, "I've gone the road I'm supposed to go. Follow my steps. Let's meet in heaven."

He died at 9.30 pm on 13 April 1944. One of his sons did indeed follow in his footsteps, both in his firm faith and in his death, for he was martyred under the Communists.

Lord, we pray for your church in every part of the world, the great family of which we are a part. We pray for those who are denied freedom in their religious beliefs, for those called to the suffering of imprisonment, and for those few who are called to martyrdom itself. May their courage set faith alight in other lives.
Intercessions, 31 March 2002, Easter Sunday, St Mark's Church, Bedford, UK

*Return to the LORD your God, for he is gracious and compassionate,
slow to anger and abounding in love.* Joel 2:13b

Demetrios (1803)
Re-committed to Christ

Demetrios, a Greek Christian, converted to Islam after falling into the company of a Muslim barber who gave him accommodation when he went to work as a builder in Tripolis. He had not previously encountered Islam, and it made a strong impression on him. But after a little while, Demetrios came to a realisation of what he had done and deeply regretted his conversion. So he fled to the city of Smyrna, where he resolved to return to Tripolis, hand himself over to the Muslim authorities and confess his decision to turn back to Christ. Back in Tripolis, the authorities tried to make him deny Christ, using a combination of bribery and torture, but he refused. On 14 April 1803 he gave his life for Christ.

*Almighty God, Father of our Lord Jesus Christ, grant, we pray, that
    we may be grounded and settled in your truth by the coming of your
    Holy Spirit into our hearts.*
What we do not know, reveal to us;
What is lacking within us, make complete;
That which we do know, confirm in us;
And keep us blameless in your service, through Jesus Christ our Lord.
Clement of Rome (martyred c. 100)

Out of the depths I cry to you, O Lord; O Lord, hear my voice. Let your ears be attentive to my cry for mercy. Psalm 130:1-2

Adana Massacre (1909)
Pillaged and Destroyed

In April 1909, around 20,000 Christians, mostly Armenians, were killed in a two-stage massacre by the Turks in Adana and the surrounding region. A Christian minister described the first outbreak of violence on 14 April:

> People were firing from roofs, windows and minarets: the bullets fell thick as hail on roofs, streets and houses. It was a cross-fire that began all at once, as if a flash of electricity had armed all the inhabitants of Adana at the same time... Leaving the mosque, Muslims who usually did not wear turbans were seen wearing mullahs' headgear, so that they would not be mistaken for Christians. Finally, there was something like the smell of blood in the air.

Thousands of people took refuge in churches and Christian buildings as the Armenian quarter, including shops and homes, was set alight. The violence intensified over the next two days, leaving a trail of devastation and carnage. Armenian villagers in the surrounding region were also targeted.

Calm was restored by the morning of 17 April, but it was short-lived. On the 25th, Adana was again besieged for three days. Gangs rampaged through the city, slitting people's throats and torching churches and Armenian schools.

American missionary Herbert Adams Gibbons, who was in Adana at the time, described the aftermath in an article for the *New York Times* on 28 April: "Adana is in a pitiable condition. The town has been pillaged and destroyed... It is impossible to estimate the number of killed. The corpses lie scattered through the streets. Friday, when I went out, I had to pick my way between the dead to avoid stepping on them. Saturday morning I counted a dozen cartloads of Armenian bodies in one-half hour being carried to the river and thrown into the water."

The 1909 Adana massacre was part of the mass genocide of Armenian Christians throughout Turkey between 1894 and 1923 (see July 5).

The saint never knows the joy of the Lord in spite of tribulation, but because of it.
Oswald Chambers (1874-1917)

April 16

If we have been united with him in a death like his, we will certainly also be united with him in a resurrection like his. Romans 6:5

Simeon Barsabba'e (341)
Crucified

On Good Friday 341, Simeon – the chief bishop – and others were put to death on the cross at Ctesiphon, Persia. This happened during a time of great persecution of Christians under King Shapur II. Simeon was accused of collaborating with the Christian Roman Emperor Constantius II. He was ordered to follow the Persian religion, Zoroastrianism, but he would not accept this.

Two of Simeon's successors as bishop of Seleucia-Ctesiphon were also martyred. Shahdost was tortured and beheaded along with others in 342 and Barbasymas (see January 14) was killed in 346. During this time thousands of other Christians were killed and many fled abroad.

Lord Jesus you prayed for those who placed you
upon the cross and told us to pray for our enemies.
Stephen, your deacon, prayed for those who put him to death,
and you received his spirit.
Receive the souls of my brothers and receive my spirit with theirs.
Set us among the martyrs who have come before us and have
received the crown of victory;
Set us among the holy apostles and blessed prophets.
Lord, bring to faith those who persecute us and put us
to death, and do not count this against them as sin.
May they come to the knowledge that you are God.
Simeon's prayer

So will it be with the resurrection of the dead. The body that is sown is perishable, it is raised imperishable; it is sown in dishonour, it is raised in glory; it is sown in weakness, it is raised in power; it is sown a natural body, it is raised a spiritual body. 1 Corinthians 1:42-44a

Donan (618)
Killed by Raiders

Every one of the 52 monks at a monastery founded by Irishman Donan on the Scottish island of Eigg, in the Inner Hebrides, was martyred at Easter 618. Christian missions in Celtic lands rarely suffered violent opposition at this time, but a group of armed men turned up on this evening as the monks were celebrating communion. The assailants agreed to Donan's request to let the monks finish the service, but then took them into a building and set fire to it. Those who survived were killed later by the sword. It is thought that local chieftains, who resented the presence of the monks, may have been responsible for their murders or that it may have been a Viking raid.

O Merciful God, the Father of our Lord Jesus Christ, who is the Resurrection and the Life; in whosoever believeth shall live though he die; and whosoever liveth and believeth in him shall not die eternally: We bless thy holy name for all thy servants departed this life in thy faith and fear, especially those most dear to us; beseeching thee to give us grace so as to follow their good examples that with them we may be partakers of thy heavenly kingdom. Grant this, O Father, for Jesus Christ's sake, our only Advocate and Redeemer.
Parish Prayers (no. 303), based on the *Book of Common Prayer*

In the fear of the LORD one has strong confidence.
Proverbs 14:26a (NRSV)

Isma Dogari (2011)
Prepared for Martyrdom

"I am not a pagan, but a servant of the living God. You need Jesus in your life." This was the bold response of Nigerian missionary pastor Isma Dogari when radical Muslims posing as police pulled over the van he was travelling in and asked, "Is there any pagan amongst you?" This happened in Bauchi state on 18 April 2011 as Muslim rioters were rampaging through Northern Nigeria, savagely attacking Christians, using the re-election of Christian President Goodluck Jonathan as a pretext to vent their hostility.

The men who stopped Isma's van pulled him out of the vehicle and took him to a mosque by the roadside. They gave him a Quran and told him to renounce Christ. But he refused, saying, "I have since passed that level a long time ago" and repeating, "You need Jesus in your life."

They beat him and gouged his eyes out, asking him again to denounce his faith, but he persisted in his plea, "You need Jesus." The pastor was then stabbed and burnt to death. Other Christians who were with Isma, a married father of seven, testified to his courageous martyrdom, describing him as a great hero of the faith.

It seems that the Lord had prepared Isma ahead of time. Not long before his death he had a dream in which he heard a voice saying, "Men were killed in a war leaving a good number of women as widows." From that day, he constantly reminded his family of that revelation and urged them to stand firm in their faith no matter what. In the final sermon he preached, just the day before his death, he warned that it was time for Christians to stop living carelessly and be prepared, if the Lord willed, to lay down their lives for Christ's sake.

The sight of any trouble strikes terror into the heart of those who do not have faith, but those who trust Him say, "Here comes my food!"
Watchman Nee (1903-72)

...so that, having been justified by his grace, we might become heirs having the hope of eternal life. Titus 3:7

Tilman Ekkehart Geske, Necati Aydin, and Ugur Yuksel (2007) Murderers Forgiven

"Father, forgive them, for they do not know what they are doing" (Luke 23:34a). This was the verse Tilman's widow read during a TV interview in which she publicly forgave the men who had killed her husband. Necati's widow also publicly expressed her forgiveness. Their husbands, along with Ugur, who was single, were killed on 18 April 2007, in Malatya, eastern Turkey.

The three men were found in the publishing house where Necati and Ugur worked, which printed Bibles and other Christian literature. Each man had been bound to a chair by his hands and feet; they had been stabbed and had their throats cut. Ugur was still alive when they were found, but died later in hospital. German national Tilman worked for a Christian translation company; Necati and Ugur were both converts from Islam.

Five men suspected of involvement in the murders had been to a church service led by Necati, and two of them had been out with him giving away New Testaments on the street. They had arranged to meet with him on the morning of the attack to learn more about the Bible.

> *Oh, what their joy and their glory must be,*
> *Those endless Sabbaths the blessed ones see;*
> *Crowns for the valiant, for weary ones rest:*
> *God shall be all, and in all ever blest.*
> *There, where no trouble distraction can bring,*
> *We the sweet anthems of Zion shall sing,*
> *While for thy grace, Lord, their voices of praise*
> *Thy blessed people eternally raise.*
> Peter Abelard (1079-1142)
> Translated by John Mason Neale (1818-1866)

The gospel is bearing fruit and growing throughout the whole world.
Colossians 1:6

Habil (1933)
Singled Out

In April 1933 the emir of the region of Eastern Turkestan (now Xin-jiang, an autonomous region in China) threatened Christian missionaries who had established a fruitful ministry in his territory. He arrested many of the indigenous converts to Christianity and treated them roughly, accusing them of preaching against Islam and forsaking their religion. Habil, the son of a Muslim in Kashgar, was singled out and shot while the others were imprisoned. Some of the girls were seized for the emir's harem. Shortly afterwards the emir was killed by his own rebels, and so great was the hatred against him that for half a year his skull was kicked about in the bazaar like a football.

The work of missionaries from the Swedish Mission Covenant in Eastern Turkestan and the Chinese Province of Sinkiang bore much fruit over a period of 40 years. From 1892 they established mission stations at Kashgar, Yarkand and Yengi-Hessar, which included medical work and schools with hostels for the pupils to live. Many converts were won, and by 1933 the church had around 500 members, including the children in the hostels. But in 1940 the Swedish missionaries had to leave, and in the ensuing years the church building was destroyed and the Christians were scattered. Most of them are believed to have been killed.

The wind that blows can never kill
The tree God plants;
It bloweth east, it bloweth west,
The tender leaves have little rest,
But any wind that blows is best.
The tree that God plants
Strikes deeper root, grows higher still,
Spreads greater boughs, for God's good will
Meets all its wants.

There is no storm hath power to blast
  The tree God knows;
No thunderbolt, nor beating rain,
Nor lightning flash, nor hurricane;
When they are spent, it doth remain,
  The tree God knows,
Through every tempest standeth fast,
And from its first day to its last
  Still fairer grows.
Annie Johnson Flint (1866-1932) from *Streams in the Desert*

April 21

The God who made the world and everything in it is the Lord of heaven and earth and does not live in temples built by human hands. And he is not served by human hands, as if he needed anything. Rather, he himself gives everyone life and breath and everything else. Acts 17:24-25

Apollonius (c. 185)
Excellent Apologist

Apollonius was a Roman senator, denounced as a Christian by one of his own slaves. An authentic account of his examination by the magistrate was found in an Armenian text in 1874. He was told to sacrifice to Roman emperor Commodus' statue and other "gods", but he refused. Three days later, Apollonius was asked if he had changed his mind. He replied with a passionate defence of the one true God, and thus is remembered by historians as one of the best early Christian apologists for the faith. Apollonius is reported to have said:

I am aware of the Senate's decree, but my God whom I serve is not made with human hands. I can never worship gold or iron or bronze or silver, or any deaf and dumb idols. You are wrong on many counts to indulge in such worship...

Man's decrees have no power over God's decrees. The more you kill these poor, innocent people, the more God will raise up more of them. Everyone is in God's hands; kings and senators, to free men and slaves. After we die we come to the time of judgment. We do not think that it is difficult to die for the God of truth.

Apollonius was beheaded on 21 April c. 185.

O God, Thou in whom all things live, who commandest us to seek thee, and art ever ready to be found: To know thee is life, to serve thee is freedom, to praise thee is our soul's joy. We bless thee and adore thee, we give thanks to thee for thy great glory; through Jesus Christ our Lord. Augustine of Hippo (354-430), *Parish Prayers* (no. 1519)

April 22

Do not suppose that I have come to bring peace to the earth. I did not come to bring peace, but a sword. For I have come to turn a man against his father, a daughter against her mother, a daughter-in-law against her mother-in-law – a man's enemies will be the members of his own household. Matthew 10:34-36

David Abdulwahab Mohamed Ali (2008) Killed by his Cousin

David's conversion from Islam to Christianity was strongly opposed by his Somali Muslim family. Consequently he had not seen them for many years when, in April 2008, he travelled back to Somalia from Ethiopia, where he had been living since 2000, to visit his sick mother.

On 22 April, one of David's cousins came to him with two members of the Islamic militant group al-Shabaab, to question him about his faith. They asked him if he was a Muslim or an infidel, to which he replied, "Neither. I am a follower of the Messiah." David's cousin, to avenge the family's honour, pulled out a gun and shot the 29-year-old. The other two did the same. They dragged his body to a mosque, praising Allah that "an apostate was dead".

David was described as a gifted evangelist who led many to the Lord. He was a linguist and philosopher who shared his faith and thoughts through blogs. Some Somalis called him "The Great Thinker".

I know the sorrow I will bring to my family.
It has cost me tears of blood to take such a step
and give those I love such pain.
Who is there who cared for home
and family more than I?
All my earthly happiness was to be found there.
But you, O God, who united us with such
tender affection,
weaned me from what I loved that
I might serve you.
Theophane Venard (martyred 1861)

April 23

For our struggle is not against flesh and blood, but against the rulers,
against the authorities, against the powers of this dark world and against
the spiritual forces of evil in the heavenly realms. Ephesians 6:12

George (303)
A Patron Saint

According to tradition, George, a secret believer in Jesus Christ, began his adult life as a Roman soldier, and it is thought that he achieved a high rank in the army. In 303 the Emperor Diocletian began a systematic persecution of Christians, and, as a soldier, George would have had to participate in this. But he refused, and, declaring his faith openly, George was tortured and executed in Palestine on or around 23 April 303.

Later he became patron saint of England and many other European countries. George is also a very important figure for Christians in Egypt and the Middle East. He is often associated with the legend of slaying a dragon, which has been regarded as a symbol of the Christian's daily spiritual battle.

Onward, Christian soldiers, marching as to war,
With the cross of Jesus going on before.
Christ, the royal Master, leads against the foe;
Forward into battle see His banners go!

At the sign of triumph Satan's host doth flee;
On then, Christian soldiers, on to victory!
Hell's foundations quiver at the shout of praise;
Brothers lift your voices, loud your anthems raise.

What the saints established that I hold for true.
What the saints believèd, that I believe too.
Long as earth endureth, men the faith will hold,
Kingdoms, nations, empires, in destruction rolled.

Crowns and thrones may perish, kingdoms rise and wane,
But the church of Jesus constant will remain.
Gates of hell can never gainst that church prevail;
We have Christ's own promise, and that cannot fail.
Sabine Baring-Gould (1834-1924)

April 24

The bloodthirsty hate the blameless, and they seek the life of the upright.
Proverbs 29:10 (NRSV)

Hridoy Roy (2003)
Bangladesh's First Martyr?

Just after midnight, early in the morning of 24 April 2003, Hridoy was returning home after showing a film version of Luke's Gospel. As he approached his house seven or eight people attacked him, stabbing him seven times. He died instantly.

Hridoy was a Bangladeshi evangelist and regularly showed the "Jesus Film". He is believed to be the first martyr in modern Bangladesh to die in such a premeditated way. Local believers were in a state of deep shock, mourning and great fear following his death. They felt that he would not be Bangladesh's last martyr, and tragic events in the ensuing years would seem to prove their fears to be well-founded (see July 29).

Under sharia law, conversion from Islam to another faith (apostasy) is punishable by death. This law is the fundamental reason for the hostility that most Muslims hold towards those who try to evangelise in their communities.

Dark is the sky! and veiled the unknown morrow!
  Dark is life's way, for night is not yet o'er;
The longed-for glimpse I may not meanwhile borrow;
  But, this I know, HE GOETH ON BEFORE.
Dangers are nigh! and fears my mind are shaking;
  Heart seems to dread what life may hold in store;
But I am His - He knows the way I'm taking,
  More blessed still - HE GOETH ON BEFORE.
Doubts cast their weird, unwelcome shadows o'er me;
  Doubts that life's best - life's choicest things are o'er;
What but His Word can strengthen, can restore me,
  And this blest fact; that still HE GOES BEFORE.
HE GOES BEFORE! Be this my consolation!
  He goes before! On this my heart would dwell!
He goes before! This guarantees salvation!
  HE GOES BEFORE! And therefore all is well.
J. Danson Smith

April 25

In this world you will have trouble. But take heart! I have overcome the world. John 16:33b

Nigerian Christians (2010)
"We killed them all"

Two journalists from a Nigerian Christian magazine, *The Lightbearer*, were en route to interview a local politician on 24 April 2010 when they were pulled from their motorbike and stabbed to death in a predominantly Muslim suburb of Jos, Plateau State.

Deputy editor Nathan Dabak and reporter Sunday Gyang Bwede were just two of the Christians martyred during intense anti-Christian violence in the early part of 2010. After the pair went missing, a friend called

126

Nathan's phone, only to hear the voice of a stranger say in reply, "We killed them all – you can do your worst."

Their deaths followed the murders of Christian pastor Ishaya Kadah and his wife Selina, whose bodies were found on 15 April, two days after they were kidnapped in Boto village, Bauchi State. Four days later, the mutilated bodies of two elderly Christian farmers were found in the village of Rim, south of Jos.

Lord Jesus Christ, creator of heaven and earth;
you will never abandon those who put their trust in you.
We give you thanks,
you have prepared us to live in your heavenly city
and share in your kingdom.
We give you thanks:
you have strengthened us to overcome the serpent
and crush its head.
Grant rest to your servants,
let the violence of their enemies be placed upon me.
Grant peace to your Church;
may it be delivered from the oppression of the Wicked One.
Theodotus of Ancyra (martyred c. 303)

April 26

But thanks be to God! He gives us the victory through our Lord Jesus
Christ. 1 Corinthians 15:57

Kosmos Aitolos (1779)
Passionate about Education

Kosmos, a travelling preacher who taught the Christian faith throughout Greece, Albania and Turkey for 19 years, was passionate about social justice, equality and education. Few Christians at the time were educated in their faith, so many of them were converting to Islam. As a result of his preaching and teaching, schools were established in more than 200 villages and towns. His work angered Muslims, and in Berat, Albania, they seized Kosmos and charged him with various imaginary crimes. From there, he was taken to a nearby village and hanged.

Almighty God, the Father of mercies and God of all comfort, come to my help and deliver me from this difficulty that besets me. I believe Lord, that all trials of life are under Your care and that all things work for the good of those who love You. Take away from me fear, anxiety and distress. Help me to face and endure my difficulty with faith, courage and wisdom… I trust in Your love and compassion. Blessed is Your name, Father, Son and Holy Spirit, now and forever. Amen.
Greek Orthodox Prayer

April 27

Where two or three gather in my name, there am I with them.
Matthew 18:20

Gu Xianggao (2004)
House Church Raids

Xianggao, a 28-year-old Christian who worked as a teacher, was beaten to death in custody in Heilongjiang Province, China, on 27 April 2004. He had been arrested the previous day in a series of raids targeting the Three Grades Servants House Church to which he belonged. His parents were given the equivalent of around £15,000 not to speak about what had happened.

Unregistered churches or "house churches" suffer frequent harassment and persecution from the Chinese authorities. They refuse to register with the state, so are regarded as unstable social elements that need to be suppressed. The government allows Christianity to be practised only under the authority of the registered churches. The worship and activities of these churches are tightly controlled by the state, and many Chinese Christians find them too restrictive. However, those who belong to house church congregations can face discrimination, detention, violence – and even death – at the hands of the authorities. The Church in China is one of the fastest growing in the world.

All is Silent.
In the still and soundless air,
I fervently bow
To my almighty God.
Hsieh Ping-Hsin, China

Start children off on the way they should go, and even when they are old
they will not turn from it. Proverbs 22:6

Felicitas and her Seven Sons (2ⁿᵈ century)
Faithful Family

Felicitas was a widow with seven sons who lived in Rome during the reign of Emperor Antoninus (138-61). Many people became followers of Christ as a result of the faithful witness of Felicitas and her family, while other Christians were encouraged likewise to share their faith with others. This angered the Roman priests, who complained to the emperor that Felicitas was drawing people away from worshipping their gods. They argued that these gods were the protectors of the empire and were offended and angry; in order to appease them, the priests said, Felicitas and her children must sacrifice to the gods.

Antoninus was superstitious, so he issued an order to the prefect of Rome, Publius, to see that this was done. Publius called Felicitas and her sons before him and tried to persuade the mother to carry out the sacrifice to prevent him from penalising the whole family. She refused, stating confidently that they "will live eternally with Christ if they are faithful to him".

Felicitas urged her sons to stand firm before they were brought before the judge one by one; he used a mixture of promises and threats to attempt to persuade them to worship pagan gods, but they all refused. The brothers were whipped and detained. The emperor issued an order that they be sent to different judges and condemned to different deaths: Januarius was scourged to death with whips, Felix and Philip were beaten with clubs, Sylvanus was thrown head first down a steep precipice, while the

129

three youngest, Alexander, Vitalis and Martialis, were beheaded. Felicitas was executed four months later.

Almighty God, we praise your holy name for all the saints throughout the ages who have kept the lamp of faith burning brightly. Grant that we who are following in their steps may keep that light shining, that the darkness of this world may be lit by him who is the light of the world, even your Son, our Saviour Jesus Christ. Amen.
William Hampson (*More Prayers for Today's Church*, no. 296)

April 29

The righteous will flourish like a palm tree, they will grow like a cedar of Lebanon. Psalm 92:12

Paul and Priscilla Johnson (1952)
"Bless Them, Lord"

In April 1952 Paul and Priscilla, missionaries from America working in Thailand, were holding church services in Ban Dong Mafai village, where several people had become Christians. One Friday, seven children prayed to receive Christ. During the evening, the couple were singing hymns when gunshots rang out. Priscilla was hit in the chest; she ran for shelter but collapsed and died. Paul was shot in the abdomen.

He was taken to hospital in Bangkok, where he was operated on. He sang a prayer for his fellow workers and the Thai Christians whom he left behind, "Bless Them, Lord and Make Them a Blessing". A few minutes later he lost consciousness and then died.

God is more anxious to bestow his blessings on us than we are to receive them.
Augustine of Hippo (354-430)

130

For though we live in the world, we do not wage war as the world does.
The weapons we fight with are not the weapons of this world. On the
contrary, they have divine power to demolish strongholds.
2 Corinthians 10:3-4

Mariam Hdago (1954)
"I won't take your oath"

Mariam was a Kenyan Christian, but her husband Samuel was a Mau Mau guerrilla. For some reason he reported to the other militants in his group that his wife was a Christian, and they decided to kill her. In April 1954 Mariam was sitting with her daughter and some other women when the Mau Mau appeared, asking them to come and take their oath of loyalty. Mariam replied, "I have taken the blood of Jesus, and no matter what you do I won't take your oath."

The men took the women into the forest, leaving the child behind, and continued to threaten them with death if they did not take the oath. Mariam stood firm and gave her testimony, even as she watched them dig her own grave. The guerrillas threw her into the grave, covering her with soil up to her neck, but she continued to praise God and witness to her attackers, asking God to forgive them. Finally they killed her and covered the grave. Her husband later died in the fighting. Her daughter survived.

Soul of Christ, sanctify me,
Body of Christ, save me.
Blood of Christ, fill me.
Water from the side of Christ, wash me.
Passion of Christ, strengthen me.
O good Jesus, hear me.
Within your wounds hide me.
Suffer me not to be separated from you.
From the malicious enemy defend me.
In the hour of death call me.
And bid me come unto you.
That with your saints I may praise you.
For ever and ever.
14th-century Prayer

You shall not be intimidated by anyone, for the judgement is God's.
Deuteronomy 1:17b (NRSV)

Ashur Yacob Issa and Arkan Jehad Jacob (2011) Kidnap Targets

These two Iraqi Christians were killed within the space of just over two weeks in May 2011.

Ashur Yacob Issa, a 29-year-old construction worker, was kidnapped in Kirkuk on 13 May. The captors contacted Ashur's family the day after his disappearance and demanded a $100,000 ransom for his release. When they failed to pay this hefty sum, Ashur's decapitated body was found dumped on the morning of the 16th. The husband and father had clearly been subjected to extensive torture by his attackers. A senior Iraqi church leader, who suspected that radical Islamists were behind the crime, said, "The murder was meant to intimidate Christians so that in the future they will more readily pay ransom demands."

Iraqi Christians are frequently targeted in this manner. Before his death, the second victim, Arkan Jehad Jacob, had managed to evade two kidnapping attempts by assailants who seemingly wanted to extort ransom money from his family. The deputy director of a cement factory was shot dead in Mosul, northern Iraq, on the morning of 30 May. He was killed instantly by unidentified gunmen who fired at him repeatedly, using weapons fitted with silencers, before fleeing the scene. It appeared that they had been lying in wait to execute Arkan, a married father of four, as he drove to work.

Christians are frequent victims of such ransom attempts because it is known that they will not retaliate and are thus considered easy targets for gaining money. The attacks are also part of a wider Islamist campaign to "cleanse" the country of all Christians by intimidation and violence.

Always keep in mind the grievous afflictions of those stricken with sorrow and tribulations, that you may render due thanks for the small and insignificant adversities, which may happen to you, and be able to bear them with joy.
Isaac of Syria (7th century)

Let all who take refuge in you be glad; let them ever sing for joy. Spread your protection over them that those who love your name may rejoice in you. Psalm 5:11

Ravi Murmu (2010)
Evangelist Murdered

"The peace of God still reigns in this house and in this family." This was the calm response of Ravi's brother when asked how the family was coping with his murder.

Ravi, a Christian evangelist from Jamalpur, Bihar State, India, was killed on 2 May 2010 after showing the "Jesus Film" in nearby Laxmanpur. He was working as part of a team of evangelists and either stayed behind to fix the generator at the end of the film or became separated from the others on the way back. When he did not return home that night, a search was organised; his body was found with his right hand severed and deep cuts on his neck and other parts of his body. Ravi's personal belongings, including his watch, mobile phone and motorbike, were found with the body, so it was clear that that robbery was not the motive for the attack. Ravi was married with an eight-year-old daughter.

O God, mighty to save, infinite in compassion towards the nations that know thee not, and the tongues which cannot speak thy name: We humbly thank thee that thou hast made the Church of thy dear Son the chariot of the gospel, to tell it out among the nations that thou art king, and to bear thy love unto the world's end; and for all thy servants who counted not their lives dear unto them on this employment, and for all peoples newly praising thee, we praise and bless thee, Father, Son and Holy Spirit, one Lord and God for ever and ever.
Parish Prayers (no. 754), from *After the Third Collect*

Submit yourselves for the Lord's sake to every human authority: whether to the emperor, as the supreme authority, or to governors, who are sent by him to punish those who do wrong and to commend those who do right. For it is God's will that by doing good you should silence the ignorant talk of foolish people. 1 Peter 2:13-15

Ahmed Kalphas (1682)
A Slave's Witness

Ahmed's high status as a secretary in the office of the Chief Secretary of the Islamic Ottoman Empire enabled him to have slaves. One of them was a pious Christian woman, and slowly, over time, Ahmed became interested in her faith, eventually starting to attend church. Finally he decided to be baptised. At first he tried to keep his faith a secret. However, he could not keep it under wraps for long, and, taking confidence from his faith, he began to defend Christianity in front of friends. It soon became obvious to them that he had changed religion, and consequently he was brought before the authorities, who found him guilty of apostasy. He was immediately sentenced to death and on 3 May 1682 was executed in Constantinople.

Lord Jesus Christ, you faced temptation with confidence in God; suffering with serenity; loneliness with the assurance that your Father would not forsake you; and the cross with an inner spirit of peace. You endured all things that we might be saved... Prepare us for whatever life brings of joy or sorrow so that, being sure of your love, we may be confident of your eternal presence. Amen.

"For my thoughts are not your thoughts, neither are your ways my ways,"
declares the LORD. Isaiah 55:8

Egyptian Christians (1992)
Under Siege

On 4 May 1992 in the village of Manshyet El-Nasr, Dairout, Assiut, gangs of radical Muslims attacked and murdered twelve Egyptian Christians. Some attackers sat in wait for ten farmers to begin working in their fields before opening fire on them. Another group killed a teacher after bursting into a primary school, while a doctor who was coming out of his home on his way to work was shot by a different gang. Five other people were wounded. One of them, a child, suffered gunshot wounds and died of his injuries a day later.

Egyptian Christians face much discrimination in daily life and in recent years have been increasingly facing physical violence directed against themselves and their property.

Be mindful, O God, of all who stand in need of Thy great tenderness
of heart, whether friend or foe or stranger; for Thou are the help for the
helpless, the Saviour of the tempest tossed, the haven of those that sail,
and the God and Father of our Lord Jesus Christ. Amen.
From the Coptic Liturgy of St Basil, 4th century

Do not repay anyone evil for evil. Be careful to do what is right in the eyes of everyone. If it is possible, as far as it depends on you, live at peace with everyone. Do not take revenge, my dear friends, but leave room for God's wrath, for it is written: "It is mine to avenge; I will repay," says the Lord. Romans 12:17-19

Angelo (1220)
Prayed for Murderers

Angelo, the son of Jewish converts to Christianity, was born in Jerusalem and set out for Sicily as a result of a vision. Many people became Christians through his teaching and miracles during the journey, including over 200 Jews at Palermo. While he was preaching at Leocata he was killed by a gang who were offended by his message. He was still praying for his murderers as he died at the scene of the attack.

As the first martyr Stephen prayed to thee for his murderers, O Lord, so we fall before thee and pray: forgive all who hate and maltreat us and let not one of them perish because of us, but may all be saved by thy grace, O God the all-bountiful.
Eastern Church

Jerusalem the glorious! Glory of the elect!
O dear and future vision that eager hearts expect!
Even now by faith I see thee, even here thy walls discern;
To thee my thoughts are kindled, and strive, and pant, and yearn.
Jerusalem, the only, that look'st from heaven below,
In thee is all my glory, in me is all my woe!
And though my body may not, my spirit seeks thee fain,
Till flesh and earth return me to earth and flesh again.
Bernard of Morlaix (fl. 1146)
Translated by John Mason Neale (1818-1866)

Follow God's example, therefore, as dearly loved children and walk in the way of love, just as Christ loved us and gave himself up for us as a fragrant offering and sacrifice to God. Ephesians 5:1-2

Bahram Dehqani-Tafti (1980)
Victim of the Revolution

Bahram's father was a bishop of the Episcopal Church in Iran, who left the country because of the 1979 Islamic Revolution. There was no place for Christianity in the new Islamic Republic, and a harsh crackdown on the Church later ensued. Despite this, Bahram chose to remain in his homeland. On the afternoon of 6 May 1980, after leaving college, Bahram was driving home when he was stopped by two men in a car. They got into his vehicle and forced him to drive to a secluded location, where they shot him and fled the scene. The murderers were members of the Iranian Revolutionary Guard.

Let us pray: In the Church, with the Church, for the Church.
For there are three things that preserve the Church and belong to the
  Church:
Firstly: to teach faithfully.
Secondly: to pray constantly.
Thirdly: to suffer reverently.
Martin Luther (1483-1546)

When the perishable has been clothed with the imperishable, and the mortal with immortality, then the saying that is written will come true:
"Death has been swallowed up in victory."
"Where, O death, is your victory? Where, O death, is your sting?"
1 Corinthians 15:54-55

Jamil Ahmad al-Rifai (2003)
Hero Neighbour

Jamil was killed in a bomb blast as he came to the aid of a neighbouring missionary family whose home had been targeted with the explosives. Initially the police stated that Jamil (28), a Jordanian convert to Christianity, had himself planted the bomb at the property in Tripoli, northern Lebanon. But it became apparent that he was killed while helping the Dutch missionary, Gerrit Griffioen (52), and his family.

At 11.30 pm on the night of the incident in May 2003, Griffioen's German wife, Barbel, realised there was an intruder in their garden. The Dutchman called to Jamil, his next door neighbour, for help. By the time they entered the garden the intruder had fled. Griffioen proceeded to extinguish the fuse and then gave chase, while Jamil carried the couple's three children out of the house. After this he returned to the garden, where a 2kg bomb detonated as he was trying either to defuse it or simply to move it further away. Griffioen has been repeatedly threatened during his 20 years of Christian work in Lebanon.

He whose head is in heaven need not fear to put his feet into the grave.
Matthew Henry (1662-1714)

But even if I am being poured out like a drink offering on the sacrifice and service coming from your faith, I am glad and rejoice with all of you. Philippians 2:17

Victor Maurus (c. 303)
Lived Faithfully

Victor was a Mauritanian who put his faith in Christ at a young age. He became a soldier in the elite Roman Praetorian Guard and lived a long life of faithful Christian obedience during dangerous times. In Milan, in about 303, he was imprisoned and tortured severely on the orders of the Emperor Maximianus, which included having molten lead poured onto his skin. But Victor, who was an old man by this time, remained steadfast in his faith and was beheaded.

The Son of God goes forth to war,
A kingly crown to gain;
His blood red banner streams afar:
Who follows in His train?
Who best can drink His cup of woe,
Triumphant over pain,
Who patient bears his cross below,
He follows in His train.
A noble army, men and boys,
The matron and the maid,
Around the Saviour's throne rejoice,
In robes of light arrayed.
They climbed the steep ascent of Heav'n,
Through peril, toil and pain;
O God, to us may grace be given,
To follow in their train.
Reginald Heber (1783-1826)

For the message of the cross is foolishness to those who are perishing, but to us who are being saved it is the power of God. 1 Corinthians 1:18

Ishtiaq Masih (2009)
Hostile Discrimination

On 9 May 2009, Pakistani Christian Ishtiaq Masih was stoned to death for innocently ordering tea from a "Muslim-only" stall.

Ishtiaq had disembarked from a bus that had stopped in Machharkay village, Punjab province, to give the passengers an opportunity for rest and refreshment. A sign hung on the roadside tea stall, which read, "All non-Muslims should introduce their faith prior to ordering tea. This stall serves Muslims only." Ishtiaq failed to see this sign and paid for the mistake with his life. When he went to pay for his tea, the owner noticed his necklace with a cross on it and called on his employees to punish the Christian for not abiding by the sign. A group of men then beat Ishtiaq severely with whatever they could lay their hands on, including stones from the ground on which he lay.

Villagers and bus passengers managed to intervene to break up the beating, but Ishtiaq died from his extensive injuries at a rural health centre. Police said that they were treating the crime as a faith-based murder.

Fence me about, O Lord, with the power of thine honourable and life-giving cross, and preserve me from every evil.
Eastern Orthodox Prayer

Forgive, and you will be forgiven. Luke 6:37b

Christians in India (1857)
Mutiny Martyrs

Ali Wallayat was martyred in Delhi on the first day of the Sepoy Mutiny (Indian Mutiny), which erupted on 10 May 1857. He was killed while trying to save his missionary colleague, John Mackay, from the sepoy rebels, who were targeting Christians.

The sepoys, Indians trained by the British as soldiers, rebelled because of discontent over British rule and the rumour that rifles were being greased with pork lard and beef fat; this was objectionable to Muslims, who consider pigs unclean, and Hindus, to whom cows are sacred. During the rebellion the Indian Church lost countless members; the roll call of martyrs for 1857 included both Indian believers and foreign missionaries and clergy.

Ali, who was born in Agra to a Muslim family, became a Christian after coming into contact with a British colonel. He was severely persecuted by his family but went on to serve the Lord as pastor of a Baptist church in Delhi. He had been working there for twelve years when he was murdered by the sepoy rebels. Ali's wife Fatima, who had also become a Christian, said that her husband, when faced with death, refused to recant his faith; his final words were, "Father, lay not this sin on their charge."

The Reverend John McCallum, chaplain of Shahajanpore, was also martyred during the Sepoy Mutiny. He was worshipping with his congregation when they were surrounded by the rebels. John initially managed to escape, but only after the loss of one of his hands. Later that same day, he was attacked by labourers in a field and decapitated.

God forgave us without any merit on our part; therefore we must forgive others, whether or not we think they merit it.
Lehman Strauss (1911-1997)

The earth is the LORD's, and everything in it, the world, and all who live in it. Psalm 24:1

Maluku Christians (1999-2001)
"Butchered and Killed"

"Are you a follower of Christ? Then you will also follow him in his death." These words were spoken by an Islamic extremist to an Indonesian Christian who was then crucified and left to die, like his Lord, amid a campaign of severe anti-Christian violence in the province of Maluku between 1999 and 2001.

In May 2000 Islamic extremists sent a 3,000-strong militia to the area to launch a jihad against the Christian population. Over 1,000 people were butchered in a single attack that completely destroyed a town. In another massacre over 200 were slaughtered, their bodies being horribly mutilated. In one incident three children were tied up and dragged to their deaths behind a speeding vehicle. The entire Christian population of Ternate, the capital of North Maluku, was driven from the city, and over 25,000 Christian refugees arrived in Manado on Sulawesi Island to escape the atrocities.

During the anti-Christian attacks in Maluku province at least 450 church buildings were destroyed as well as an estimated 55,000 homes.

While Christian and Muslim leaders called for international intervention, Ustad Attamimi, leader of the Islamic militant Laskar Jihad forces in Ambon, declared on 11 May 2001, "We will have no reconciliation before all Christian infidels and their leaders are butchered and killed."

Let nothing disturb us, nothing alarm us:
while all things fade away
God is unchanging.
Help us be patient
so that we gain everything:
for with God in our hearts
nothing is lacking,
God meets our every need
Teresa of Avila (1515-82)

Don't let anyone look down on you because you are young, but set an example for the believers in speech, in life, in love, in faith and in purity.
1 Timothy 4:12

Pancras (304)
Young Martyr

Pancras was orphaned as a young child; his mother Cyriada died during childbirth, and his father Cleonius passed away when Pancras was just eight years old. Pancras was entrusted to the care of his uncle Dionysius, and they moved to Rome. Both converted to Christianity, and Pancras became a zealous follower of Christ.

They were arrested during Emperor Diocletian's persecution in 304. According to tradition, Pancras was brought before the authorities and asked to perform a sacrifice to the Roman gods, but he refused. Diocletian was impressed with the boy's steadfastness and promised him wealth and power if he would make the sacrifice, but Pancras could not be swayed. He was beheaded aged just 14 years old.

Thanks be to God.
O Christ, Son of God,
deliver your servants
by the power of your name.
O God most high,
do not consider the actions of
my persecutors as sin.
God, have pity on them.

Lord, for the sake of your name,
grant me strength to endure what I must.
Release your servants from the captivity of this world.
My God, I thank you,
though I cannot thank you as I should.
Thelica of Abitine (martyred c. 304)

Although he causes grief, he will have compassion according to the abundance of his steadfast love; for he does not willingly afflict or grieve anyone. Lamentations 3:32-33 (NRSV)

Yan Weiping (1994)
Seized at Home

Yan Weiping, a priest and administrator of the Diocese of Yixian, Hebei, was arrested on 13 May 1994 by Chinese security forces. They burst into his home, where he was worshipping with fellow Christians, and took him away for interrogation. That same evening he was found dead in a Beijing street. As he had no known health problems, the local Christian community see the security police as his murderers.

In China the authorities often crack down on Christians, especially those in the underground "house church" movement, often with the aim of closing down these unregistered groups. Christians can be beaten, arrested, imprisoned, tortured or even killed.

Against the persecution of a tyrant the godly have no remedy but prayer. John Calvin (1509-64)

Now then, stand still and see this great thing the Lord is about to do before your eyes! 1 Samuel 12:16

Javaid Anjum (2004)
Tortured Teenager

Javaid, a 19-year-old Christian student, was on his way to visit his grandfather in Punjab Province, Pakistan. While waiting at a bus stop, he felt thirsty and drank from a tap belonging to an Islamic seminary. It was an act that would prove fatal.

He was spotted by seminary students, who quizzed Javaid about who he was and what he was doing. When they discovered that he was a Christian, they abducted him and took him into the seminary, where they tried to force him to renounce Christ and recite the Islamic creed. He refused, so they tortured him for five days, giving him electric shocks and pulling out his nails. They then took Javaid to the police, accusing him of theft. He died of his injuries two weeks later. The doctors who examined him said he was covered in wounds, his kidneys had failed and his right arm and fingers were broken.

How happy would you be if your hearts were but persuaded to close with Jesus Christ! Then you would be out of all danger: whatever storms and tempests were without, you might rest securely within; you might hear the rushing of the wind, and the thunder roar abroad, while you are safe in this hiding-place. O be persuaded to hide yourself in Christ Jesus! What greater assurance of safety can you desire? He has undertaken to defend and save you, if you will come to him: he looks upon it as his work; he engaged in it before the world was, and he has given his faithful promise which he will not break; and if you will but make your flight there, his life shall be for yours; he will answer for you, you shall have nothing to do but rest quietly in him; you may stand still and see what the Lord will do for you.
Jonathan Edwards (1703-58)

May 15

For the Lord is righteous, he loves justice; the upright will see his face.
Psalm 11:7

Indian Church Leaders (2001)
Defied Threats

Three Indian church leaders were shot dead at a training centre in the north-eastern state of Manipur on 15 May 2001 amid a systematic extortion campaign against Christians.

Around 20 separatist groups who were fighting for self-determination in the region were funding their war against the government by demanding money from church schools and using violence when their "tax" was not paid, according to Christian leaders. The three murdered church leaders had received an extortion threat from one of these groups. Other church leaders were killed and Christian schools were closed because they refused to pay up. Hostility towards Christians was fuelled by militant Hindu groups who falsely claimed that church workers were supporting the rebels, whereas in fact they were falling victim to them.

O Lord our God, in whose hands is the issue of all things, and who requirest from thy stewards not success but faithfulness: Give us such faith in thee and in thy sure purposes, that we measure not our lives by what we have done or failed to do, but by our obedience to thy holy will; through Jesus Christ our Lord.
Parish Prayers (no. 34), from *Daily Prayer*

May 16

Now, Lord, consider their threats and enable your servants to speak your word with great boldness. Acts 4:29

Abdul Karim (1906)
Enthusiastic Evangelist

Abdul, an enthusiastic evangelist, had both arms sliced off by an Afghan mob who went on to kill him when he refused to renounce Christ.

Before being martyred, Abdul had already suffered significantly for his faith. When he became a Christian he was rejected by his Muslim family and, when word spread that he had converted, was unable to find anyone who would work on his land, his sole source of income. But he began work as an evangelist to his people in the North-West Frontier, then part of British-ruled India, now the Pakistani province of Khyber Pakhtunkhwa.

Abdul was so passionate about telling others of Christ that he decided one morning in May 1906 to take the Gospel message over the border into Afghanistan. After he had left, the authorities in his home town,

Quetta, learnt that Abdul had been detained in the city of Kandahar. He was then taken to the capital, Kabul, where, after the intervention of the British authorities, his release was obtained. This news caused fury among the local people, and he was seized by a crowd. Given the choice to renounce Christ or die, he stood firm in his faith. The mob cut off his arm and asked him again. Still he refused and his other arm was sliced off. Yet he refused to deny Christ, and was killed.

Catch on fire with enthusiasm and people will come for miles to watch you burn.
John Wesley (1703-91)

May 17

Pursue peace with everyone, and the holiness without which no one will see the Lord. Hebrews 12:14 (NRSV)

Musa and Alexander Bakut (1992)
Nigerian Riots

This father and son were martyred together when Muslim rioters went on an anti-Christian rampage in Nigeria's Kaduna state in May 1992. They had both dreamed about their deaths before they were murdered.

During an evening service at their church on 17 May, Musa led the congregation in praying about the rioting in Zangon Kataf, Kaduna. The Christians were told not to retaliate even if they were attacked. Musa went home but had to return to the church because it had been set on fire. He came home weeping.

At 1 am stones were thrown at Musa's house, and attackers returned later to pour petrol on the property. He went outside to talk with them and found 15 men waiting with sticks, guns and arrows. They ordered Musa to take them to someone who could identify him. His wife begged them not to take her husband, but they responded by wounding her. Their eldest son, Alexander, followed them but could not save his father. One group killed Musa by pouring petrol on him and setting him alight while the other group beheaded Alexander.

Father in heaven, often have we found that the world cannot give us peace. Oh but make us feel that you are able to give peace; let us know the truth of your promise; the whole world may not be able to take away your peace.
Soren Kierkegaard (1813-1855)

May 18

The arrogant mock me unmercifully, but I do not turn from your law.
Psalm 119:51

Peregrinus (c. 261)
Preached Against Idolatry

Peregrinus was the first bishop of Auxerre, France, and his preaching saw most of the city's inhabitants convert to Christianity. Furthermore, he built a church and began to evangelise the surrounding area. When a new temple to Roman god Jupiter was being dedicated at Interanum, south-west of Auxerre, Peregrinus went to the town and appealed to the people to give up their idolatry. He was seized and brought before the governor. He was tortured and then beheaded in c. 261.

Thanks to you, Lord Jesus Christ,
for all the benefits which you have won for us,
for all the pains and insults which you have borne for us.
O most merciful Redeemer, Friend and Brother,
may we know you more clearly,
love you more dearly,
and follow you more nearly,
day by day.
Richard of Chichester (1197-1253)

Christ is faithful as the Son over God's house. And we are his house, if indeed we hold firmly to our confidence and the hope in which we glory.
Hebrews 3:6

The Perez Family (1954) Attacked at Home

Pastor Perez, his wife and six of their seven children were killed when an armed gang burst into their family home on 19 May 1954. They were among at least 120 Christians killed in the 1940s and 1950s in Colombia, which became notorious for its persecution of Christians during this period. Evangelical churches were burnt and their members were targeted because they were thought to be helping revolutionaries against the government.

Pastor Perez and his son Bernardo, aged 12, were arrested in November 1953 and questioned about aiding the revolutionaries; their lives were threatened.

On 19 May 1954, without warning, an armed gang burst into the Perez family home and shot dead Pastor Perez and his wife. Their seven children were also attacked with machetes, and tragically only one child, David, survived the attack. He overcame the devastating loss and trauma and followed in his father's footsteps by becoming a pastor.

God, I pray Thee, light these idle sticks of my life, that I may burn for Thee. Consume my life, my God, for it is Thine. I seek not a long life, but a full one, like you, Lord Jesus.
Jim Elliot (1927-56) (see January 10)

I consider my life worth nothing to me; my only aim is to finish the race and complete the task the Lord Jesus has given me – the task of testifying to the good news of God's grace. Acts 20:24

George, Ellen and James Gordon (1861 and 1872) The last martyrs of "Martyr Island"

George and Ellen Gordon served in a dangerous mission field: the South Pacific island of Erromanga where the first two missionaries had lasted only a few hours before being killed and eaten (see November 20).

The Gordons were very concerned by the brutality of white traders, taking Erromanga's sandalwood.

After nearly four years, the Gordons had led around 40 people to the Lord. Then sandalwood traders deliberately introduced measles to the island. Hundreds died of the unfamiliar disease. George cared diligently for the sick and only two of his patients died; unfortunately they were both children of a chief, who believed that George had killed them by magic. In revenge, he and some warriors killed George and Ellen on 20 May 1861.

George's younger brother, James, offered to continue the work, reaching Erromanga, by then often called "Martyr Island", in the mid-1860s. The island was so depleted of sandalwood trees that the traders had begun trading in men, taking the Erromangans as indentured labourers to Fiji, New Caledonia and Australia where they were often worked to death. It was almost a slave trade.

Many Erromangans opposed James' ministry. During a time of sickness on the island, two children died after James had given them medicine, and the feeling grew that the disease and deaths were his fault. On 7 March 1872 James was on his veranda, translating the book of Acts. He had almost reached the words: "Lord, do not hold this sin against them" (Acts 7:60) when two islanders arrived, one of them the father of the children who had recently died. He struck James a fatal blow in the face with his hatchet.

And then came the faithful few, men and women whose hearts had been softened by the gentle deeds of the Missionary and his winsome wife, and their holy words about Jesus. There was awe in the presence of so great a sacrifice for their sakes. "Like Jesus," they felt. "Just what Jesus did. He died that we might live."
A.K. Langridge, describing the Erromangan Christians coming to take the bodies of George and Ellen Gordon

In him the whole building is joined together and rises to become a holy temple in the Lord. And in him you too are being built together to become a dwelling in which God lives by his Spirit. Ephesians 2:21-22

Nigerian Christians (2001)
Further Violence

At least 150 people (many more according to local estimates) were killed in an outbreak of inter-communal violence in the city of Kaduna in Northern Nigeria, which began on 21 May 2001. Thousands of people fled their homes as dozens of houses, churches and shops were burnt and militias barricaded several roads. Christians were actively targeted and killed in cold blood. Among the victims were the Reverend Aniyo Bobai, Pastors Paul Chickira, David Maigari and Adamu Seko, and the Reverend Clement Ozi Bello.

The violence followed four days of similar religious violence in February that year, which left thousands dead and 80,000 refugees. Those riots began when Muslims attacked a peaceful, if rowdy, Christian demonstration against moves to extend the scope of sharia in the Northern and Middle Belt states of Nigeria. Relations between Muslims and Christians in the city had previously been relatively harmonious but remained tense after the attacks, which have sadly recurred over the ensuing years.

Draw your Church together, O God, into one great company of disciples, together following our Lord Jesus Christ into every walk of life, together serving him in his mission to the world, and together witnessing to his love on every continent and island.
A New Zealand Prayer Book

Precious in the sight of the LORD is the death of his faithful servants.
Truly I am your servant, LORD; I serve you just as my mother did; you
have freed me from my chains. Psalm 116:15-16

Julia of Carthage (439)
Brave Slave

When the Germanic Vandals attacked Carthage, in modern-day
Tunisia, Julia was taken prisoner and sold as a slave to a Syrian named
Eusebius. She frequently went with her master on his voyages, and on
one occasion they went to Corsica.

When she refrained from taking part in an idol feast because she was
a Christian, Eusebius complained about this to the Corsican governor,
Felix. The latter questioned Julia, who remained firm in her Christian
faith. Felix tried to bribe Eusebius to induce Julia to change her faith,
without success. He then invited Eusebius to a dinner, made him drunk
and summoned Julia. Felix told her that if she sacrificed to the gods she
would be freed. But she refused and was beaten and later hanged.

I worship you O Christ,
and I thank you that I have been
counted worthy to suffer for your name.
Let me grasp the greater crown.
As you showed mercy to Rahab,
and received the penitent thief,
turn not your mercy from me.
Theodota of Philippopolis (martyred c. 318)

Rulers persecute me without cause, but my heart trembles at your word.
Psalm 119:161

Desiderius (607)
Challenged Corruption

Desiderius, Bishop of Vienne (France), was a model church leader who supported missionary activity, cared for the sick, enthused his clergy and challenged the ungodly lifestyle of the secular rulers of his day. This made him many enemies.

Desiderius' chief persecutor was Queen Brunhildis, whose grandsons, Theodebert and Theodoric, were kings of Austria and Burgundy respectively.

Desiderius was accused of being too worldly because he read the great Latin classics and gave lessons in grammar. Despite being cleared by Pope Gregory the Great, Brunhildis brought a series of fictitious charges against him and had him expelled for four years.

On his return, Desiderius strongly condemned King Theodoric's lifestyle to the court. For this, the king ordered three of his hired men to beat the bishop on the way back to his house. He was attacked so severely that he died as a result of his injuries.

O Lord, who by triumphing over the power of darkness, didst prepare our place in the New Jerusalem: Grant us, who have this day given thanks for thy resurrection, to praise thee in that city whereof thou art the light; where with the Father and the Holy Spirit thou livest and reignest, world without end.
William Bright (1824-1901), *Parish Prayers* (no. 295)

Be wise in the way you act towards outsiders; make the most of every opportunity. Colossians 4:5

K Isaac Raj and K Daniel (2005)
Preachers Pursued

Pastor Isaac of Rock Church went missing on the night of 24 May 2005 and was found murdered in Skaikpet near Hyderabad, India, on 2 June. His body was not easily recognisable, but his wife Satyaveni and son Satya Prakash formally identified it. Pastor Isaac had left his family home with someone claiming to be taking him to a prayer meeting.

The sudden disappearance and eventual murder of Pastor Isaac followed a similar incident involving Hyderabad Christian preacher and teacher K Daniel earlier in May. He also went missing from his home and was found murdered a few days later. Before his death he had been warned by Hindu extremists not to proclaim Jesus or distribute Bibles. And afterwards, an anonymous letter sent to a local newspaper claimed that the murders were carried out by an organisation called the "Anti-Christian Forum".

Almighty God who in many and various ways, didst speak to thy chosen people by thy prophets, and hast given us, in thy Son our Saviour Jesus Christ, the fulfilment of the hope of Israel: Hasten, we beseech thee the coming of the day when all things shall be subject to him, who liveth and reigneth with thee, and the Holy Spirit, ever one God, world without end.
Church of South India, *Parish Prayers* (no. 20)

It is better, if it is God's will, to suffer for doing good than for doing evil.
1 Peter 3:17

Safwat Zakher Saleh (1995)
Kindness Kills

Safwat was killed and his Christian neighbour injured in an attack on Christians in Upper Egypt in late May 1995. The incident in Hoor village, near Assiut, occurred when Safwat and his brother Nabeel, who were both doctors, were at home taking a break from their work. They were disturbed by a phone call from their clinic, complaining that some patients had been waiting a long time to see a doctor. Nabeel said that the patients could come over to the house. When they arrived, the "patients" pulled their guns on Safwat and shot him dead. Nabeel managed to hide while their courageous neighbour, who heard the gunshots, was wounded as he ran towards the house.

The perpetrators of this crime were Islamic extremists who had threatened the life of Nabeel if he did not pay them a large sum of money because he was a Christian. The *jizya* is a tax paid by non-Muslims according to sharia as a sign of their subjugation to Muslims.

Even if it's a little thing, do something for those who have need of help, something for which you get no pay but the privilege of doing it.
Albert Schweitzer (1875-1965)

Indeed, all who want to live a godly life in Christ Jesus will be persecuted. But wicked people and impostors will go from bad to worse, deceiving others and being deceived. 2 Timothy 3:12-13 (NRSV)

Zhang Xiuji (1996)
Family Bribed

Zhang Xiuji was killed by police in Henan province, China in May 1996, aged 36. Xiuji was dragged out of her home at night and beaten to death the next day. When the police handed over Xiuji's body to her family, they also gave them $600 to keep quiet. The police's official statement said that Xiuji was killed in an accident when she jumped from a car.

Christians in China continue to face violent persecution by the authorities; those who belong to unregistered "house churches" are particularly vulnerable. They are viewed as a threat to the Communist regime, which demands supreme loyalty to the state.

Brief life is here our portion,
Brief sorrow, short lived care;
The life that knows no ending,
The tearless life is there.

There God, our King and Portion,
In fullness of His grace,
We then shall see forever,
And worship face to face.
Bernard of Cluny (12th century)

Praise be to the God and Father of our Lord Jesus Christ! In his great mercy he has given us new birth into a living hope through the resurrection of Jesus Christ from the dead. 1 Peter 1:3

Winnie Davies (1967)
Taken by Rebels

From humble beginnings in Wales, Winnie went to Nebobongo in the Congo to serve as a missionary in 1946. She had trained as a nurse and studied at Bible college for two years before embarking on this endeavour. Winnie re-opened a maternity centre in Nebobongo, where she worked until a rebellion broke out against the Congolese central government in 1964. Winnie and her fellow workers were evacuated in 1961, but she returned shortly afterwards.

Winnie was taken into captivity by the rebels in the summer of 1964, and there were reports at irregular intervals that she was alive. But on 27 May 1967 she was killed by the rebels after trying to escape. Four other missionaries, Jim Rodger, Bill McChesney, Cyril Taylor and Muriel Harman, were killed in the 1964 uprising.

The most eloquent prayer is the prayer through hands that heal and bless. The highest form of worship is the worship of unselfish Christian service. The greatest form of praise is the sound of consecrated feet seeking out the lost and helpless.
Billy Graham (1918-2018)

Blessed are you when people insult you, persecute you and falsely say all kinds of evil against you because of me. Matthew 5:11

Samuel Masih (2004)
Murdered in Hospital

Samuel, a young Christian man, died from severe head trauma after a Muslim police constable struck him with a hammer while he lay defence-less in hospital.

He was admitted to hospital on 22 May 2004, having contracted tuberculosis in prison, where he had been detained since August 2003 under Pakistan's controversial "blasphemy laws" for allegedly defiling a mosque.

In the early hours of 24 May, police constable Faryad Ali entered Samuel's hospital room and – despite the presence of a police guard – assaulted Samuel with a brick-cutter's hammer. Samuel went into a coma and died on 28 May. Faryad sought to kill Samuel because of the accusation of blasphemy. He was arrested for attempted murder, which was changed to formal murder charges after Samuel died.

The "blasphemy laws" are often misused by Pakistani Muslims to get revenge in personal disputes, especially against Christians. A man called Muhammad Yaqoob had filed charges against Samuel, claiming that he saw Samuel spit on the wall of the mosque near the library.

See from his head, his hands, his feet,
Sorrow and love flow mingled down;
Did e'er such love and sorrow meet,
Or thorns compose so rich a crown?
Isaac Watts (1674-1748)

I want to know Christ – yes, to know the power of his resurrection and participation in his sufferings, becoming like him in his death, and so, somehow, attaining to the resurrection from the dead. Philippians 3:10

Raphael Aka Kouame (2011)
Crucified Peasant

Raphael and his younger brother, Kouassi Privat Kacou, were brutally crucified in imitation of Christ's suffering. The incident happened in the Ivory Coast on 29 May 2011. It was one of many atrocities committed against Christians as forces loyal to the new Muslim President, Alassane Ouattara, sought to establish his authority in the country following a disputed election that saw his Christian predecessor, Laurent Gbagbo, ousted. Raphael died of his injuries; incredibly, Kouassi survived the ordeal.

The pair were badly beaten and tortured before being crudely nailed to cross-shaped planks by their hands and feet with steel spikes. The brothers were falsely accused of hiding weapons in their home village of Binkro, which was being targeted by Ouattara supporters as the birthplace of a key enemy. The brothers repeatedly denied any involvement in a weapons cache, but their pleas were ignored. After crucifying the brothers, Ouattara's men carried out an extensive search of Binkro, but they found only a store of medical equipment and supplies, which they looted. The seriously wounded pair were then taken to prison in Oumé, where Raphael died in the night.

There is a green hill far away
Outside a city wall,
Where the dear Lord was crucified,
Who died to save us all.

We may not know, we cannot tell
What pains he had to bear;
But we believe it was for us
He hung and suffered there.
Cecil Frances Alexander (1823-95)

*The LORD is king for ever and ever; the nations shall perish from his
land. O LORD, you will hear the desire of the meek; you will strengthen
their heart, you will incline your ear to do justice for the orphan and the
oppressed.* Psalm 10:16-18a (NRSV)

Lebanese Christians (1860) Massacred by Islamists

Between 30 May and 26 June 1860, rioters from the Druze, an Islamic
sect, burned and pillaged Christian villages in Lebanon. In one inci-
dent Emmanuel Ruiz, guardian of a monastery at Damascus, was killed
together with seven of his community and three laymen. They were given
the choice of accepting Islam or dying; they stood firm in their faith.

The Druze were systematically massacring Christians in an uprising
against the Maronite Church. They were angry that they did not have
equal rights with Christians at that time. On 9 July 3,000 men were
slaughtered in Damascus.

Loving Deliverer,
who gathered the prayers of your blessed martyrs
in the cup of the sufferings of Christ,
guide us by the hand of your mercy
that we may offer no other service
but that which is pleasing in your sight.
We ask this in the Name of Jesus Christ our Lord.
For All the Saints (Canada)

See, I am sending you out like sheep into the midst of wolves; so be wise as serpents and innocent as doves. Beware of them, for they will hand you over to councils and flog you in their synagogues.
Matthew 10:16-17 (NRSV)

Chou Wen-Mo (1801)
Handed Over

This missionary was twice betrayed to the Korean authorities before being condemned to death and executed on 31 May 1801. Chou Wen-Mo, a Chinese orphan, had been helped to enter Seoul by two Koreans in December 1794. He began to pastor Christians there until he was arrested, having been reported to the authorities by a convert. On this occasion he was able to escape with the help of some friends and went on to have several successful years as an "underground" pastor.

During the 1801 persecution in Korea that saw around 300 Christians martyred, he was again betrayed by someone he thought to be a fellow believer. After his execution, Wen-Mo's body was secretly buried by the authorities so that no Christian would ever discover it.

Lord Jesus Christ, who came to this world as a man
and suffered your passion, allowing your hands to be nailed to the cross
*   for our sins, give me the strength to endure my passion.*
It comes not from my enemies, but from my own brother:
Yet, Lord, do not account it to him as sin.
Boris of Kiev (martyred 1015)

We demolish arguments and every pretension that sets itself up against the knowledge of God, and we take captive every thought to make it obedient to Christ. 2 Corinthians 10:5

Justin Martyr (c. 165)
Persuasive Writer

Justin was one of the greatest early Christian apologists and philosophers, and his skill in arguing persuasively for the Christian faith led to his martyrdom. He was born at Flavia, Neapolis, to Greek parents in around 100 and became a Christian aged around 30 while studying at Ephesus. There Justin witnessed and was impressed by the faithfulness of the Christian martyrs and also met an elderly Christian man whose character made an impression upon him. The man spoke to him about how Jesus was the fulfilment of God's promises to the Jews. Justin described his reaction: "Straightaway a flame was kindled in my soul, and a love of the prophets and those who are friends of Christ possessed me."

Justin was well educated, and he engaged in debates with non-Christians of various beliefs. He opened a school of Christian philosophy first at Ephesus and then later in Rome. Three of his writings survive, two *Apologies* and the *Dialogue with Trypho;* they persuasively contend for the Gospel and were intended to convince pagans to turn to Christ.

Justin was arrested following a debate in Rome with a celebrated Cynic philosopher, Crescens. It is thought that Crescens lost the debate and denounced Justin to the authorities out of spite. He was charged with practising an unauthorised religion and brought for trial before the Roman prefect Rusticus. Justin refused to renounce Christ, so he was executed along with six of his students in c. 165.

No one makes us afraid or leads us into captivity as we have set our faith on Jesus. For though we are beheaded, and crucified, and exposed to beasts and chains and fire and all other forms of torture, it is plain that we do not forsake the confession of our faith, but the more things of this kind which happen to us the more are there others who become believers and truly religious through the name of Jesus.
Justin Martyr (c. 100-c. 165)

For whoever wants to save their life will lose it, but whoever loses their life for me will find it. Matthew 16:25

Iraqi Christians (2007)
Frequent Targets

Church leaders are frequently targeted by Islamist militants in Iraq to send a message to Christians that their faith is not welcome in the country. On Sunday 3 June 2007 a minister and three deacons were shot dead as they drove away from their church in Mosul, northern Iraq, after the evening service. They were about a hundred metres from the church when the gunmen opened fire.

Ordinary Iraqi Christians are also killed by militants; the week before the shooting, Christian couple Hazim and Amal were beheaded by an Islamic militant.

> *O God, who hast appointed unto men once to die, but hast hidden from them the time of their death: Help us to so live in this world that we may be ready to leave it; and that, being thine in death as in life, we may come to the rest that remaineth for thy people; through him who died and rose again for us, thy Son Jesus Christ our Lord.*
> *Parish Prayers* (no. 867)

> *O sweet and blessèd country, the home of God's elect!*
> *O sweet and blessèd country, that eager hearts expect!*
> *Jesus, in mercy bring us to that dear land of rest,*
> *Who art, with God the Father, and Spirit, ever blessed.*
> Bernard of Morlaix (fl. 1146)
> Translated by John Mason Neale (1818-1866)

Rejoice always, pray continually, give thanks in all circumstances; for this is God's will for you in Christ Jesus. 1 Thessalonians 5:16-18

Buganda Martyrs (1885-87)
Praising Him on the Way to the Fire

This date is set aside as a public holiday in Uganda to commemorate the country's martyrs, in particular the 45 Buganda martyrs.

Christianity arrived in Uganda (Buganda) in 1877 after British explorer and journalist Henry Stanley shared the Gospel with King Mutesa, who then appealed for missionaries to come to the country. However his successor King Mwanga did not share King Mutesa's enthusiasm for Christianity. Rather he became increasingly angry that converts were putting their loyalty to Christ above the traditional loyalty to the monarch and eventually resolved to wipe out Christianity.

Martyrdoms began in 1885; the first to die, on 31 January, were Mark Kukumba, Yusuf Rugarama and Noah Seruwanga. The next year, on 3 June, 26 court pages were burned to death on the orders of King Mwanga, because they were Christians (see also November 15). But rather than crushing the new faith as the king intended, the example of these youths – who walked to their deaths singing hymns and praying for their enemies – inspired many of the bystanders to find out more about Christianity. A total of 45 Christians were executed during the persecution under King Mwanga, but within a few years the original handful of converts had multiplied and spread far beyond the court.

Daily, daily, sing the praises, of the city God hath made;
In the beauteous fields of Eden, its foundation stones are laid:
O, that I had wings of angels, here to spread and heav'nward fly:
I would seek the gates of Sion, far beyond the starry sky!
S Baring-Gould (1834-1924)
This hymn is known as the "Uganda Martyrs' Hymn" because it is believed that some sang it in Swahili as they went to their death: *Bulijjo tutendereza ekibuga kyaffe. Ekyakubibwa mu Ggulu, Yesu kyeyazimba. Singa mbadde n'ebiwaawa nga Bamalayika, Nandibuuse, nandituuse eri mu Sayuni.*

We have come to share in Christ, if indeed we hold our original conviction firmly to the very end. Hebrews 3:14

Sanctus (177)
"I am a Christian"

Sanctus was one of a number of Christians who stood firm in his faith throughout a series of horrendous tortures during an outbreak of anti-Christian persecution in the Roman province of Gaul in the second century. A contemporary letter said that he "endured all cruelty with superhuman courage".

Sanctus was tortured in an attempt to extract information from him, but he refused to answer any questions. When asked his name, race, city of origin and whether he was slave or free, Sanctus unashamedly proclaimed in response to every question, "I am a Christian."

Angered by this, the governor and torturers increased the pressure on Sanctus, pressing red-hot plates of brass against the most tender parts of his body, but he was unmoved. Sanctus, swollen and inflamed, was brought out again after a few days for further torture. This time he was put on a rack but, rather than destroying his fragile body, it served to straighten out his contorted physique. After this, Sanctus was taken with a number of other Christians to a special public exhibition, where they were subjected to more suffering, including being mauled by beasts. But Sanctus responded only with the same confession that he had made at the beginning until finally he was put to death.

Give us, O Lord, a steadfast heart, which no unworthy affection may drag downwards; give us an unconquered heart, which no tribulation can wear out; give us an upright heart, which no unworthy purpose may tempt aside. Bestow upon us also, O Lord, our God, understanding to know you, diligence to seek you, and faithfulness that may finally embrace you; through Jesus Christ our Lord. Amen.
Thomas Aquinas (1225-1274)

Ruth replied...“Your people will be my people and your God my God.”
Ruth 1:16

Daw Pwa Sein (1942)
Stood By Hated Tribe

Daw Pwa Sein was hacked to death when she chose to stand with a Christian tribe during a raid by the Burmese. The daughter of a Buddhist, she became a Christian as a teenager and went on to become headmistress of a Christian school in Kemendine, Burma. The country was invaded in 1941, and along with her school she was evacuated to Nyaugn-ngu. The inhabitants of this village were Karens, a tribe that includes many Christians and is hated by the Burmese majority.

On 5 June 1942 the village was raided by the Burmese, and although Daw Pwa Sein was not a Karen, she stood with her fellow-believers. The Burmese raiders chose her and her companions, namely Daw Sein Thit, Daw Aye Nyein, Hilda, Ann and Ma Tin Shwe, to be killed. All were given a few moments to pray before being hacked to death.

Thy way, not mine, O Lord,
   However dark it be;
Lead me by Thine own hand,
   Choose out the path for me.

Take Thou my cup, and it
   With joy or sorrow fill,
As best to Thee may seem;
   Choose Thou my good and ill.

Choose Thou for me my friends,
   My sickness or my health.
Choose Thou my cares for me,
   My poverty or wealth.

Not mine, not mine the choice,
  In things both great and small;
Be Thou my guide, my strength,
  My wisdom and my all.
Horatius Bonar (1808–1889)

June 6

All our steps are ordered by the LORD. Proverbs 20:24a (NRSV)

Carl Heine (1944)
Led by Love

Falling in love – first with the Marshall Islands in the Pacific Ocean, and then with a Christian woman he met there – led Carl to finding faith in Christ. He went on to become known as the foremost Protestant missionary of the Marshalls.

His travels with the merchant navy took Carl from his home in New South Wales, Australia, to the Marshalls, Micronesia, in 1892. Tragically, the beloved wife whom he met there died after a short period. Carl left the island and joined a mission organisation, with which he was ordained a minister. From then on he dedicated his life to the furtherance of the Gospel in the Marshalls and eventually assumed the leadership of the church there.

With the outbreak of the Second World War, the Japanese military arrived on the Islands. All the missionaries there were taken out by their missionary organisations except Carl, who chose to stay faithful to his post. In early 1944 Japanese soldiers found Carl and took him and his eldest son, Claude, to be executed.

O God, who art the author of peace and lover of concord, in knowledge of whom standeth our eternal life, whose service is perfect freedom: defend us thy humble servants in all assaults of our enemies; that we, surely trusting in thy defence, may not fear the power of any adversaries; through the might of Jesus Christ our Lord.
Book of Common Prayer 1549, Morning Prayer

For it is by grace you have been saved, through faith – and this not from yourselves, it is the gift of God – not by works, so that no one can boast.
Ephesians 2:8-9

George Kuzhikandum and Vijay Ekka (2000)
Murder Witness Killed

George was a teacher and church leader in a part of India where tensions between Hindus and Christians are always near the surface. He was attacked by a group of Hindus, who beat him with iron rods until he died. This happened on 7 June 2000 while George was on the campus of the school where he taught, Brother Polus Memorial School, near Mathura, Utter Pradesh. The incident was witnessed by another Christian called Vijay Ekka, who died in police custody in suspicious circumstances three days later.

Vijay gave a statement at the police station about George's murder and was promised by police that he would be released on the same day, but he was detained for questioning for several days. When his friends visited him after two days, Vijay told them that the policemen were torturing him. After he died, the police reported that Vijay had committed suicide, but a post-mortem revealed that he had been beaten and given electric shock treatment, which caused his death. Vijay left a pregnant wife.

As a Hindu I endured the self-discipline and much study for one purpose – to better myself, to achieve heaven by my own deeds. Christianity starts with man's weakness. It asks us to accept our selfishness and inabilities, then promises a new nature.
Paul Krishna, a former Hindu

For it is to your credit if, being aware of God, you endure pain while suffering unjustly. 1 Peter 2:19 (NRSV)

Mitrophan (Chi-Sung) (1900)
"It does not hurt to suffer for Christ"

In June 1900, proclamations were posted on walls across Beijing calling for the slaughter of all Christians. The following day, groups of Boxer rebels went around the city forcing Christians to bow to idols, torturing and killing any who refused.

Among those hunted down was Mitrophan, a Chinese minister whose Chinese name was Chi-Sung.

One evening he, his wife, three sons and dozens of other Christians gathered together for protection. But the group was found and surrounded by Boxers. They grabbed Chi-Sung's son Isaiah and began to cut him with swords in an attempt to persuade the father to renounce his faith. They taunted him, but Chi-Sung replied, "It does not hurt to suffer for Christ." Faced with his staunch declaration of faith, the rebels executed him quickly.

In total 222 Christians were killed in the Beijing parish during the Boxer rebellion.

Stand up, stand up for Jesus!
The strife will not be long;
This day the noise of battle,
The next the victor's song.
To him that overcometh
A crown of life shall be;
He with the king of glory
Shall reign eternally
George Duffield (1818-88)

You will shine among them like stars in the sky as you hold firmly to the word of life. Philippians 2:15b-16a

Esther Ethan (2003)
Stabbed at Home

On 9 June 2003 Esther was stabbed to death in her own home on her return from engaging in street evangelism. As she walked the short distance to her home in Numan, a Christian-majority town in north-eastern Nigeria, a man named Mohammed Salisu followed close behind. Esther's children saw him emerge from the house carrying a knife covered with blood.

Esther's murder triggered a lengthy period of sectarian unrest that resulted in the deaths of three other Christians. Christians are in the minority in the northern part of Nigeria and face the constant threat of persecution.

We are the Bibles the world is reading;
We are the creeds the world is needing;
We are the sermons the world is heeding.
Billy Graham (1918-2018)

Our days may come to seventy years, or eighty, if our strength endures; yet the best of them are but trouble and sorrow, for they quickly pass, and we fly away. Psalm 90:10

Maximus (250)
Homeward Bound

When Maximus was called before the consul Optimus under the persecution of Emperor Decius, he provided his name, profession (a merchant)

and identity as a Christian. A decree had required people to venerate a statue of the emperor or else face torture and death. Maximus was given a choice by the consul: either to sacrifice to the statue and save his life or die in torment. He said, "This is what I have always wanted. This is why I presented myself to you, so I could exchange this miserable temporal existence for eternal life." Despite being tortured on the rack and beaten with rods, Maximus still refused to obey the decree, so Optimus ordered him to be taken outside the city walls and stoned to death.

Blessed Creator,
Thou hast promised thy beloved sleep...
May my frequent lying down make me familiar with death,
the bed I approach remind me of the grave,
the eyes I now close picture to me their final closing.
Keep me always ready, waiting for admittance to thy presence.
Weaken my attachment to earthly things.
May I hold life loosely in my hand,
knowing that I receive it on condition of its surrender.
As pain and suffering betoken transitory health,
may I not shrink from a death that introduces me
to the freshness of eternal youth.
From "Sleep", *Puritan Prayers*

June 11

The whole assembly became silent as they listened to Barnabas and Paul telling about the signs and wonders God had done among the Gentiles through them. Acts 15:12

Barnabas (c. 61)
Son of Consolation

Barnabas, a Jewish Cypriot, was one of the earliest Christian disciples in Jerusalem. His name means "son of consolation", and he was known for his encouraging nature, always willing to help and share with those around him. Indeed, in Acts 4:36-37 we are told that he "sold a field he owned and brought the money and put it at the apostles' feet".

Much of what we know about him is taken from the book of Acts, in which we read that he was well-regarded in the Jerusalem church, which eventually entrusted him with the task of leading the church in Antioch. Luke, the author of Acts, described Barnabas' fruitful ministry in Antioch thus:

> When he arrived and saw what the grace of God had done, he was glad and encouraged them all to remain true to the Lord with all their hearts. He was a good man, full of the Holy Spirit and faith, and a great number of people were brought to the Lord.
> (Acts 11:23-24)

Paul joined him in Antioch, and they embarked upon a missionary journey to Cyprus and Asia Minor, where they "proclaimed the word of God in the Jewish synagogues" (Acts 13:5b). On one occasion, in Pisidian Antioch, "almost the whole city gathered to hear the word of the Lord" (Acts 13:44b). The Jews were jealous and opposed the pair, who then turned their attention to the Gentiles, and "the word of the Lord spread through the whole region" (Acts 13:49). The persecution from the Jews intensified as the Gospel message rang out, attracting large numbers of followers. They then returned to Antioch before setting off on separate missionary journeys. Barnabas went back to Cyprus, this time with his cousin John Mark.

Barnabas is regarded as the founder of the church in Cyprus, which is where he was later martyred at Salamis, in around the year 61. According to tradition, he was dragged by Jews out of the synagogue, where he was preaching the Gospel, and stoned to death.

The son of consolation, moved by thy law of love,
forsaking earthly treasures, sought riches from above.
As earth now teems with increase, let gifts of grace descend,
that thy true consolations may through the world extend.
Horatio Nelson (1823- 1913)

My bones suffer mortal agony as my foes taunt me, saying to me all day long, "Where is your God?" Why, my soul, are you downcast? Why so disturbed within me? Put your hope in God, for I will yet praise him, my Saviour and my God. Psalm 42:10-11

Missionaries to China (1900)
Hunted Down

During the Boxer Rebellion in China, a group of missionaries took shelter from a bloodthirsty crowd in the house of a Chinese magistrate who had offered them protection. They were there under armed guard for 18 days, during which time Stewart McKee's wife gave birth. There were two couples and two single women in the group, and the newborn brought the total number of children to five.

On 12 June a local official arrived at the house and took a list of all those present. A short time later, a troop of 300 soldiers arrived, and Stewart went out to see what they wanted. He was stabbed to death by the angry soldiers, who proceeded to torch the house. Only one child, Alice, escaped, but even she was hunted down and killed by the rebels, who wanted to kill all the Christians that they could find.

*I asked the Lord for a bunch of fresh flowers but instead he gave me an
   ugly cactus with many thorns.
I asked the Lord for some beautiful butterflies but instead he gave me
   many ugly and dreadful worms.
I was threatened, I was disappointed, I mourned.
But after many days, suddenly, I saw the cactus bloom with many
   beautiful flowers and those worms became beautiful butterflies fly-
   ing in the spring wind.
God's way is the best way.*
Kao Chun-Ming, written from a Taiwanese prison where he was
jailed from 1980 to 1984

Trust in the LORD with all your heart and lean not on your own understanding; in all your ways submit to him, and he will make your paths straight. Proverbs 3:5-6

Ashish Prabash Masih (2000)
Hindu Hostility

Ashish was a 23-year-old preacher who was found murdered at his house in Jalandhar city, Punjab state, India, in June 2000. The Punjab Christian Association believes that his killing was the outcome of a concerted campaign against the Christian community by Hindu nationalists.

Christians in India face much hostility from Hindu extremists. At the time of Ashish's murder, a minister was killed in the city of Mathura, Uttar Pradesh state, and there were bomb attacks outside churches in Andhra Pradesh and Karnataka.

Should pain and suffering, sorrow, and grief, rise up like clouds and overshadow for a time the Sun of Righteousness and hide Him from your view, do not be dismayed, for in the end this cloud of woe will descend in showers of blessing on your head, and the Sun of Righteousness rise upon you to set no more for ever.
Sadhu Sundar Singh (1889-1929)

Love your enemies, do good to them... Then your reward will be great, and you will be children of the Most High. Luke 6:35

Chris Leggett (2009)
"Infidel" Assassinated

"Two knights of the Islamic Maghreb succeeded Tuesday morning at 8 am to kill the infidel American Christopher Leggett for his Christianizing activities."

A recording of this statement, reportedly from al-Qaeda, was played on Al-Jazeera television following the assassination of American Christian Chris Leggett in Mauritania in June 2009. Two attackers had tried to kidnap him, and when he resisted they shot him several times in the head.

Following his death, his parents released the following statement: "In a spirit of love, we express our forgiveness for those who took away the life of our remarkable son. Chris had a deep love for Mauritania and its people, a love that we share. Despite this terrible event, we harbour no ill will for the Mauritanian people. On a spiritual level, we forgive those responsible, asking only that justice be applied against those who killed our son."

Leggett, his wife and four children lived for seven years in the impoverished El-Kasr neighbourhood of Nouakchott, where he directed an aid agency that provided training in computer skills, sewing and literacy, and he also ran a micro-finance programme. Despite his humanitarian works in Mauritania, Leggett was perceived as an enemy by the Islamic radicals.

People are often unreasonable, illogical, and self-centered...
*   forgive them anyway*
If you are kind, people may accuse you of selfish ulterior motives...
*   be kind anyway*
What you may spend years building, someone may destroy overnight...
*   build anyway*
The good you do today, people will often forget tomorrow...
*   do good anyway*
Give the world the best you have, and it may never be enough...
*   give the world the best you have anyway*
Mother Teresa (1910-1997)

June 15

Just as sin reigned in death, so also grace might reign through righteousness to bring eternal life through Jesus Christ our Lord. Romans 5:21

Bantu Masih (1992)
Blasphemy Charge

Bantu, a 65-year old Christian, was accused of blasphemy by a man named Shehzad Ahmed after a quarrel over money in Lahore. Pakistan's "blasphemy laws" are often used by Muslims to settle personal grudges; Christians and other non-Muslims are particularly vulnerable to false accusations.

A procession of *maulvis* (Muslim preachers) took place, protesting against Bantu, and the police took him into custody on 4 May 1992. Some Muslim friends stood as guarantee for Bantu, but while they were signing the affidavit, Shehzad went to the police station and stabbed him. Bantu was taken to hospital, and a police document called an FIR (First Information Report) was registered against Shehzad.

On 8 May, Shehzad registered his own FIR against Bantu under Section 295-C of the Pakistan Penal Code, which carries a mandatory death sentence for "defiling the name of Muhammad". Meanwhile Bantu was prevailed upon to withdraw his case against Shehzad. He spent 21 days in hospital but did not fully recover and later died.

O Lord of life, where'er they be,
Safe in Thine own eternity,
Our dead are living unto Thee:
Hallelujah!

Thy word is true, Thy ways are just;
Above the requiem, 'Dust to dust'
Shall rise our psalm of grateful trust:
Hallelujah!

O happy they in God who rest,
No more by fear and doubt oppressed,
Living or dying they are blest:
Hallelujah!
F L Hosmer (1840-1929)

Now if we are children, then we are heirs – heirs of God and co-heirs with Christ, if indeed we share in his sufferings in order that we may also share in his glory. Romans 8:17

The Scillitan Martyrs (c. 180)
Embraced Death

The Scillitan Martyrs were seven men and five women from Scillium in North Africa who were arrested, taken to Carthage and brought before the Roman proconsul Saturninus. Speratus, their spokesman, was asked what he carried in his bag. He answered, "The sacred books and the letters of a righteous man named Paul."

They were given one month to give up their Christian beliefs, but they refused and so were sentenced to immediate death by the sword. At hearing this, Speratus cried, "Thanks be to God." They died around the year 180.

O God, who dost inspire us to confess thy holy name by the witness of thy martyrs: Grant that thy Church, encouraged by their example, may be ready to suffer fearlessly for thy cause, and to strive for the reward of thy heavenly glory; through Jesus Christ our Lord.
W H Frere (1863-1938), *Parish Prayers* (no. 590)

I will show you my faith by my deeds. James 2:18

Bernard Mizeki (1896)
Stood by the Suffering

Bernard is regarded by many as the first indigenous Christian martyr of Southern Africa. He started to work among the Mashona people of Zimbabwe (then Rhodesia) in 1891, and through his linguistic, musical and teaching gifts he brought the Gospel to them in their own language and culture. This society was dominated by traditional religions and, at a time when the Europeans were making military and commercial advances into Southern Africa, Bernard was regarded by some as an agent of the imperialists.

The Mashona rebelled against the British, and Bernard could have left, but he chose to stay. He was advised to abandon his station and was hesitating when he saw a man covered with sores, whom he had taken in. Bernard realised that if he went, that man would be left to starve. He wrote of his decision, "I cannot leave my people now in a time of such darkness."

On the night of 17 June 1896 he was attacked and wounded by warriors but was able to crawl to a nearby hillside, where he died. Bernard's wife and another woman went to look for him, but the body had gone. The site of his martyrdom has been a place of pilgrimage for many Christians from all over southern Africa.

Lord, if any have to die this day, let it be me, for I am ready.
Billy Bray (1794-1868)

June 18

This is my gospel, for which I am suffering even to the point of being chained like a criminal. But God's word is not chained. Therefore I endure everything. 2 Timothy 2:8b-10a

Jiang Zongxiu (2004)
Dying for Bibles

This 34-year-old Chinese Christian woman was arrested on 18 June for "spreading rumours and inciting to disturb the social order" after distributing Bibles on the street. She died the same afternoon in police custody, according to a report in China's state-run *Legal Daily* newspaper.

Tan Dewei, Zongxiu's mother-in-law, was arrested at the same time but later released. Dewei told reporters that Zongxiu was repeatedly kicked and struck by police during her interrogation. When police released her body to relatives they noticed that it was bruised and blood-stained. But the police told them that Zongxiu, a farmer from China's south-western Uizhou province, had suddenly been taken ill. Her husband and other villagers said that Zongxiu did most of the family's farm work and she was in good health before the arrests.

God's book of "grace" is just like his book of nature; it is his thoughts written out. This great book, the Bible, this most precious volume is the heart of God, made legible; it is the gold of God's love, beaten out into gold leaf, so that therewith our thoughts might be plated, and we also might have golden, good and holy thoughts concerning him.
John Bunyan (1628-88)

June 19

The God of all grace, who called you to his eternal glory in Christ, after you have suffered a little while, will himself restore you and make you strong, firm and steadfast. To him be the power for ever and ever. Amen.
1 Peter 5:10-11

Harry Goehring (1966)
Poisoned for Christ

In 1963 Harry and his wife went to East Pakistan (now Bangladesh) as part of a missionary team which was to build a hospital, start a school and be involved in Bible translation and literature distribution. Harry's contribution to the mission was as a translator and educator. He had been studying in Tennessee when the Lord spoke to him about mission through Ephesians 3:8: "Although I am less than the least of all the Lord's people, this grace was given me: to preach to the Gentiles the boundless riches of Christ."

The school and translation work went well, and Harry led a tribal chief to commit his life to Christ.

In June 1966 he was reading Colossians and reflecting on Christ's sufferings, and he was beginning to sense the powers of darkness more than ever before. One day his kidneys stopped working, and the doctors felt that he should go back to the USA. The next day he seemed better, but the following day his heart began to fail. The doctors tried to save him, but Harry gasped, "Let me go," and died. A post-mortem revealed that his kidneys had stopped because of poisoning, though it was unclear how he had been poisoned. Many Bengalis attended his funeral.

Whom shall we trust but you, O God?
Where rest but on your faithful word?
None ever called on you in vain:
Give peace, O God, give peace again.
Henry Williams Baker (1821-1877)

June 20

But thanks be to God, who always leads us as captives in Christ's triumphal procession and uses us to spread the aroma of the knowledge of him everywhere. 2 Corinthians 2:14

Korean Family (1950s)
Buried Alive

During the Korean War in the early 1950s, hundreds of Christian leaders were captured and killed, and around 2,000 churches were destroyed. One church leader and his family who were seized in Inchon, Korea, were subjected to a harrowing public ordeal. The Communists dug a large hole and put the pastor, his wife and several of their children in it. He was accused of "misleading the people with the superstition of the Bible" and was told that if he would denounce it before the crowd, he, his wife and their children would be freed. "But if you persist in your superstitions," the Communist leader added, "all of your family is going to be buried alive. Make a decision!"

The pastor's children cried out, "Oh Daddy! Daddy! Think of us! Daddy!" He was greatly shaken and started to speak: "Yes, yes, I'll do it. I am going to denounce…" But his wife stopped him, saying, "Daddy! Say NO!"

She comforted the children with the words, "Tonight we are going to have supper with the King of kings, the Lord of lords!" and led them in singing the Christian hymn, "In the Sweet By and By". The Communists began to bury them, but they all continued singing until the soil came up to their necks. Many of the people who witnessed their calm confidence in the face of execution became Christians.

There's a land that is fairer than day,
And by faith we can see it afar;
For the Father waits over the way
To prepare us a dwelling place there.

In the sweet by and by,
We shall meet on that beautiful shore;
In the sweet by and by,
We shall meet on that beautiful shore.

We shall sing on that beautiful shore
The melodious songs of the blessed;
And our spirits shall sorrow no more,
Not a sigh for the blessing of rest.
Sanford Fillmore Bennett (1836-1898)

June 21

And this is the testimony: God has given us eternal life, and this life is in his Son. 1 John 5:11

Maulawi Assadullah (2004) "Propagating Christianity"

After former Muslim cleric Maulawi Assadullah converted to Christianity in the Awdand district of Ghazni Province, Afghanistan, he began to share his new faith. This was incredibly brave given that the country is strongly Islamic and most Muslims there believe – in line with Islamic teaching – that converts should be killed. Maulawi suffered this penalty in June 2004.

Announcing his death, Taliban spokesman Abdul Latif Hakimi said, "A group of Taliban dragged out Maulawi Assadullah and slit his throat with a knife because he was propagating Christianity. We have enough evidence and local accounts to prove that he was involved in the conversions of Muslims to Christianity."

Lord God of all times and places, we pray for your Church... Help her to proclaim boldly the coming gospel of her Lord. Fill her with the prophet's scorn of tyranny, and with a Christ-like tenderness for the heavy laden and downtrodden. Bid her cease from seeking her own life, lest she lose it. Make her valiant to give up her life to humanity, that like her crucified Lord, she may mount by the path of the cross to a higher glory; through the same Jesus Christ our Lord. Amen.
Walter Rauschenbusch (1861-1918)

June 22

Very rarely will anyone die for a righteous person, though for a good person someone might possibly dare to die. But God demonstrates his own love for us in this: While we were still sinners, Christ died for us.
Romans 5:7-8

Alban (year unknown)
First British Martyr

Alban was a soldier at Verulamium (now named St Albans after him), one of the Roman towns that guarded Britannia in the third century. Though a pagan, Alban concealed a Christian clergyman, Amphibalus, who was fleeing persecution in the Roman Empire. When Alban saw Amphibalus praying, he started to question him about Christianity and soon after made a commitment to Christ and was baptised.

Soldiers heard that a clergyman was being concealed, and came to Alban to arrest their suspect. But Alban donned the clerical clothes and allowed himself to be arrested in Amphibalus' place. He was brought before a judge and ordered to sacrifice to the pagan gods, but he refused, saying, "I confess Jesus Christ, the son of God, with my whole being. Those whom you call gods are idols; they are made by hands." Alban further enraged the court when he refused to reveal where Amphibalus had gone.

He was condemned to death, but on the way to the execution site the soldier who had been ordered to carry out the penalty refused because he too had become a Christian. Both Alban and the Roman soldier were beheaded.

Alban is celebrated on 22 June as the first British Christian martyr; the year of his death has never been firmly established.

O the deep, deep love of Jesus, vast, unmeasured, boundless, free!
Rolling as a mighty ocean in its fullness over me!
Underneath me, all around me, is the current of Thy love
Leading onward, leading homeward to Thy glorious rest above!
Samuel Francis (1834-1925)

June 23

Open your eyes and look at the fields! They are ripe for harvest.
John 4:35

Elim Mission Workers (1978)
Guerrilla Onslaught

"On Friday 23 June 1978 is the day and date we reached Ngue Mission on Vumba Area near Matondo Camp in Zimunya District. Time of operation from 6.30 to 9.00 pm... Total number of comrades who were there, 21... Weapons used, axes and knobkerries. Aim: to destroy the enemies. We killed 12 whites including 4 babies..."

This chilling account was recorded in the diary of one of the guerrillas who attacked a Christian mission in Zimbabwe (then Rhodesia). The killers took the Christians into the bush and killed every one, including the children.

Those martyred were: Catherine Picken, a nurse; Mary Fisher, a teacher; Wendy White, a social worker; Peter McCann, a science teacher at the Elim Secondary School at Caterere; his wife Sandra and baby Joy; Roy Lynn, a maintenance man, and his wife Joyce, the hospital matron, and baby Pamela; Philip and Sue Evans with their three children. Mary Fisher was found alive, but she later died of her wounds. Their funeral was attended by 800 Europeans and Africans.

The world will see that killing one Christian is actually multiplying us.
The blood of the Church martyrs is actually the seed for new Christians.
In this way the Church will triumph when it is oppressed and progress
when it is despised. Now I believe that it is my duty to spread the gospel.
African Christian reflecting on the savage incident

June 24

Do not fear, for I am with you; do not be dismayed, for I am your God.
I will strengthen you and help you; I will uphold you with my righteous
right hand. Isaiah 41:10

Victor, Montanus, Lucius and Flavian (259)
Falsely Accused

This quartet were part of a group of eight African martyrs arrested on
false charges of being involved in a revolt against the Roman procurator
at Carthage. Some of them were clergy under Cyprian, who had been
executed the year before.

The group were interrogated and remained in custody, where they
received short rations and suffered from hunger and thirst. The priest,
Victor, was brought out to be killed immediately; the rest were in prison
for several months before being condemned to death. Lucius went to the
place of execution first since he felt weak and thought he would not keep
up with the others. Montanus felt stronger, and as he went to his death
he preached to the non-Christian bystanders and encouraged his broth-
ers. One of the prisoners, Flavian, had his sentence repealed until he was
discovered to be a deacon. He was then also beheaded.

Eternal God, who rulest the world from everlasting to everlasting:
Speak to our hearts when men faint for fear, and the love of many grows
cold, and there is distress of nations upon earth. Keep us resolute and
steadfast in all things that cannot be shaken; and make us to lift our eyes
and behold, beyond the things that are seen and temporal, the things that
are unseen and eternal; through Jesus Christ our Lord.
Parish Prayers (no. 26)

I chose you and appointed you so that you might go and bear fruit – fruit that will last. John 15:16b

William E Simpson (1932)
Natural Evangelist

Born to American missionary parents in the border country of Tibet and China, William followed in his father's footsteps as an evangelist to the Tibetan people. He travelled 4,000 miles a year on horseback, going from camp to camp, sharing the Gospel with the Tibetans. He built a small school on the Tibetan border, where he taught the Bible to children. It was here that he was martyred one day in June 1932, when a horde of Muslim army deserters attacked the Christian school. William was 29 years old.

News of the incident was sent to his father who lived nearby, and he immediately rushed to the school, where he found his son's mangled body on the floor. Under William's body he found a note smeared with blood that said, "In remembrance of Me."

William's father, who was also called William, remained in China until 1949. He continued to evangelise widely and also focused his efforts on the training of Chinese clergy.

Are not all the trials, the loneliness, the heartache, the weariness and pain, the cold and fatigue of the long road, the darkness and discouragements, and all the bereavements, temptations and testings, deemed not worthy to be compared with the joy of witnessing to this "glad tidings of great joy"?
William Simpson (martyred 1932)

Now it is God who makes both us and you stand firm in Christ.
2 Corinthians 1:21

John and Paul (c. 362)
Brothers in Faith and Life

These martyrs were brothers from a noble family and held high office in the Roman Army. Following the accession of the Emperor Julian "the Apostate", they were accused of being Christians and given ten days in which to consider whether they would give up their faith and bow to pagan idols or die as martyrs. They chose to die and were executed in their own home. They are reputed to be the last to have suffered in Rome for refusing to worship idols.

Through the night of doubt and sorrow
Onward goes the pilgrim band,
Singing songs of expectation,
Marching to the Promised Land.
Clear before us, through the darkness,
Gleams and burns the guiding light.
Brother clasps the hand of brother,
Stepping fearless through the night.
Bernhardt S. Ingemann (1789-1862)
Translated by Sabine Baring-Gould (1834-1924)

Thanks be unto thee, O God, for revealing thyself to man, and for sending forth thy messengers in every age. Thanks be unto thee for the first apostles of Christ, sent forth into all the world to preach the gospel; for those who brought the good news to our land; for all who, in ages of darkness, kept alive the light, or in times of indifference were faithful to their Lord's command; for all thy followers in every age who have given their lives for the faith; for those in our own day who have gone to the ends of the earth as heralds of thy love for the innumerable company who now praise thee out of every kindred and nation and tongue. With these and the whole company of heaven we worship thee; through Jesus Christ our Lord.
Parish Prayers (no. 755)

Surely he took up our pain and bore our suffering, yet we considered him punished by God, stricken by him, and afflicted. But he was pierced for our transgressions, he was crushed for our iniquities; the punishment that brought us peace was on him, and by his wounds we are healed.
Isaiah 53:4-5

Gregory Nikolsky (1918)
Shot in the Mouth

On 27 June 1918, the Reverend Gregory Nikolsky of Mary Magdalene monastery in Russia was taken out through the gates by the Communist troops. They forced him to open his mouth and shouted, "We will also give you the sacrament." They then shot him in the mouth.

When the Communists came to power in 1917 they launched an all-out attack on Orthodox churches and Christians. Gregory's death is one example of the type of atrocities that took place.

Christ is a substitute for everything, but nothing is a substitute for Christ.
Henry Allan Ironside (1876-1951)

Answer me when I call to you, my righteous God. Give me relief from my distress. Psalm 4:1a

Irenaeus (c. 304)
Refused to Sacrifice

When Irenaeus, Bishop of Sirmium (Serbia), was arrested and taken before the prefect Probus, he was ordered to sacrifice to pagan gods. But he refused, quoting Exodus 22:20: "Whoever sacrifices to any god other than the LORD must be destroyed."

Irenaeus' position as a senior Christian leader during a time of great persecution under Roman emperor Diocletian made his response all the more significant. His father, mother, wife, children and friends urged him to carry out the pagan sacrifice in order to save his own life, but he stood firm in his faith. He was imprisoned, tortured and beheaded.

Lord grant me this crown for which I have longed;
For I have loved you with all my heart and all my soul.
I long to see you, to be filled with joy, and to find rest.
Then I will no longer have to witness the suffering of my congregation, the destruction of your churches, the overthrow of your altars, the persecution of your priests, the abuse of the defenceless, the departure from truth, and the large flock I watched over diminished by this time of trial.
I no longer wish to see those I considered my friends change within their hearts, becoming angry and seeking my death; or have those who are my true friends taken from me by this persecution, while their killers order us about.

Simon of Seleucia (martyred c. 340)

June 29

"Very truly I tell you, when you were younger you dressed yourself and went where you wanted; but when you are old you will stretch out your hands, and someone else will dress you and lead you where you do not want to go." Jesus said this to indicate the kind of death by which Peter would glorify God. Then he said to him, "Follow me!" John 21:18-19

Peter the Apostle (c.64)
Destined to be a Martyr

Peter, who is traditionally honoured on this day, was a simple fisherman called Simon when Jesus called him and his brother Andrew to "fish for people" (Matthew 4:18-19). He went on to become a central figure in the spread of the Gospel and the formation of the Church. Indeed, it was his testimony about Jesus' identity, "the Messiah, the Son of the living

God", that Jesus described as the rock upon which He would build His Church (Matthew 16:15-18). When Jesus was arrested, a fearful Peter denied that he knew him three times, as predicted by his Lord (Luke 22:54-62). But Peter was graciously and wonderfully restored by Jesus in an encounter following the resurrection that has encouraged faltering believers throughout the generations.

Peter was transformed by the Holy Spirit, and throughout Acts he is recorded as speaking boldly for the Lord he previously disowned. It was through Peter that the Gentiles first heard the Gospel (Acts 15:7), but he was principally called to reach the Jews while the apostle Paul went to the Gentiles (Galatians 2:7). After King Herod had James killed and saw that this pleased the Jews, he resolved to "seize Peter also" (Acts 12:3). Peter was apprehended and jailed but miraculously freed by an angel.

He spent his final part of his life in Rome, where he was martyred under Emperor Nero. Detained with the apostle Paul, the pair converted two captains of the guard and 47 others to Christianity during their time in prison. After nine months, Peter was brought for execution, and after being severely flogged, he was crucified with his head downwards. He had been prepared for his martyrdom by the risen Lord in their final meeting, in which Jesus restored Peter and put him in charge of tending the flock (John 21:18-19).

Dear friends, do not be surprised at the fiery ordeal that has come on you to test you, as though something strange were happening to you. But rejoice inasmuch as you participate in the sufferings of Christ, so that you may be overjoyed when his glory is revealed. If you are insulted because of the name of Christ, you are blessed, for the Spirit of glory and of God rests on you. If you suffer, it should not be as a murderer or thief or any other kind of criminal, or even as a meddler. However, if you suffer as a Christian, do not be ashamed, but praise God that you bear that name.
Peter the Apostle (1 Peter 4:12-16)

In peace I will lie down and sleep, for you alone, Lord, make me dwell in safety. Psalm 4:8

Missionaries and Chinese Converts (1900) "I don't fear if God wants me to suffer the death of a martyr"

During the infamous Boxer rebellion in China, ten Swedish missionaries were massacred near So-p'ing on 29 June 1900 after a violent mob looted and torched their mission premises. Chinese Christians and others friendly to the missionaries were thrown into the fire and burnt to death. The missionaries had escaped but were later captured, manacled and killed.

Among those who died during this incident were: Nathaniel Carleson, who was the senior member of the mission group; Ernst Peterson, the youngest and shortest-serving missionary; and a Chinese mother and daughter. One of the four young Swedish women who died, Mina Hedlund, had written poignantly in her last letter, "I don't fear if God wants me to suffer the death of a martyr".

The following day, missionaries Edith Searell and Emily Whitchurch also fell victim to the Boxers at Hiao-i, Shan-si. Emily had gone to China in 1884 after hearing of the country's need from Hudson Taylor, founder of the China Inland Mission. Edith, one of the first missionaries to China from New Zealand, worked alongside Emily for four years, and they spoke of Jesus to many at a refuge for opium smokers. About Emily, a fellow worker wrote, "God has graciously owned and blessed her service of love; and the many precious souls saved, demons cast out, sick ones healed, opium smokers reclaimed, testify how mightily God can use one yielded life."

From the human standpoint all are equally unsafe, from the point of view of those whose lives are hid with Christ in God all are equally safe! His children shall have a place of refuge, and that place is the secret place of the Most High... "A mighty fortress is our God" and in Him we are safe for time and for eternity.

Edith Searell wrote this in one of her last letters, dated just two days before her martyrdom in 1900

Everyone will hate you because of me. But not a hair of your head will perish. Stand firm, and you will win life. Luke 21:17-19

Shamimu Muteteri Hassan (2007)
A Defiant Daughter

When Ugandan 16-year-old Shamimu Muteteri Hassan converted from Islam to Christianity in 2007, her radical Muslim father was enraged. He was famous in his village for his extremism, and he tried to make Shamimu deny Christ, threatening his daughter with death if she refused.

The church began making plans to help her escape the family home, but before the plans were complete her father attacked and killed her with a large hammer on 1 July, two months after her conversion. He burned the body with paraffin and buried it. Police arrested him, but were later bribed by wealthy Muslims to set him free. Shamimu's grieving fiancé Ivan, a pastor's son who had led her to Christ, was also arrested and held by the police for a few days.

There is no safety – human safety, worldly safety – apart from the true safety I found with the Lord Jesus Christ.
Nagla Al-Imam, Egyptian lawyer and human rights' activist, who was interrogated and beaten in 2010 by security personnel because of her Christian faith

We who are alive are always being given over to death for Jesus' sake, so that his life may also be revealed in our mortal body. 2 Corinthians 4:11

Tateos Michelian (1994)
Prophesied Martyrdom

In his final sermon, delivered three days before he was last seen alive, Iranian church leader Tateos stressed that the Christian Church had given many martyrs throughout its history and that Iranian Christians should not be perplexed about or afraid of martyrdom, but should be prepared to face it. They were prophetic words, for Tateos left home on 29 June 1994 and was killed sometime between that date and 2 July.

His son Galo was called by the Iranian authorities to identify his body, and saw he had been shot several times in the head. Tateos, who had served the Iranian Church for over 40 years, had received threats from the authorities on several occasions prior to his death. He was an exceptionally gifted translator, author and apologist.

O God, the God of all goodness and grace,
who art worthy of a greater love
than we can either give or understand:
Fill our hearts, we beseech thee, with such love towards thee
that nothing may seem too hard for us to do or suffer
in obedience to thy will;
and grant that thus loving thee,
we may become daily more like unto thee,
and finally obtain the crown of life
which thou hast promised to those that love thee;
through Jesus Christ our Lord.
Bishop Westcott (1825-1901)

July 3

The Lord knows how to rescue the godly from trial, and to keep the unrighteous under punishment until the day of judgement.
2 Peter 2:9 (NRSV)

Christian Farmer (2002)
Unremembered Martyr

A Christian farmer, who had recently returned to his home in Kayamanya, near Poso in Central Sulawesi, Indonesia, was murdered in July 2002 when he went to tend his plantations. His wife had died the previous year when the family was living in a refugee camp. They left behind five children.

This farmer was one of many often-unremembered Christians who lost their lives during the turmoil in Central Sulawesi. The Poso district in particular had been the scene of much anti-Christian violence since 1998. The district where this farmer lived exploded into sectarian violence at the end of 2001, when organisations such as Laskar Jihad, an Islamist terrorist group, began to send militants to the area from all over Indonesia. Their activities, which involved destroying numerous Christian villages, killed many thousands and created around 50,000 refugees.

O Lord, we beseech you to deliver us from the fear of the unknown future, from fear of failure, from fear of poverty, from fear of sickness and pain, from fear of age and from fear of death. Help us, O Father, by your grace to love and fear you only. Fill our hearts with cheerful courage and loving trust in you; through our Lord and Master Jesus Christ.
Akanu Ibaim (1906-1995)

July 4

Where can I go from your Spirit? Where can I flee from your presence? If I go up to the heavens, you are there; if I make my bed in the depths, you are there. If I rise on the wings of the dawn, if I settle on the far side of the sea, even there your hand will guide me, your right hand will hold me fast. Psalm 139:7-10

Sayid Ali Sheik Luqman Hussein (2008) Courageous Christian

Sayid, from Somalia, converted from Islam to Christianity in 2004 and became active in telling people in his community about his faith. In July 2008 two Islamic extremists approached Sayid and asked him whether he faced Mecca when praying. He answered that as a Christian he did not have to face a specific direction to pray, as God is everywhere. The two Muslims returned two days later, armed with guns, and shot Sayid dead in the town of Afgyoye. His wife, who was pregnant at the time, went into premature labour when she heard about her 28-year-old husband's death. The baby was stillborn.

Somalia is a highly dangerous place to be a Christian and many converts from Islam are martyred for their faith. Most violence and abuses against Christians are committed by al-Shabaab, a radical Islamist militia group that controls most of southern Somalia. The tiny Christian community, all converts from Islam, meet in secret or follow Jesus in isolation.

My dearest Lord,
be thou a bright flame before me,
be thou a guiding star before me,
be thou a smooth path beneath me,
be thou a kindly shepherd behind me,
today – tonight – and forever.
Columba (521-97)

July 5

Of the greatness of his government and peace there will be no end. He will reign on David's throne and over his kingdom, establishing and upholding it with justice and righteousness from that time on and forever. The zeal of the LORD Almighty will accomplish this. Isaiah 9:7

Armenian Christians (1894-1923)
Genocide

Around 1.5 million Armenian Christians were massacred under the Ottoman government of Turkey between 1894 and 1923. Along with other Christian groups such as the Assyrians, Armenian Christians were a despised minority under Islamic Ottoman rule. Mass killings took place periodically (see April 15) throughout the three decades but 1915 was by far the bloodiest year. Around 800,000 Armenian Christians were killed; many of the men were executed without trial, while women and children were deported with many dying on the way, either slaughtered or from starvation. By 1923 the formerly growing minority of Armenian Christians had been reduced to only about 50,000.

The mass killings were religiously, rather than ethnically, motivated. The fact that Christians from other ethnic groups were targeted (around

250,000 Assyrian Christians were exterminated) and that those who were willing to convert to Islam were spared from deportation, serve to demonstrate this. Also, the Kurds, who were Muslim but non-Turkic, were not attacked but rather used by the Turks to carry out the atrocities. A serious attempt was made to destroy every vestige of Christian identity in the region, including destroying church buildings or turning them to other uses such as barns.

Turkey still vigorously denies that this was genocide, despite the fact that the Kurds have both admitted their role in the massacres and officially apologised. The country acknowledges that many Armenians died but cites the much lower figure of 300,000 and claims that the deaths resulted from inter-ethnic violence in which many Turks also died.

In memory of those who have had to make the supreme sacrifice for owning the name of Christ, O God give us grace to be better Christians, and bless us with a peace in times of trouble through Jesus Christ our Lord.

July 6

By their fruit you will recognise them. Do people pick grapes from thornbushes, or figs from thistles? Likewise every good tree bears good fruit, but a bad tree bears bad fruit. Matthew 7:16-17

Michael Zhizhilenko (1931)
Willing Servant

While working as medical superintendent at the Tanganka prison, Moscow, Michael, a physician and psychiatrist, was influenced by a Christian inmate who encouraged him to become a priest. For fear of being caught by the Communist authorities he did this in secret. He was eventually made Bishop of Serpukhov.

In 1929 he was arrested for his Christianity and sent to the Solovki Labour Camp. Here, with other Christians, he conducted secret services in the cells or in the nearby forest. This continued until he was taken by the camp guards and executed on 6 July 1931.

Do little things as though they were great, because of the majesty of Jesus
Christ who does them in us, and who lives our life: and do the greatest
things as though they were little and easy, because of His omnipotence.
Blaise Pascal (1623-62)

Fear not, O little flock and blest,
The lion that your life oppressed!
To heavenly pastures ever new
The heavenly Shepherd leadeth you;
Who, dwelling now on Zion's hill,
The Lamb's dear footsteps follow still;
By tyrant there no more distressed,
Fear not, O little flock and blest.
The Venerable Bede (673-735)
Translated by John Mason Neale (1818-1866)

July 7

Whoever does not take up their cross and follow me is not worthy of me.
Whoever finds their life will lose it, and whoever loses their life for my
sake will find it. Matthew 10:38-39

Aron and Companions (1994)
Crucified

Three Christians were crucified in the Nuba mountains of Sudan
during the summer of 1994. They were identified as Aron, a pastor, and
two other Christians from Akon. According to a visitor who conducted
a fact-finding visit to the area, six-inch nails were used for the crucifix-
ion. Anglican Bishop Daniel Zindo of Yambio said about the killings,
"There is no clear reason except that they are Christians."

The Nuba mountains are in South Kordofan state, on the border of
what is now the independent nation of South Sudan. Many Nuba people
allied with the South during the long and bloody civil war (1983-2005)
in which the North fought to Islamise and Arabise the South. Christians
were frequently harassed by the regime (see 28 March).

Blessed are you Lord Jesus Christ, Son of God, for you have, in your
mercy, been so kind as to allow me a death like yours.
Papylus of Thyateira (martyred late 2nd or early 3rd century)

July 8

The fear of others lays a snare, but one who trusts in the LORD is secure.
Proverbs 29:25 (NRSV)

Kilian (c. 689)
Challenged the Powerful

Celtic Christian Kilian left Ireland with eleven others to spread the
Gospel in Europe. They made their way to the region near the mouth of
the river Rhine named Franconia and East Thuringia, where they were
welcomed by the Governor of Wurtzburg, Gozbert. He was converted
and encouraged his people to listen to Kilian's teachings.

Gozbert was married to his brother's widow, Geilana, which was not
considered acceptable by the Church at the time. When Kilian chal-
lenged the governor about his marriage, Gozbert decided to give up his
wife. Geilana was greatly angered by this and, in revenge, had Kilian and
two of his companions beheaded. Before they were killed, Kilian encour-
aged the others by reminding them that they need not fear those who
could only kill the body but had no power over the soul (Matthew 10:28).

Come, Lord,
and cover me with the night.
Spread your grace over us
as you assured us you would do.
Your promises are more than
all the stars in the sky;
your mercy is deeper than the night.
Lord, it will be cold.
The night comes with its breath of death.
Night comes; the end comes; you come.
Lord, we wait for you day and night.
Prayer from Ghana

Therefore my heart is glad and my tongue rejoices; my body also will rest secure, because you will not abandon me to the realm of the dead, nor will you let your faithful one see decay. You make known to me the path of life; you will fill me with joy in your presence, with eternal pleasures at your right hand. Psalm 16:9-11

Sabo Yakubu and George Orjih (2009)
"Tell my brothers that I died well"

These two pastors were brutally murdered amid a series of coordinated anti-Christian attacks that began in July 2009 in Northern Nigeria. When asked to convert to Islam, Sabo and George refused and were beheaded.

Sabo, a father of seven, was killed with a machete. George preached to the leader of the militants about Christ before his own martyrdom. A fellow kidnap victim, who was later released, reported, "While we were lying there, tied up, George turned to me and said, 'If you survive, tell my brothers that I died well, and am living with Christ. And if we all die, we know that we die for the Lord.'" One eye witness said that George was singing and praying all through the ordeal and encouraging the believers not to give up, even unto death.

Islamist militants targeted Christians and the local police during these attacks, setting fire to churches and homes of local Christians as the violence spread across several states. At least twelve churches were torched; five police officers and twelve Christians were killed.

I'll praise my Maker while I've breath
And when my voice is lost in death,
Praise shall employ my nobler powers:
My days of praise shall ne'er be past
While life, and thought, and being last
Or immortality endures.
Isaac Watts (1674-1748)

If you are to be taken captive, into captivity you go; if you kill with the sword, with the sword you must be killed. Here is a call for the endurance and faith of the saints. Revelation 13:10 (NRSV)

Francis, Abdel-Mohti and Raphael Massabki (1860) Brothers Betrayed

These three brothers were killed in a massacre of Christians in Damascus on 10 July 1860, when Syria, then part of the Ottoman Empire, was under the tyrannical rule of Ahmed Pasha. On the previous day, many of his men had drawn crosses in the streets of Damascus in order to cause unrest among the Muslims and Christians. On 10 July they started a riot, which quickly turned into a bloodbath in front of a church. Many Christians were massacred, their homes destroyed and their goods plundered.

After finding safety for Francis and Abdel-Mohti's wives and children, the Massabki brothers headed to a nearby convent where they hid with other Christians. But they were betrayed and the rioters burst in. The brothers were killed in the ensuing pandemonium; each refused to renounce their faith at the demand of the attackers.

Whate'er my God ordains is right:
Though now this cup, in drinking,
May bitter seem to my faint heart,
I take it, all unshrinking.
My God is true; each morn anew
Sweet comfort yet shall fill my heart,
And pain and sorrow shall depart.

Whate'er my God ordains is right:
Here shall my stand be taken;
Though sorrow, need, or death be mine,
Yet I am not forsaken.
My Father's care is round me there;
He holds me that I shall not fall:
And so to Him I leave it all.
Samuel Rodigast (1649-1708)
Translated by Catherine Winkworth (1827-78)

I care very little if I am judged by you or by any human court; indeed, I do not even judge myself... It is the Lord who judges me. Therefore judge nothing before the appointed time; wait till the Lord comes. He will bring to light what is hidden in darkness and will expose the motives of the heart. At that time each will receive their praise from God.
1 Corinthians 4:3-5

Rashid and Sajid Emmanuel (2010) Blasphemy Charge

Christian brothers Rashid (32), a pastor, and Sajid (24), a graduate student, were falsely accused of blasphemy in Pakistan, where there is a mandatory death sentence for "defiling the name of Muhammad". They were alleged to have produced a derogatory pamphlet against the prophet of Islam and were due to appear in court to face the blasphemy charge. The week before their first hearing, on 10 and 11 July, a mob of thousands of Muslim protestors descended on the majority-Christian part of Faisalabad where the brothers lived, demanding the pair be given the death penalty.

The court heard from police on 19 July that there was no evidence to support the charge against the brothers and a report from a handwriting expert found that the writing on the pamphlet did not match that of either of the accused. However, as the brothers were being escorted from the court by police, the case not yet concluded, they were shot dead by masked gunmen. Rumours had spread that the Emmanuels would be found innocent and released, so Islamist extremists took matters into their own hands.

Local Christians took to the streets in protest over the murders, prompting calls from mosques for Muslims to come out to "fight rampaging" Christians. Shops were looted, and vehicles and homes were vandalised with at least ten people reported injured.

O God our Father, whose blessed Son, being falsely accused, answered nothing; being reviled not again: Give us faith, when others accuse us falsely, to go quietly on our way, committing ourselves to you, who judge righteously, after the pattern of our Lord and Saviour Jesus Christ.
Eric Milner-White (1884-1963) and G W Briggs (1875-1959)

The Lord will rescue me from every evil attack and will bring me safely to his heavenly kingdom. To him be glory forever and ever. Amen.
2 Timothy 4:18

Manuel Amador (1995)
Shot Dead

"When I heard the shots, my heart dropped to the floor. I could hear people screaming, and there was chaos and confusion. Against the counsel of my neighbours, I ran to see what had happened. I found my husband lying on the floor in a pool of blood. I picked him up, hoping he had some last words for me; but it was too late... he was gone."

This is how Manuel's wife recalled the dreadful night that her husband, a pastor in Uraba, Colombia, was shot dead. The Association of International Christian Ministers had called a meeting on 3 July 1995, with Manuel as one of the leaders, to discuss the massacres that were happening in the Uraba area. Many people had left Uraba, fearing for their safety, but Manuel and others decided to stay. A second meeting was planned for 13 July after which they intended to send an SOS to the church worldwide, revealing the violence in Uraba. Manuel was shot the night before the second meeting. He had been a pastor for only four years, and was well-known and well-loved in the area.

In the storm the tree strikes deeper roots in the soil; in the hurricane the inhabitants of the house abide within, and rejoice in its shelter. So by suffering the Father would lead us to enter more deeply into the love of Christ.
Andrew Murray (1828-1917)

True instruction was in his mouth and nothing false was found on his lips. He walked with me in peace and uprightness, and turned many from sin. Malachi 2:6

Dennis of Paris (c. 250)
Powerful Preacher

When Dennis, who was bishop in Paris, went to Gaul in 250 as a missionary, he preached so powerfully and so many were converted as a result that he was arrested on the orders of the Roman governor Fescenninus Sisinnius.

He was imprisoned for a lengthy period and then beheaded at Montmartre, or "Martyrs Hill", in Paris. A priest, Rusticus, and a deacon, Eleutherius, are believed to have been executed with him.

Lord God of truth and love, "thy kingdom come", we pray
Give us thy grace to know thy truth and walk thy way:
That here on earth thy will be done
'Till saints in earth and heaven are one.
Howard Charles Adie Gaunt (1902-1983)

O God our heavenly father, who hast manifested thy love towards mankind in sending thine only Son into the world, that all might live through him: We pray thee to speed forth these good tidings of great joy to every nation, that the people who sit in darkness and in the shadow of death may see the great light, and may come, with us, to worship him whose name is called Wonderful, even our Lord and Saviour Jesus Christ.
Frank Colquhoun (1909-1997)

The eternal God is your refuge, and underneath are the everlasting arms. Deuteronomy 33:27a

Mehdi Dibaj (1994)
"But from the arms of my God to whom can I return?"

Iranian evangelist Mehdi, who had converted from Islam to Christianity in his late teens, endured nine years in prison where he faced torture and solitary confinement before eventually being brought to trial at a Revolutionary Court in 1993, charged with apostasy from Islam.

In a written defence at his trial Mehdi wrote:

I would rather have the whole world against me but know that the Almighty God is with me, be called an apostate but know that I have the approval of the God of glory... They tell me 'Return!' But from the arms of my God to whom can I return? Is it right to accept what people are saying instead of obeying the Word of God? It is now 45 years that I am walking with the God of miracles, and His kindness upon me is like a shadow and I owe Him much for His fatherly love and concern...

...I am not only satisfied to be in prison for the honour of His Holy Name, but am ready to give my life for the sake of Jesus my Lord and enter His kingdom sooner, the place where the elect of God enter everlasting life, but the wicked to eternal damnation.

He was sentenced to death but released in January 1994 following an international outcry, though his sentence was not repealed. He disappeared in June 1994 and died in mysterious circumstances. On 2 July Mehdi's family were contacted by the Iranian authorities to come and identify his body, which was reported to have been found that day in a forest, west of Tehran.

Truly fearless, truly fortunate martyrs, called and chosen to glorify our Lord Jesus Christ! If any man magnifies the Lord, honours and adores

him, these are the models for him. If he reads about them, he will find that though they are modern, they are not inferior to the ancient ones: they will edify the Church just as much. These new examples of virtue will prove that it is one and the same Holy Spirit who was active then and is active now, one and the same omnipotent God the Father and His Son, Jesus Christ, our Lord, whose glory and power are boundless and always will be, age after age. Amen.
Tertullian (c. 160-c. 225)

July 15

For everyone born of God overcomes the world. This is the victory that has overcome the world, even our faith. 1 John 5:4

Artur Suleimanov (2010)
Dynamic Leader

This dynamic Christian leader was shot in the head as he was leaving his church in the strongly Islamic republic of Dagestan, in the Russian Federation, on 15 July 2010. A gunman approached and opened fire as the pastor got into a car. He died from his wounds in hospital around an hour later, leaving behind his wife Zina and five children.

Another Christian was sitting in the car with Pastor Suleimanov when he was killed, strongly indicating that the latter was singled out for assassination. The 49-year-old pastor, himself a convert from Islam, had been involved in outreach to Muslims and his life had been threatened on several previous occasions. Pastor Suleimanov's church was one of the largest Protestant churches in Dagestan and very active in the community. His murder was seen as an attempt to put further pressure on Christian converts in the republic. The population is 98 per cent Muslim, and the Church faces harassment and intimidation from various groups.

God has called us to shine. Let no one say that he cannot shine because he has not so much influence as some others may have. What God wants you to do is to use the influence you have.
Dwight L Moody (1837-99)

The LORD is my rock, my fortress and my deliverer; my God is my rock, in whom I take refuge. Psalm 18:2a

China Inland Missionaries and Chinese Christian (1900) Deceived

A group of China Inland Missionaries from Great Britain and their Chinese Christian servant were brutally murdered by soldiers on 16 July 1900. They were travelling to Ho-tsin in a bid to escape the Boxers, who were rampaging through the country killing foreigners and Christians. After a band of men stopped the group and stole their possessions, mounted soldiers overtook them and led them to understand that they had been sent to escort them to safety. The soldiers directed them along a quiet road, promising that a ferry boat would be provided for their escape. But when the Christians arrived, they discovered that they had been deceived.

The soldiers said that they had not in fact come to protect them but to murder them unless they stopped worshipping God and preaching against idolatry. George McConnell was dragged from his mule and killed with a sword, his wife Isabella and their young son Kenneth meeting a similar end. Annie King pleaded with the soldiers to stop, saying, "We have come to do you good". But seeing they were relentless, she held on to Elizabeth Burton and the pair were put to death in one another's arms. At the same time, a man and his wife, believed to be John and Sarah Young were also killed as they embraced. Their Chinese servant, K'eh-t'ien-hsuen, refused to deny his Christian faith and also met a violent death.

The winds may blow, and the waves may roll high; if we keep our eyes off them to the Lord we shall be all right.
Sarah Young, from one of her last letters, dated 5 July 1900

Are not five sparrows sold for two pennies? Yet not one of them is forgotten by God. Indeed, the very hairs of your head are all numbered. Don't be afraid; you are worth more than many sparrows. Luke 12:6-7

Holy Land Converts (2002-03) Targeted by Extremists

Converts to Christianity in the Palestinian Authority area and local Christians who support them have been targeted by Islamic extremists.

A man who headed into a mountainous region of the area in mid-July 2003 carrying Christian materials including cassettes, videos and Bibles, was one such victim. After he had been missing for approximately ten days, during which his friends and family received no word from him, his body was returned. He had been brutally killed and his body carved into four pieces as a warning to other converts. He left behind a wife and two small children.

In a separate incident in 2002, a local Christian received a phone call telling him that a convert from Islam was in a serious condition in hospital. He immediately set off and on the way his car was deliberately driven off the road by another vehicle. The phone call later proved to be a hoax designed to lead him into the trap.

Jesus lover of my soul,
Let me to Thy bosom fly,
While the nearer waters roll,
While the tempest still is high;
Hide me, O my saviour, hide,
Till the storm of life is past;
Safe into the haven guide,
O receive my soul at last.
Charles Wesley (1707-88)

And this gospel of the kingdom will be preached in the whole world as a testimony to all nations, and then the end will come. Matthew 24:14

Susianty Tinulele (2004)
Shot in the Pulpit

Susianty Tinulele was shot dead while speaking from the pulpit of her church in Central Sulawesi in Palu, Indonesia, on Sunday 18 July 2004. Four masked men opened fire with machine guns on the preacher and worship team. Susianty was shot in the head and died instantly. Four teenage worshippers were hospitalised with serious injuries and one 17-year old girl died.

Susianty was a victim of what appears to have been a campaign to assassinate Christian leaders in Central Sulawesi that began in November 2003. When police arrested suspected members of militant group Jemaah Islamiyah they found detailed descriptions of church services and lists of Christian leaders.

Violence was also directed against Sulawesi Christians who were not church leaders. The night before Susianty's death, Mrs Helmy Tombiling died from nine stab wounds to her chest and stomach inflicted by attackers outside her home in Poso, Central Sulawesi.

May we be strengthened in our faith, live the rest of our lives in following your Son, and be ready when you call us to eternal life. Lord in your mercy, hear our prayer.
The Alternative Service Book, 1980

He made himself nothing by taking the very nature of a servant, being made in human likeness. And being found in appearance as a man, he humbled himself by becoming obedient to death – even death on a cross!
Philippians 2:7-8

Grand Duchess Elizabeth (1918)
Devoted to Others

Born of royal blood (the grand-daughter of Queen Victoria), Grand Duchess Elizabeth of Russia laid aside a life of luxury and poured out herself – and her wealth – in caring for the poor and lowly, motivated by her faith in Christ. She said, "I want to work for God and in God for suffering mankind." When the Revolution broke out in 1917, the Grand Duchess, as a member of the country's aristocracy, was vulnerable but she turned down an offer from a Swedish Cabinet Minister to leave the country, preferring to stay and continue her humanitarian work.

She had totally devoted herself to serving others following the assassination of her husband, the Grand Duke Sergei in the Russo-Japanese War of 1904-05. The Grand Duchess bought a house and a large piece of land in Moscow and established a community with several women from all classes of society devoted to tending the sick, helping the poor and taking care of the street children of Moscow. She also founded a rent-free hostel for young women workers and students, a hospice, a hospital, a clinic, a school for nurses and a soup kitchen. All her personal fortune was devoted to such good works.

Following the outbreak of revolution, the rebels regularly visited the community and tried to arrest the Grand Duchess a number of times. There were also threats to kill her but nothing happened. She was taken into captivity with other members of the Imperial Family in May 1918. On the night of 18 July, following the execution of Tsar Nicholas II, they were taken to a mine, blindfolded, and thrown alive into the shaft. Hand grenades were then thrown into the shaft, but after the explosions, the horrified murderers heard singing, the hymn "O Lord, Save Thy People", coming from the shaft. They filled it with brush and set it ablaze, finally killing the Grand Duchess and the others. Her life and martyrdom were commemorated with a statue in Westminster Abbey in London in 1998.

> *He that is down needs fear no fall*
> *He that is low, no pride:*
> *He that is humble shall*
> *Have God to be his Guide.*
> John Bunyan (1628-88)

July 20

If we died with him, we will also live with him; if we endure, we will also reign with him. If we disown him, he will also disown us; if we are faithless, he remains faithful, for he cannot disown himself.
2 Timothy 2:11b-13

Tahir Iqbal (1992)
"I found the truth"

Tahir was a Christian convert from Islam who died in mysterious circumstances whilst in prison in Pakistan, having been arrested on blasphemy charges.

He was born in 1959 into a Muslim family and as a young man became an Islamic extremist. In 1982 he contracted meningitis, which left the lower part of his body paralysed and brought an end to his career in the Pakistan Air Force. He received support from a local group of Christians, who helped him acquire a wheelchair.

Tahir began a comparative study of Islam and Christianity which led to his conversion. He was rejected by his family, received anonymous threats and was pressurised by some influential people to re-convert to Islam. A case of blasphemy was filed against him by a local imam, the evidence being Tahir's copy of the Quran, which was marked on several pages. Tahir was thrown into prison where he was mistreated and was under constant pressure to renounce Christ. But he told his persecutors, "You want me to say that I changed my religion because somebody pushed me into it for the sake of money, to get a job, or to have women. But you are lying. You should know that I changed because I found the truth. I will kiss the rope that hangs me, but I will never deny my faith."

On 23 April 1992 an application was made to the court, seeking Tahir's execution. The court refused, on the basis that conversion from Islam is not a crime under Pakistani law. On 21 June Tahir told his counsel that he feared for his life and also sent letters to the highest authorities in the land appealing for protection. He died mysteriously in prison on 20 July 1992, aged 33, having been described as in good health at his last court hearing a week before. The Christian community was certain that he was murdered – a charge denied by the prison authorities. Tahir's body was given to his stepmother without a post-mortem or investigation being conducted. He was buried in Faisalabad according to Islamic rites.

Thank you, Lord Jesus that you will be our hiding place whatever happens.
Corrie Ten Boom (1892-1983)

July 21

As you go, proclaim this message: "The kingdom of heaven has come near". Matthew 10:7

Goda Israel, Manzoor Ahmad Chat
Pau Za Khen (2007)
Active Evangelists

These three men, who were all active in evangelism in India, were killed within the space of a few months of each other in 2007.

On 20 February 2007, 29-year-old church minister Goda Israel was found stabbed to death in Andhra Pradesh state. A news report quoted a comment that he had no personal enemies but he had previously been threatened by Hindu extremists due to his involvement in preaching the Gospel in the area.

Islamic extremists were thought to have been responsible for the abduction and beheading of Manzoor Ahmad Chat in Jammu and Kashmir state. His head was left in a plastic bag outside a mosque on 14 April.

210

The convert from Islam, who sometimes hosted a house church gathering, had disappeared the previous day, not arriving for a prayer meeting he was due to lead.

In July a Burmese Lutheran pastor, Pastor Pau Za Khen (62), was kidnapped and later found beheaded in Manipur state. He had previously worked as a pastor in a church in Chin state, Burma.

Almighty God, thank you for the vast and varied land of India. Thank you that the gospel of Christ has been proclaimed there from the days of the Apostle Thomas. Thank you for those that still seek to live for you in that country of many religions. Grant to your people, O Lord, the freedom of religion which India's constitution guarantees, for peace in their land and for good in their government. May this be accomplished though Jesus Christ our Lord. Amen.

July 22

We are hard pressed on every side, but not crushed; perplexed, but not in despair; persecuted, but not abandoned; struck down, but not destroyed.
2 Corinthians 4:8-9

Lucian Tapiedi and British Missionaries (1942) Revered Martyrs

When the Japanese army reached Papua New Guinea in the summer of 1942 and ordered people to leave the northern coast, some missionaries chose to stay. Lucian Tapiedi, a Papuan evangelist, refused to abandon the missionaries with whom he worked. He was the son of a sorcerer but had converted to Christianity. After graduating in 1941 he joined the mission team as teacher and evangelist, carrying out a lot of work among his own people.

Before the group was forced to flee their mission station at Gona for the jungle in July, he shared the Eucharist together with the missionaries for the last time. They were captured by Orokaiva tribesmen with whom Lucian pleaded on behalf of the missionaries. But it was in vain and he was struck down with an axe and killed by one of the Orokaiva, a man named Hivijapa. The others were handed over to the Japanese, and were beheaded on Buna beach.

Their example led to the growth of a strong Papuan church, which particularly remembers Lucian's witness. His killer converted to Christianity, took the name Hivijapa Lucian, and built a church dedicated to the memory of his victim at Embi.

O Lamb of God, who takest away the sin of the world, look upon us and have mercy upon us; thou who art thyself both Victim and Priest, thyself both Reward and Redeemer, keep safe from all evil those whom thou hast redeemed, O Saviour of the world.
Irenaeus of Lyon (c. 130-200)

July 23

Love your enemies, do good to those who hate you, bless those who curse you, pray for those who mistreat you. Luke 6:27b-28

Phocas the Gardener (303)
Dug his own Grave

A group of Roman soldiers were sent to find and execute a man named Phocas, a hermit and skilled gardener, who had been sentenced to death without trial during the persecutions under the Roman Emperor Diocletian. On arriving at his hermitage they met Phocas, and not knowing they were speaking to their target, asked him if he knew where Phocas was. He said that he would take them to him but first offered them food and shelter for the night, and the soldiers agreed.

After serving the men with food and showing them where to sleep, Phocas went out and dug his own grave, and then spent time preparing himself for his imminent death. In the morning he led the soldiers to the grave he had prepared and revealed who he was. Shocked by his announcement they hesitated, but Phocas urged them to carry out their assignment and they beheaded him.

Force may subdue, but love gains: And he that forgives first, wins the laurel.
William Penn (1644-1718)

If we are thrown into the blazing furnace, the God we serve is able to deliver us from it, and he will deliver us from Your Majesty's hand. But even if he does not, we want you to know, Your Majesty, that we will not serve your gods or worship the image of gold you have set up.
Daniel 3:17-18

Christina (4ᵗʰ century)
Mercilessly Tortured

Christina, the Christian daughter of a rich and powerful pagan magistrate in Bolsena, Italy, suffered unimaginable tortures because of her faith. Her ordeal began after she broke a number of golden idols belonging to her father and gave away the pieces to the poor.

He was outraged, and had Christina whipped with rods and then thrown into a dungeon. She refused to repent, so her father ordered that she be torn by iron hooks, then tied to a rack and held over a blazing fire. She was later tied to a heavy stone and thrown into a lake. Incredibly, she survived all these tortures and even outlived her merciless father. But the judge who succeeded him continued the persecution and had Christina thrown into a burning furnace where she remained – unhurt – for five days. She was thrown among snakes and had her tongue cut out before eventually her ordeal ended when she was killed by being pierced with arrows.

O God, Father of all mercies, give to all Christian people courage to confess your name. In your mercy strengthen those who are being persecuted for their witness to your gospel, so that, as they stand fast for your holy word, they may be sustained by it; through Jesus Christ our Lord.
After Prayers of 1585

The cords of the grave coiled around me; the snares of death confronted me. In my distress I called to the LORD; I cried to my God for help. From his temple he heard my voice; my cry came before him, into his ears.
Psalm 18:5-6

Pierre (1959)
Poisoned by Pagans

Pierre was a member of the Diola tribe in Senegal, who mysteriously fell ill shortly after proclaiming his new found faith in Christ at a pagan fetish feast. The local missionaries gathered up their medicine and made their way to his home, where they were shocked to find Pierre unconscious, his face swollen and his breathing heavy. They rushed him to the nearest hospital but within a few minutes of arriving Pierre died. This happened one Sunday morning in July 1959.

Pierre had been a healthy young man, and his sudden death perplexed the missionaries who knew him. They traced his recent movements and, considering his symptoms, concluded that he must have been poisoned at the pagan feast where he proclaimed his new faith in Christ.

Bless us, O God the Father, who hast created us
Bless us, O God the Son, who hast redeemed us.
Bless us, O God the Holy Spirit, who sanctifieth us
O Blessed Trinity, keep us in body, soul and spirit unto everlasting life.
Parish Prayers (no. 1683)

Though sinners do evil a hundred times and prolong their lives, yet I know that it will be well with those who fear God, because they stand in fear before him. Ecclesiastes 8:12 (NRSV)

Banja Villagers (1970)
Military Massacre

On July 26 1970, many Sudanese Christians were massacred in the village of Banja on the Sudan-Congo frontier. It was one of the many attacks made upon settlements in Southern Sudan as part of the long-running civil war between the Islamic government of the North and the rebels of the largely-Christian South.

Soldiers from the North burst into a church in the village and attacked while the Christians were praying. They held the pastor and congregation captive by tying them to chairs while they scoured the village, killing everyone in sight. Once they had finished massacring the villagers, their attention returned to the worshippers. The soldiers shot the Christians and set the church ablaze. As they did so, the commander shouted, "We're shooting you in your church. Let your God come and save you." Everyone inside died. Reports of the massacre came from the 14 villagers who survived.

God bless Sudan, the largest country in Africa. Guide her rulers and grant her peace based on justice and freedom. Renew the Church and give your children the power to be peacemakers. Have compassion on the suffering Church. Bring about reconciliation, stability and a hunger for your Word, for your name's sake. Amen.

Everyone who has left houses or brothers or sisters or father or mother or wife or children or fields for my sake will receive a hundred times as much and will inherit eternal life. Matthew 19:29

Raheela Khanam (1997)
Family Honour

Raheela was gunned down by her brother after she was considered to have dishonoured the family by converting from Islam to Christianity.

The 18-year-old from Lahore, Pakistan, had been befriended by a 17-year-old Christian girl, Saleema, who gave her a Bible. Intrigued by the faith that she saw in her new friend, Raheela decided to attend church with her and on hearing about Jesus, Raheela made a profession of faith.

When Raheela's parents found out, they were furious and immediately demanded she recant. In a bid to ensure that she would not remain a Christian, they quickly found a Muslim man for her to marry, but Raheela refused and fled to her Christian friends for refuge. Her friend Saleema was arrested, and for three days she and her pastor, who was also detained, were tortured and beaten in an attempt to find the whereabouts of Raheela. A few weeks later, in July 1997, she was found in a woman's shelter. Her brother, Altaf, shot her dead to avenge the family's lost honour.

Live near to God, and so all things will appear to you little in comparison with eternal realities.
Robert Murray McCheyne (1813-43)

I became a servant of this gospel by the gift of God's grace given me through the working of his power. Ephesians 3:7

Christodoulos (1777)
Concern for Convert

When Christodoulos, a tailor in the village of Valta, Greece, heard that a Bulgarian man was converting to Islam, he was greatly concerned and decided to try to persuade him not to leave Christianity. At the sound of the drums which signalled the beginning of the conversion ceremony, Christodoulos rushed from his shop to the nearby coffee house where the Bulgarian was sitting. He began to plead with the man not to convert but some Ottoman soldiers, who were present in the crowd that had gathered to witness the ceremony, grabbed Christodoulos and threw him out of the shop.

Undeterred, he returned a second time, but was bound and beaten by the soldiers and taken to the local magistrate. Despite the demands of the soldiers and Christodoulos' refusal to convert to Islam, the magistrate would not condemn him to death, but gave him to the soldiers to do with as they liked. From here the soldiers took Christodoulos to a high government official who also tried to convert him. He refused, so the soldiers were allowed to thrash his feet 200 times and then take him to be hanged. On 28 July 1777 he was killed. His body hung for two days until some Christians paid for its burial.

Lord, I am coming as fast as I can. I know I must pass through the shadow of death, before I can come to Thee. But it is but a mere shadow, a little darkness upon nature: but Thou, by Thy merits and passion, hast broken through the jaws of death. So, Lord, receive my soul, and have mercy upon me; and bless this kingdom with peace and plenty, and with brotherly love and charity, for Jesus Christ His sake, if it be Thy will.
William Laud (1573-1645)

"You must go to everyone I send you to and say whatever I command you. Do not be afraid of them, for I am with you and will rescue you," declares the Lord. Jeremiah 1:7b-8

Liplal Mardy and Tapan Roy (2005)
Broadcast Jesus

These two evangelists in Bowalmari District, Faridpur, Bangladesh, were stabbed to death around midnight on 29 July 2005. Liplal, 35, and Tapan, 30, had been showing a film about Jesus, as well as health education films, in villages around the area. For this they had received at least two verbal threats from the head of the local madrassa (Islamic religious school), telling them to stop. After the second threat they ceased their work and were planning to leave the area, but were murdered before they could do so. This incident is chillingly similar to the killing of Hridoy Roy in 2003 (see 24 April).

Lord,
it sometimes feels
as if I have to give up my life
before I'm ready.
It hurts to let go.
Give me the courage
to take a step forward into the unknown,
trusting that your love will be there somewhere,
giving me new life.
Amen.
Prayers for Today's World (no. 308)

The Son of Man must suffer many things and be rejected by the elders, the chief priests and the teachers of the law, and he must be killed and on the third day be raised to life. Luke 9:22

Abdon and Sennen (c. 303)
Killed by Gladiators

These Persian noblemen were brought to Rome as prisoners of the Emperor Diocletian after his campaign in Persia. They had been openly practising their Christian faith, ministering to other persecuted Christians and burying the bodies of martyrs. When they were arrested they were asked to sacrifice to pagan gods, but refused to do so. Consequently, they were thrown to wild animals in the Colosseum and then killed by the gladiators.

Under Diocletian, the Roman Empire was at war with Persia in the latter part of the third century. The conflict was over influence in southeast Europe, especially Armenia. The Romans won a decisive victory in the Battle of Satala in 298 and, after this, moved into Persian territory, taking the capital Ctesiphon.

Diocletian began his violent persecution of Christians in 303. Churches were destroyed, the scriptures burnt and Christians ordered to sacrifice to the gods or die. They suffered merciless torture and brutal deaths. Under Constantine, the first Roman Emperor to convert to Christianity, there was peace for Christians from 313 when he proclaimed religious freedom across the empire.

Jesus, the very thought of thee
With sweetness fills the breast;
But sweeter far thy face to see,
And in thy presence rest.

Jesus, our only joy be thou,
As thou our prize wilt be;
Jesus, be thou our glory now,
And through eternity.
Bernard of Clairvaux (1090-1153)
Translated by Edward Caswell (1814-78)

No-one can lay any foundation other than the one already laid, which is Jesus Christ. 1 Corinthians 3:11

Magdi Ayad Moussad (2000)
"Over his dead body"

Magdi, an Egyptian Christian, was shot dead and five others injured in July 2000 over a dispute about the construction of a much-needed church building in the village of Sool.

Magdi had bought the land in 1990 and the work was completed in April 2000, despite objections from some of the Muslims in the village. Although the security services had persuaded representatives of Muslim families to sign a document approving of the church building, both Magdi and the church minister had received threats prior to the shooting and one Islamic extremist, suspected of involvement in the incident, was known to have said that the church would be built "over his [Magdi's] dead body".

At the time of the shooting there were five mosques for Sool's 25,000 Muslims while this was the only church building for the village's 6,000 Christians.

Christ is made the sure foundation,
Christ the head and cornerstone,
chosen of the Lord, and precious,
binding all the Church in one;
holy Zion's help for ever,
and her confidence alone.
John Mason Neale (1818-1866), translated from a Latin hymn dating from the seventh or eighth century

Because of the LORD's great love we are not consumed, for his compassions never fail. They are new every morning; great is your faithfulness. I say to myself, "The LORD is my portion; therefore I will wait for him." Lamentations 3:22-24

Minhas Hameed's Family (2009)
Muslim Mob

Minhas Hameed lost seven members of his family when a mob of more than 800 Muslims went on the rampage in a Christian settlement in the town of Gojra, Pakistan, on 1 August 2009. Homes were looted and at least 50 houses were burned to the ground as the attackers threw petrol bombs and fired indiscriminately. Hameed's 75-year-old father was the first victim when he was shot in the head. The son rushed his father to hospital while the rest of his family stayed in the house, thinking they would be safe there. But as the mob began to torch the homes of Christians, six other members of Hameed's family were burned to death.

These attacks were part of a spate of violence against Christians in Pakistan. Two days earlier some 50 Christian homes were destroyed by Muslims in the nearby village of Korian after rumours spread that a Quran had been burned during a Christian wedding ceremony. Muslims lay down in front of the fire engines to prevent them reaching the blazing houses. More than a quarter of Korian's Christians were left homeless.

The previous month, around 600 Muslims used petrol bombs to attack at least 117 Christian homes in Bahmani Walla, another village in Punjab. Acid was thrown at some Christians as they fled, leaving nine women and four children scarred.

Sometimes I say to myself,
I am a believer for nothing.
But in the hour when I say,
I'm quitting, Jesus says to me again:
"Believe me, little son, Please follow me.
To my Father's house,
I wish to lead you, little son,
To a beautiful country."
Jim Elliot (1927-1956) (see January 10)

No lion will be there, nor any ravenous beast; they will not be found there. But only the redeemed will walk there, and those the LORD has rescued will return. They will enter Zion with singing; everlasting joy will crown their heads. Gladness and joy will overtake them, and sorrow and sighing will flee away. Isaiah 35:9-10

Filipino Christians (2001) Taken Hostage

"They just barged into our houses and grabbed us at gunpoint."

These were the words of a survivor from a vicious raid in which 35 Christians were kidnapped from their homes in Lamitan, the Philippines, on 2 August 2001. Black-hooded militants from the Abu Sayyaf Islamist group swept through the town seizing hostages; they set fire to a school and hacked to death one Christian man with machetes. Of the 25 hostages who survived, 13 were rescued from their nightmare by the Filipino army on 5 August. Ten were later found beheaded.

Several days before the raid, Abu Sayyaf, which wants to establish an Islamic state in the southern Philippines, had warned that they would deliberately target local Christians in response to the Philippines' army's campaign against them. Lamitan is a Christian-majority community on the predominantly Muslim island of Basilan.

O Jesus, be mindful of your promise; think on us your servants; and when we leave this world, speak these loving words to our souls; "Today you will be with me in joy." O Lord Jesus Christ, remember us your servants who trust in you, when our tongue cannot speak, when our eyes cannot see and when our ears cannot hear. Let our soul always rejoice in you, and be joyful about your salvation, which you have brought for us through your death.
Miles Coverdale (1488-1568)

Therefore, since we are surrounded by such a great cloud of witnesses, let us throw off everything that hinders and the sin that so easily entangles. And let us run with perseverance the race marked out for us, fixing our eyes on Jesus, the pioneer and perfecter of faith. For the joy set before him he endured the cross, scorning its shame, and sat down at the right hand of the throne of God. Consider him who endured such opposition from sinners, so that you will not grow weary and lose heart.
Hebrews 12:1-3

Nasrullah Khan (1908)
Witnessed Martyrdom

When Nasrullah Khan saw the face of a Christian man, Abdul Karim (see May 16), radiant with the light of Christ as he was violently martyred in Afghanistan in 1906, it left a lasting impression on him. He was not a Christian at the time of Abdul's horrific murder, which involved torture at the hands of an angry mob, but Nasrullah told a missionary that he could not forget the picture of serenity he saw on Abdul's face. It made such an impact that when Nasrullah later heard the Gospel, he became a Christian.

Because he had been born a Muslim, Nasrullah's conversion put him too at risk of death. This caught up with him in August 1908 when he was killed by his own nephew because he would not deny Christ, his Saviour.

We thank you O God for the example of the saints. Help us to follow in their footsteps with courage and with hope, so that your work on earth may be faithfully continued and your holy name be praised until the end of the world, through Jesus Christ our Lord. Amen.
William Hampson (*More Prayers for Today's Church*, no. 179)

Do not be afraid of those who kill the body but cannot kill the soul.
Rather, be afraid of the One who can destroy both soul and body in hell.
Matthew 10:28

Ia (360)
Successful Slave Evangelist

Ia, a Greek slave in Persia, was arrested because of her success in converting the Persian women amongst whom she lived to Christianity. She was tortured by King Shapur II's forces, who stretched her limbs and beat her cruelly. Ia was then thrown in jail for several months in a bid to get her to deny her faith in Christ. But she remained steadfast, so eventually her hands were tied and she was lashed to death, her flesh torn to the bone. The soldiers then cut off her head and threw the corpse away.

They face the trials of broken bones for Jesus.
They take the pain that others won't endure.
Yet in their hearts they sing of His salvation;
They know His love
They live His way
Their faith in Him is sure.
Andrew Fleet © 2009

O Lord Jesu, our only health and our everlasting life, I give myself wholly unto your will; being sure that the thing cannot perish which is committed unto your mercy. You, merciful Lord, were born for my sake; you did suffer both hunger and thirst for my sake; you did preach and teach, pray and fast for my sake; and finally you gave your most precious body to die and your blood to be shed on the cross, for my sake. Most merciful Saviour, let all these things profit me which you have freely given me. O Lord, into your hands, I commit my soul.
Primer of 1559

Though you have not seen him, you love him; and even though you do not see him now, you believe in him and are filled with an inexpressible and glorious joy, for you are receiving the end result of your faith, the salvation of your souls. 1 Peter 1:8-9

Mary Wangechi (c. 1953)
"I could never turn my back on [Jesus]"

Mary's decision to become a Christian greatly angered her husband and mother; she was beaten and excluded from the family. They lived in the Njumbi region of Kenya during the time of the Mau Mau rebellion and were friends of a pastor, Elijah Gachanja, and his family. Mary, a mother of three, became a Christian during a weekend retreat organised by Pastor Elijah. After this she was often beaten and finally told that she could not eat in either her husband's or mother's house – even though she had grown and prepared the food they ate. Mary therefore went every day to the pastor's house for a meal.

At this time the Mau Mau strategy of making people take oaths of loyalty began. Mary was a strong witness for her faith and her family did not know what to do. Her father told her to go to her husband, her husband told her to go to her father. Mary said, "One thing I am not ever going to do is to take this oath. Jesus is my Saviour and I could never turn my back on Him."

This declaration was reported to the Mau Mau. One night, in the darkness, tribe members strangled her to death and disposed of her body in a pit latrine. The people of her church searched for Mary for a week, not realising she was dead, until finally her body was found. Despite the opposition of Mary's family to her Christian faith, over time several relatives, including her father and three children, became believers.

O Joy that seekest me through pain,
I cannot close my heart to thee;
I trace the rainbow through the rain,
And feel the promise is not vain,
That morn shall tearless be.
George Matheson (1842-1906)

Some faced jeers and flogging, and even chains and imprisonment. They were put to death by stoning; they were sawed in two; they were killed by the sword. They went about in sheepskins and goatskins, destitute, persecuted and mistreated – the world was not worthy of them.
Hebrews 11:36-38a

Sixtus (258)
Highly Celebrated

Sixtus was martyred in 258 at a time when the Roman persecution of Christians was at its height. He was captured on 6 August by Roman soldiers whilst preaching to a group of Christians on the Appian Way, Rome. It is not certain whether he was put to death immediately or whether he was first taken away for questioning, but Sixtus was killed by the sword in the same place as he was captured. Six other Christians, Felicissimus, Agapitus and four deacons, were martyred with him.

Sixtus' body was buried in the cemetery of Callistus and his death became one of the most celebrated of the early Church in Rome.

O Holy Spirit, Who, in all ages hast comforted and strengthened martyrs and confessors; Who hast ever been the sustaining comfort and sweet refreshment of the sorrowful and the suffering; Who sheddest abroad love, joy and peace, in the hearts of the faithful and obedient followers of Christ; grant that we may be filled with all the fullness of Thy gifts of grace; that, by Thy holy inspiration, we may think those things that be good, and by Thy merciful guiding, may perform the same. Amen.
Treasury of Devotion

For thus says the Lord GOD: I myself will search for my sheep, and will seek them out. As shepherds seek out their flocks when they are among their scattered sheep, so I will seek out my sheep. I will rescue them from all the places to which they have been scattered on a day of clouds and thick darkness. Ezekiel 34:11-12 (NRSV)

Five Afghan Christians (2004)
Taliban Targets

Five converts from Islam to Christianity were killed between 1 July and 7 August 2004 in Afghanistan. Each was stabbed or beaten to death by Taliban adherents.

The first victim, a former mullah named Assad Ullah, was captured in a busy daytime marketplace and was reported dead by a Taliban spokesman on 1 July. He said: "A group of Taliban dragged out Mullah Assad Ullah and slit his throat with a knife because he was propagating Christianity. We have enough evidence and local accounts to prove that he was involved in the conversion of Muslims to Christianity."

Three of the other Christian men who were killed were accused of reading the Bible, praying to Jesus or meeting with other converts. All of them, including Assad Ullah, left behind wives and children. The fifth convert to die was Naveed ul-Rehman, whose body was discovered in his car at the same marketplace in which Assad Ullah was abducted.

Hark, my soul, it is the Lord!
'Tis thy saviour, hear his Word;
Jesus speaks, and speaks to thee,
"Say, poor sinner, lovest thou me?
'I delivered thee when bound,
And, when bleeding, healed thy wound;
Sought thee wandering, set thee right,
Turned thy darkness into light.
"Thou shalt see my glory soon,
When the work of grace is done;

Partner of my throne shalt be;
Say, poor sinner, lovest thou me?"
Lord, it is my chief complaint
That my love is weak and faint;
Yet I love thee, and adore:
O for grace to love thee more!
William Cowper (1731-1800)

August 8

And they will be upheld, for the Lord is able to make them stand.
Romans 14:4b (NRSV)

Stamatios (1680)
Unfair Taxes

As a community leader, Stamatios' mandate was to represent his village, Hagios Georgios (Saint George), before the Ottoman authorities in Constantinople. He had the unenviable task of travelling there to see a certain Muslim official and voice his complaint about the unfair collection of taxes from the village's Christians.

After attending a hearing with the official, he was arrested and brought before a magistrate. Stamatios was offered his freedom if he would renounce his faith and convert to Islam. He replied, "God forbid that I should be so foolish."

He was then incarcerated in a local jail until the magistrate felt that he should be given a second chance to deny Christ. Again Stamatios stood up for his faith. This time he was tortured, but would not give in to the pain. Finally, he was beheaded in Constantinople in August 1680.

We thank thee, O Father, Lord of heaven and earth, for all who hallow pain by triumphing over it; for sufferers whose thought is always for others; for those whose faith brings light to the dark places of life; for those whose patience inspires others to endure. And grant, we beseech thee, O loving Father, to all who are bound together in the mysterious fellowship of suffering, the sense of comradeship with each other and with their

crucified Saviour; granting them in this life the peace that passeth all understanding, which the world cannot give nor take away, and in the world to come life everlasting.
Parish Prayers (no. 1293)

Love the LORD your God with all your heart and with all your soul and with all your strength. Deuteronomy 6: 5

Franz Jagerstätter (1943)
Executed by Nazis

"I can say from my own experience how painful life often is when one lives as a halfway Christian; it is more like vegetating than living," wrote Franz Jagerstätter to his godchild. This view was one he would maintain for the rest of his short life.

Born in Austria, Franz was required to heed the call-up to the Nazi army. He managed to get out of his first summons in 1940, but in 1943 he was called up again. At the time he stated: "I believe it is better to sacrifice one's life right away than to place oneself in the grave danger of committing sin and then dying."

But he gave in to family and local pressure and reported for duty with the express wish of being able to serve in the medical corps and not in the regular army. This, however, was unacceptable to the Third Reich and Franz was imprisoned for his beliefs. He was executed aged 36 on 9 August 1943 for keeping firm to his Christian convictions.

Lord, I am willing to appear to the world and to all to have lost my life, if only I may have made it good in your sight.
Temple Gairdner (1873-1928)

Command them [the rich] to do good, to be rich in good deeds, and to be generous and willing to share. In this way they will lay up treasure for themselves as a firm foundation for the coming age, so that they may take hold of the life that is truly life. 1 Timothy 6:18-19

Lawrence (258)
True Treasure

Lawrence, a deacon in the Roman Church, was arrested along with the bishop and other deacons during a spate of persecution in August 258. As well as helping to administer the communion cup and reading the Gospel, he was in charge of the Church money and ensured that it was used for the poor and needy. All the others were beheaded but Lawrence was spared because the magistrate was aware that he kept the money. Lawrence was asked to hand over the Church's treasure, which he agreed to do in three days' time. After selling the expensive vessels and giving away all remaining Church money to the poor, Lawrence gathered together the poor and sick people who had been helped by the Church in the courtyard. He told the magistrate, "Here is the Church's treasure."

The furious magistrate immediately ordered Lawrence's execution and he was roasted slowly to death over an iron grill. In the fifth century Augustine said of Lawrence's example, "Lawrence ministered the blood of Christ to the faithful, and for the sake of Christ's name he poured out his own."

Happy the man whose hopes rely
On Israel's God; He made the sky,
And earth, and seas, with all their train,
His truth forever stands secure;
He saves the oppressed, He feeds the poor,
And none shall find His promise vain.
Isaac Watts (1674-1748)

In everything set them an example by doing what is good … so that those who oppose you may be ashamed because they have nothing bad to say about us. Titus 2:7a,8b

Alfred Sadd (1942)
Wartime Missionary

Alfred was an established missionary on the small Pacific island of Beru when the Second World War spread into East Asia. He chose to stay and continue his Christian witness even as the war was coming closer to his door.

Alfred had started his missionary work in Suva on the island of Fiji in 1933. After mastering the language, for which he had a natural flair, he moved on to Beru, which is part of the Gilbert Islands. He became minister to the new Christians of Beru, established a surgery, began teaching the local people and started to translate the Bible into their dialect.

In 1942, the Japanese began to occupy the Gilbert Islands. In August of that year the Japanese army reached Beru where they found Alfred and the other Christians on the island huddled inside their church. They captured him and the other Europeans present and took them to the island of Tarawa, where they were beheaded.

> *We pray thee, Lord, for all who minister in thy name.*
> *Strengthen them in time of weakness and trial, and direct them in all*
> *   their work.*
> *Give unto them the spirit of power, and of love, and of sound mind,*
> *that in all their work they may set forth thy glory,*
> *and set forward the salvation of souls;*
> *that so the nations may become thine inheritance,*
> *and the uttermost part of the earth thy possession;*
> *through Jesus Christ our Lord.*
> *Prayers of the Worldwide Church*

*He humbled you by letting you hunger, then by feeding you with manna,
with which neither you nor your ancestors were acquainted, in order to
make you understand that one does not live by bread alone, but by every
word that comes from the mouth of the LORD.*
Deuteronomy 8:3 (NRSV)

Euplius (304)
Scriptures Banned

Euplius was a Sicilian Christian who owned a book of the Gospels at
a time when the Emperor Diocletian forbade the scriptures. Euplius let it
be known that he possessed the book, and was ushered before the Roman
governor who questioned him about how he had got hold of it. When
asked to give it up, Euplius refused, saying that within the book was to be
found eternal life. Very much angered by this, the governor condemned
Euplius to death. He was subjected to torture and executed with the
Gospels hung around his neck on 12 August 304. His final words were:
"Thanks be to thee, O Christ. O Christ, help. It is for Thee that I suffer."

*Christ himself says to his Father, "Your Word is truth." May the almighty
God, our heavenly Father, give us the love and light of truth to shine
in our hearts through the Holy Spirit, through Jesus Christ, our Lord.*
Nicholas Ridley (c. 1500-55)

Saul, Saul, why do you persecute me?... I am Jesus, whom you are persecuting... Now get up and stand on your feet. I have appeared to you to appoint you as a servant and as a witness of what you have seen and will see of me. Acts 26:14b-16

Yi Ki-Poong (1942)
Stoner Stoned

When Ki-Poong was baptised a Christian by a Presbyterian missionary to Korea in 1894, it was a remarkable turnaround for the young man who had stoned the first foreign missionary he ever saw.

Ki-Poong was serious about his new found Christian faith and felt that he should attend a theological seminary in Pyongyang. He graduated in 1907 and was shortly afterwards ordained a minister. This led to his volunteering to be a missionary and he was sent to a remote island off the south coast of Korea as the first Korean missionary there. Here he was stoned – but this did not lead to his martyrdom. This came about during World War II when he was imprisoned and tortured by the Japanese for this faith. Ki-Poong died as a result of tortures and deprivation.

Amazing grace! How sweet the sound
That saved a wretch like me!
I once was lost, but now am found;
Was blind, but now I see.

'Twas grace that taught my heart to fear,
And grace my fears relieved;
How precious did that grace appear
The hour I first believed.

Through many dangers, toils and snares,
I have already come;
'Tis grace hath brought me safe thus far,
And grace will lead me home.
John Newton (1725-1807)

They will seize you and persecute you. They will hand you over to synagogues and put you in prison, and you will be brought before kings and governors, and all on account of my name. And so you will bear testimony to me. Luke 21:12-13

Rasalama (1837)
Defied Threats

Rasalama was Madagascar's first martyr after Christianity was outlawed in the country.

She had attended a school set up by the London Missionary Society and became part of the first Christian community on the island. As a result of the Malagasy belief that their queen was their god, Christianity came to be seen as subversive and wrong. Thus Rasalama was forced to go into hiding when Christianity was outlawed by Queen Ranavalona I.

In July 1837 Rasalama was arrested and given to a courtier as a slave. There she practised her faith openly, despite the threat of capital punishment, and was soon sentenced to death due to her uncompromising assertion of faith. On 14 August 1837 she was led to her execution and killed with a spear. Today a church stands on the spot of her martyrdom.

A noble army – young and old –
from every nation came;
some weak and frail, some strong and bold,
to win the martyr's fame.
Eternal joy to all is given
who trust you and obey:
O give us strength, great God of heaven,
to follow them today!
Reginald Heber (1783-1826)

Teach us to number our days, that we may gain a heart of wisdom.
Psalm 90:12

Lizzie Atwater, Annie Eldred and the Lundgrens (1900) No Escape

"I am preparing for the end very quietly and calmly. The Lord is wonderfully near, and He will not fail me. I was very restless and excited while there seemed a chance of life, but God has taken away that feeling, and now I just pray for grace to meet the terrible end bravely. The pain will soon be over, and oh, the sweetness of the welcome above!"

Anticipating she would not escape the violence being perpetrated against foreigners and Christians in China, missionary Lizzie Atwater wrote these lines in a letter sent shortly before her death. She was pregnant when she was brutally hacked to death alongside her husband on 15 August 1900. Fellow missionaries Annie Eldred, the Reverend Anton Lundgren and his wife Elsa were also killed in the same incident.

Following the appointment of a new and bitterly anti-foreign prefect to the city of Fen-chau-fu, all missionaries had been ordered to leave. This group was offered an escort and under this pretence of protection they left the city. When they had gone 37 miles, the soldiers who were escorting them killed the missionaries.

Annie had served in China for a year and with tremendous zeal had applied herself to studying the Chinese language. The Lundgrens worked in Kie-Hiu; Mr Lundgren spent his time between an opium refuge and preaching, even reaching several high officials with the Gospel. Mrs Lundgren was highly regarded among the Chinese women whom she took every opportunity to evangelise. She also helped at the opium refuge, teaching Bible verses and hymns to the patients.

We praise thee, our Father, that even in the hour of darkness we can come to thee with confidence and unflinching faith. We know that thou art the ruler of nations and the maker of history; we know that nothing that men can do can ever frustrate thy holy and righteous will; we know that thou canst make even the wrath of men to praise thee. Help us, Father,

to learn the lessons that have come out of conflict; help us to work for the new day that will bring us one step nearer the kingdom. Dear Lord and Father of mankind, grant that the day may not be too far off when the nations will become one, when war will be abolished, and when we shall all live peacefully together as brethren in thy holy family.
A Chinese Christian, *In His Name* (no. 212)

August 16

Am I now seeking human approval, or God's approval? Or am I trying to please people? If I were still pleasing people, I would not be a servant of Christ. Galatians 1:10 (NRSV)

Robert Jermain Thomas (1866)
Brave Bible Distributor

Welshman Robert went to Korea as a missionary following the sudden death of his wife Caroline, having previously served the Lord in China. At this time Korea was a very isolated and dangerous country, but Robert bravely distributed Bibles to the Koreans he met on two separate missionary journeys.

He negotiated his first trip with two Korean traders in 1865 and spent two and a half months there giving out Bibles. A year later he got a job as an interpreter on an American trading ship, which set sail for Korea. The country had, however, banned trade with foreigners and was actively persecuting its own national church at this time. Despite this threatening climate, Robert gave out Bibles to the Koreans he met throughout the trip up river to the city of Pyongyang. But the ship did not have permission for its journey and was attacked by Korean forces. The crew were killed and Robert was reportedly beheaded while giving a Bible to his executioner, aged just 27.

> *Eternal God, who are the light of the minds that know you, the joy of the hearts that love you, and the strength of the wills that serve you; grant us so to know you, that we may truly love you, and so to love you that we may fully serve you, whom to serve is perfect freedom, in Jesus Christ our Lord.*
> Augustine of Hippo (354-430)

Fight the battle well, holding on to faith and a good conscience.
1 Timothy 1:18b-19

Jonathan Daniels (1965)
Took a Bullet

Jonathan joined the US civil rights movement in March 1965 when Martin Luther King called for volunteers to go to Selma, Alabama, where Afro-Americans were campaigning for black voter registration. Jonathan, who three years earlier had been through a "re-conversion" experience after a period of rebellion against his Christian upbringing, initially agreed to go for a few days but stayed for longer. The seminary student lived with an Afro-American family and represented the Church Society for Cultural and Racial Unity. Jonathan wanted to help fellow white Americans accept people of another colour as equal citizens, but those who sided with Afro-Americans were often hated.

In August he joined a demonstration in Lowndes County, Alabama, which resulted in a stand-off between blacks and whites. The police moved in and Jonathan, along with many other demonstrators, was arrested. After a week in jail they were released. Jonathan, along with fellow activists and 16-year-old Ruby Sales, went from the prison to a grocery store to buy a drink. Volunteer deputy sheriff Tom L Coleman appeared with a shotgun, shouting, "Goddamn Niggers, get off this property before I blow your damned brains out!" He threatened Ruby, pointing the gun at her, and as he fired the weapon, Jonathan pulled the teenager down – taking the bullet intended for her. The 26-year-old died instantly having saved the young girl's life. Coleman was arrested, tried and acquitted by an all-white jury. In 1991 Jonathan was designated as a martyr of the Episcopal Church.

There comes a time when one must take a position that is neither safe, nor politic, nor popular, but he must take it because conscience tells him it is right.
Martin Luther King, Jr. (1929-68)

If we live, we live for the Lord; and if we die, we die for the Lord. So, whether we live or die, we belong to the Lord. Romans 14:8

Akram Kattan (2005)
The Dead of Night

Akram and his family went to bed on the night of 18 August 2005 unaware of what was to happen a few hours later. In the dead of night, three armed Islamic militants with their faces covered broke into their home in Baghdad, Iraq. They pushed Akram's wife to the floor, saying, "You are Christians. You do not deserve to live."

The militants then demanded money but the Christian family begged them to take whatever they liked from the house instead. Akram was shot dead and another person was shot in the leg. The family called the police, but they were too afraid to come to the scene, saying, "Save yourselves!"

This was one of the countless Muslim extremist attacks on Iraqi Christians that followed the US-led invasion in 2003. As a result of the intense persecution, hundreds of thousands of Christians have fled their homeland.

We pray for the people of the land of the Tigris and Euphrates. We pray for its many casualties of wars. We pray too for those within its boundaries who are persecuted and oppressed for Christ's sake. Grant them protection by the Lord himself from those who have such hatred for them. Guide them, we pray, and bring peace to their homeland, through Jesus Christ our Lord. Amen.

For I endure scorn for your sake, and shame covers my face. I am a foreigner to my own family, a stranger to my own mother's children.
Psalm 69: 7-8

Fatima al-Mutairi (2008)
"We for the sake of Christ all things bear"

Fatima, a 26-year-old Saudi woman, learned about Jesus on the internet and decided to follow Him. When, in August 2008, her family noticed the cross on her computer screensaver and discovered that she had converted from Islam to Christianity, they cut out her tongue and burned her to death.

It was considered an "honour crime"; her father worked for the Commission for Protection of Virtue and Prevention of Vice, a government agency for enforcing Islamic religious purity. In Muslim contexts, it is generally considered legitimate and even necessary for a family to kill a member who has brought perceived "shame" or "dishonour" by converting to another religion.

In the last blog that Fatima wrote before her death, she found comfort and strength in the opening verse of Psalm 27, "The LORD is my light and my salvation – whom shall I fear?" She had also written the following poem (translated from Arabic), which she posted on the internet.

And we for the sake of Christ all things bear
May the Lord Jesus guide you, O Muslims
And enlighten your hearts that you might love others
The forum does not revile the Master of the prophets
It is for the display of truth, and for you it was revealed
This is the truth that you do not know
What we profess are the words of the Master of the prophets
We do not worship the cross, and we are not possessed
We worship the Lord Jesus, the Light of the worlds
We left Muhammad, and we do not follow in his path
We followed Jesus Christ, the Clear Truth
Truly, we love our homeland, and we are not traitors

We take pride that we are Saudi citizens
How could we betray our homeland, our dear people?
How could we, when for death – for Saudi Arabia – we stand ready?
The homeland of my grandfathers, their glories, and odes – for it I am
    writing
And we say, "We are proud, proud, proud to be Saudis"
We chose our way, the way of the rightly guided
And every man is free to choose any religion
Be content to leave us to ourselves to be believers in Jesus
Let us live in grace before our time comes
There are tears on my cheek, and oh! the heart is sad
To those who become Christians, you are so cruel!
And the Messiah says, "Blessed are the Persecuted"
And we for the sake of Christ all things bear.
What is it to you that we are infidels?
You do not enter our graves, as if with us buried
Enough – your swords do not concern me, not evil nor disgrace
Your threats do not trouble me, and we are not afraid
And by God, I am unto death a Christian – Verily
I cry for what passed by, of a sad life
I was far from the Lord Jesus for many years
O History record! And bear witness, O witnesses!
We are Christians – in the path of Christ we tread
Take from me this word, and note it well
You see, Jesus is my Lord, and he is the Best of protectors
I advise you to pity yourself, to clap your hands in mourning
See your look of ugly hatred
Man is brother to man, Oh learned ones
Where is the humanity, the love, and where are you?
As to my last words, I pray to the Lord of the worlds
Jesus the Messiah, the Light of Clear Guidance
That He change notions, and set the scales of justice aright
And that He spread Love among you, O Muslims.
Fatima al-Mutairi (martyred 2008)

To the one who is victorious, I will give the right to sit with me on my throne, just as I was victorious and sat down with my Father on his throne. Revelation 3:21

Nazr Ullah Khan (1908)
"Would not deny Christ"

Nazr Ullah Khan of Chaman, Pakistan, on the border of Afghanistan, became a Christian in 1899 and lived his faith boldly, witnessing for Christ wherever opportunity availed itself. He was killed by Afghans on 20 August 1908.

A plaque in Urdu was placed over the fireplace of the church in Chaman reading: "In memory of Nazr Ullah Khan who became a Christian on 11 June 1899. He would not deny Christ, and was killed by Afghans near Chaman on 20 August 1908. He who loses his life for my sake and the Gospel's, the same shall find it."

Take up your cross and follow Christ,
nor think till death to lay it down;
for only he who bears the cross
may hope to win the glorious crown.
C W Everest (1814-77)

If our hearts do not condemn us, we have confidence before God.
1 John 3:21

Antoninus (4ᵗʰ century)
Spurned Financial Gain

Antoninus was a stonemason in Anbazus, Syria, in the fourth century and, despite the fact that the pagan practice of worshipping stone idols would have been financially advantageous to someone in his trade, he admonished those who followed this practice.

After a two year period when he retired to live as a hermit, Antoninus was driven to return to his village and destroy its pagan idols. He was chased away and fled to Apamea, Syria, where the bishop asked him to build a church, which he did. This prompted a riot by the pagan population in which Antoninus was killed.

God be in my head
and in my understanding;

God be in my eyes,
and in my looking;

God be in my mouth,
and in my speaking;

God be in my heart,
and in my thinking;

God be at my end,
and at my departing.
Book of Hours (1514)

August 22

Set your minds on things above, not on earthly things. Colossians 3:2

Pierre Claverie (1996)
Life's Worth

"Its worth is measured by my capacity to give it." These were the words of Pierre Claverie, Bishop of Oran, Algeria, describing the value of his life before he was martyred for his faith in Christ.

Bishop Pierre had been deeply involved in Christian-Muslim dialogue and was not afraid to speak out against the terrorist organisations of

Algeria; the sermons he gave were always popular. He was assassinated by militants in August 1996 when a bomb exploded next to his house. He had just returned with his driver, who was also killed, from a memorial service for seven martyred Christians.

Pierre had said, "I am not seeking martyrdom. But what would my life be worth if kept in cold storage? Its worth is measured by my capacity to give it." He was described as "steadfastly committed to the way of the cross".

My heaven is to please God and glorify Him, and to give all to Him, and to be wholly devoted to His glory; that is the heaven I long for.
David Brainerd (1718-47)

August 23

Christ died and returned to life so that he might be the Lord of both the dead and the living. Romans 14:9

Samir Yelda (2005)
Kidnapped and Killed

Iraqi Christian Samir Yelda, a lecturer at Baghdad University, was kidnapped on 23 August 2005. A ransom was demanded, and somehow his family found the money and paid it. But when they went to collect him on 24 August, they were given Samir's head in a sack.

Christians in Iraq have been targeted by Islamic militants seeking to "cleanse" the country of Christian presence, despite the fact that there have been Christians there since the first century.

When peace, like a river, attendeth my way,
when sorrows like sea billows roll;
whatever my lot, thou hast taught me to say,
It is well, it is well with my soul.

Though Satan should buffet, though trials should come,
let this blest assurance control,

that Christ has regarded my helpless estate,
and hath shed his own blood for my soul.

My sin, oh, the bliss of this glorious thought!
My sin, not in part but the whole,
is nailed to the cross, and I bear it no more,
praise the Lord, praise the Lord, O my soul!

And, Lord, haste the day when my faith shall be sight,
the clouds be rolled back as a scroll;
the trump shall resound, and the Lord shall descend,
even so, it is well with my soul.
Horatio Gates Spafford (1828-1888)

August 24

Whoever has the Son has life; whoever does not have the Son of God does not have life. 1 John 5:12

Sulaymaan Mahamed Sulaymaan and Ahmed 'Goode' Diiriye (1994) "Infidels" Targeted

Sulaymaan and Ahmed, two Somali Christians from a Muslim background, were shot dead on 24 August 1994 in Mogadishu, Somalia, by the most prominent group of Islamic radicals in the country at the time, Al-Ittihad (Islamic Unity). Sulaymaan was gunned down on a bus as he was returning home from work and Ahmed was shot near a milk factory. Ahmed had been a Christian for over 20 years and had often been persecuted for his faith. He had been a fearless witness and had shown the love of Christ in his medical work. At the time of his death, he had been working as a nurse at the eye clinic where he had been trained by a Christian group in the 1980s. Several days after the shooting, a note was found outside a relief agency that said, "Liibaan: gaal   Sulaymaan: gaal   Goode: gaal". "Gaal" is Somali for "infidel". Liibaan Xasan had been killed by Muslim extremists earlier in the year (see March 21).

Who are these like stars appearing,
these, before God's throne who stand?
Each a golden crown is wearing;
who are all this glorious band?
Alleluia! Hark, they sing,
praising loud their heavenly King.
Heinrich Theobald Schenk (1656-1727)
Translated by Frances Elizabeth Cox (1812-1897)

August 25

For I am convinced that neither death nor life, neither angels nor demons, neither the present nor the future, nor any powers, neither height nor depth, nor anything else in all creation, will be able to separate us from the love of God that is in Christ Jesus our Lord. Romans 8:38-9

Christians in Orissa (2007-08)
"Come back as Hindu or don't come back at all"

Pregnant Christian woman Kamalini Naik was cut to pieces along with her one-year-old son in front of her husband by an angry mob of Hindu extremists, when she refused to convert from Christianity to Hinduism during the horrendous anti-Christian riots that broke out in Orissa, India, in August 2008.

The large-scale violence, which continued unabated until October, followed coordinated attacks on Christians in the area the previous Christmas. At least 60 Christians were brutally murdered; some were cut to pieces, others burnt alive. Many of the dead were pastors, who were specially targeted by the attackers. A paralysed man in one village was unable to escape from a fire and so burned to death. Around 18,000 Christians were injured, many of them severely, and numerous Christian women were raped. Over 4,000 homes as well as several orphanages and hundreds of church buildings and Christian schools were destroyed. Tens of thousands of Christians were left homeless, and at least 400 villages were cleansed of all Christians. Many were too fearful to return home, threatened by the Hindu extremists: "Come back as Hindu or don't come back at all." Some of those who dared to return were forcibly converted to Hinduism or sometimes covered in petrol and set on fire if they refused to renounce Christ.

This is not our final or permanent place. We are only pilgrims here. That is our faith. Whatever may come, we will never leave our faith. In any case, we will have to die one day... I am not angry with God. I am happy with what God has given us. It is written in the Bible that you will be persecuted for your faith.
Christudas, a Christian from Kandhamal in Orissa state, whose wife, Ramani Nayak, was killed in the riots.

August 26

As long as it is day, we must do the work of him who sent me. Night is coming, when no-one can work. John 9:4

Mup (2008)
Active Minister

Mup, a Degar Vietnamese Christian preacher, was found beaten to death on 26 August 2008 outside his village of Ploi Rong Khong in the province of Gia Lai. Mup had been summoned three times by the Vietnamese security police to their headquarters in order to be interrogated regarding his religious activities, but he refused to go as he feared that he might be beaten, tortured, detained or murdered as many other Degar Christians had been. On 25 August he was on his way home after attending a funeral when he was approached by Vietnamese officials. The following morning his body was found.

Christians in the minority-ethnic Degar community, who live in the central highlands, face intense persecution at the hands of the authorities. A Degar report said, "They just kill our people any time they want to, like we are just animals for them to slaughter even for fun."

O God, the God of all goodness and of all grace, who is worthy of a greater love than we can either give or understand, fill our hearts, we beseech

you, with such love towards you, that nothing may seem too hard for us to do or suffer in obedience to your will; and grant that thus loving you we may become daily more like unto you and finally obtain the crown of life, which you have promised to those that love you; through Jesus Christ our Lord.
Farnham Hostel Manual (19th century)

August 27

The fear of the LORD is instruction in wisdom, and humility goes before honour. Proverbs 15:33 (NRSV)

Kuksha (1113)
Preached to Pagans

Kuksha was a monk but he left his monastery in Kiev (in modern day Ukraine) to begin teaching and preaching to his own Vyatichi people – a group related to the Polish – in present-day Russia. The leading Vyatichi families had set up home in towns where the Russian and Vyatichi lands met under Grand Prince Vladimir of Kiev.

Many of the people Kuksha spoke to about the Christian faith were pagans and his successful missionary activities upset the local pagan priests. They began to incite hatred toward Kuksha until eventually he was taken prisoner, tortured and beheaded on 27 August 1113.

Lord,
I am not brave.
I am not the stuff
that martyrs are made of
I would rather not hear, not see.
I would rather turn away.
I would like an undisturbed life, but there is no escape
for I cannot love you and be totally silent.
Frank Topping (1909-1997), *The Words of Christ*

"He will not let your foot slip — he who watches over you will not slumber; indeed, he who watches over Israel will neither slumber nor sleep." Psalm 121:3-4

Job Chittilappilly (2004)
Hindu Extremists

On 28 August 2004 Job, an elderly Indian church leader, was stabbed to death on the veranda of his home in the state of Kerala, south India. He had received a number of threatening phone calls because of his ministry among Hindus before he was murdered. Nothing was stolen from his house, and crime investigators said that it was most likely to have been a deliberate execution.

Christians in India face much persecution from Hindu extremists. At the time of Job's murder, there were four attacks by Hindu extremists in the space of seven days.

I bind unto myself today
The power of God to hold and lead,
His eye to watch, his might to stay,
His ear to harken to my need.
The wisdom of my God to teach
His hand to guide, his shield to ward;
The word of God to give me speech,
His heavenly host to be my guard.
Patrick of Ireland (fl. 5th century)

Truly I tell you, among those born of women no one has arisen greater than John the Baptist; yet the least in the kingdom of heaven is greater than he. Matthew 11:11 (NRSV)

John the Baptist (c. 30)
Heralded Christ

John the Baptist, the cousin of Jesus, was the last of the prophets who heralded the arrival of Jesus the Messiah. Following his birth to the aged Elizabeth and Zechariah, it was clear that John was a special arrival, and the people asked, "'What then is this child going to be?' For the Lord's hand was with him" (Luke 1:66b). His father prophesied:

...You, my child, will be called a prophet of the Most High; for you will go on before the Lord to prepare the way for him, to give his people the knowledge of salvation through the forgiveness of their sins. (Luke 1:76-77)

John himself displayed great humility about his calling. Crowds were attracted to his message and wondered if he might be the Messiah but John answered them, "I baptise you with water. But one who is more powerful than I will come, the straps of whose sandals I am not worthy to untie" (Luke 3:16a).

John spoke out against King Herod's marriage to his brother's wife, Herodias, for which he was arrested. Herodias wanted to kill John but Herod protected him; he was intrigued by the prophet's message about Jesus, and knew "him [John] to be a righteous and holy man" (Mark 6:20b). Herodias took her opportunity for revenge at a state banquet where her daughter performed a dance for Herod. He was so delighted that he promised to grant her whatever she wished. Prompted by her mother, she demanded John's head on a platter. And so, promise-bound and conscious of his guests, Herod chose to honour his word rather than his conscience, and granted her wish (Matthew 14:3-11; Mark 6:17-28). John's martyrdom is honoured on this day.

Look, the Lamb of God, who takes away the sin of the world! This is the one I meant when I said, "A man who comes after me has surpassed me because he was before me." I myself did not know him, but the reason I came baptising with water was that he might be revealed to Israel... I saw the Spirit come down from heaven as a dove and remain on him. And I myself did not know him, but the one who sent me to baptise with water told me, "The man on whom you see the Spirit come down and remain is the one who will baptise with the Holy Spirit." I have seen and I testify that this is God's Chosen One.
John the Baptist (John 1:29b-34)

August 30

Just as a body, though one, has many parts, but all its many parts form one body, so it is with Christ... If one part suffers, every part suffers with it; if one part is honoured, every part rejoices with it.
1 Corinthians 12: 12, 26

Felix and "Adauctus" (c. 304)
Shared in Suffering

Felix, a Christian leader in Rome during the reign of Emperor Diocletian, was on his way to be executed when a man in the crowd realised he was being killed for his faith. The man shouted out that he too was a Christian – an act that led to his arrest and death alongside Felix. Since his name was not known, he was referred to as "Adauctus", which means "the additional one". Pope Damasus wrote about them:

O how truly and rightly named Felix, happy, you who, with faith untouched and despising the prince of this world, have confessed Christ and sought the heavenly kingdom. Know ye also, brethren, the truly precious faith by which Adauctus too hastened, a victor, to heaven...

Suddenly I heard the words of Christ and understood them, and life and death ceased to seem to be evil, and instead of despair I experienced happiness and the joy of life undisturbed by death.
Leo Tolstoy (1828-1910)

Rejoice and be glad, because great is your reward in heaven, for in the same way they persecuted the prophets who were before you.
Matthew 5:12

Metropolitan Benjamin (1922)
Praised amid Persecution

"About myself? What can I tell you? One more thing perhaps; regardless of what my sentence will be, no matter what you decide, life or death, I will lift up my eyes reverently to God, cross myself and affirm: 'Glory to Thee my Lord; glory to Thee for everything'."

This was the powerful statement Metropolitan Benjamin made to the judge when he was put on trial as a result of Soviet persecution. The Petrograd (now St Petersburg) clergyman had joined with the Communists on a project committee called "Help for the Starving" and had approached fellow church leaders for contributions. They raised a lot of money and the Communist Central Committee in Moscow was concerned that the voluntary gifts would increase the prestige of the clergy. They ordered the Communists in Petrograd to confiscate church valuables instead of accepting them as donations. Metropolitan Benjamin and others were then put on trial with false witnesses brought in to condemn them. At the trial his defence lawyer made this appeal:

> Do not make a martyr of the Metropolitan Benjamin. The masses revere him, and if he is killed for his faith and his loyalty to the masses, he would become much more dangerous to the Soviet power... Let it remind you that true faith feeds and grows strong on the blood of the martyrs. Would you risk giving more martyrs to the restless people?

Nevertheless in August 1922, Metropolitan Benjamin and the others were executed by a firing squad. Before they were shot their beards were shaved and they were given rags to wear to disguise the fact that they were clergy.

Glory to God, and praise and love
Be ever, ever given,
By saints below and saints above,
The Church in earth and heaven.
Charles Wesley (1707-88)

September 1

The gospel must first be preached to all nations. Mark 13:10

Manuel (1999)
Gangster turned Evangelist

From a young age, Manuel and his brothers Caleb and Mario were members of illegal armed groups in the Colombian capital Bôgotá. They were endlessly in trouble with other gangs and the police. Then Manuel heard about Jesus Christ and soon gave his life to him, as too did his brothers. Their lives were suddenly transformed; from being hardcore gangsters they became ardent evangelists. Manuel would carry Bibles with him wherever he went and would keenly distribute them to his old gangland friends. Through this many came to know Jesus.

Manuel realised that his efforts to proclaim Jesus were not popular with the local gangland bosses. He received death threats on several occasions, but he remained faithful to the cause of Christ.

One night, in autumn 1999, several armed men visited Manuel's home. They took him from his wife and seven children, who pleaded for mercy. Some of the children witnessed Manuel's torture before he was driven away. Several hours later his body was recovered next to his Bible.

Thank you heavenly Father for the lands of Central and South America. Thank you for the Christians, like Manuel, who through hardship, poverty and tribulation have found you. Help the peoples of Latin America to discover you in the way Manuel did. Help them to enrich the human family in all ways which express your will, through Jesus Christ our Lord. Amen.

I love the LORD, for he heard my voice; he heard my cry for mercy. Because he turned his ear to me, I will call on him as long as I live. The cords of death entangled me, the anguish of the grave came over me; I was overcome by distress and sorrow. Then I called on the name of the LORD: "LORD, save me!" Psalm 116:1-4

Martyrs of New Guinea (1942)
Wartime Servants

New Guinea's 333 missionary martyrs, many of whom lost their lives during the Second World War, are traditionally remembered on 2 September.

Christianity came to the south-east Asian island in the 1860s. When war broke out in 1939, New Guinea became a dangerous place for European missionaries, especially once the Japanese had invaded the island. Despite the danger, Bishop Philip Scott and his mission team chose to stay, and were captured by the Japanese. He, his eight staff and two laymen were executed on 2 September 1942 in a concentration camp. Many other Christians died in these camps during the Japanese occupation, especially in Papua (eastern New Guinea). Here also, numerous Papuan Christians risked their lives to care for those wounded by attacks from the Japanese.

God of mercy,
who brought your holy martyrs of New Guinea
through the great tribulation,
grant us ever to abide in your presence,
that, whatever the calling you give us,
we may be ready for your service
and constant in the truth of your gospel.
This we ask through Jesus Christ our Lord.
For All the Saints (Canada)

In your relationships with one another, have the same mindset as Christ Jesus. Philippians 2:5

Ella Mary Schenck (1898)
"As my Saviour died for me"

"I can think of nothing that would make death more welcomed than to meet it here, to die for these dear children as my Saviour died for me. It is the suffering and dying Saviour that melts the stony heart. So with us – that which our lives cannot do, our deaths may do."

These were the words of Ella Mary Schenck when two of her missionary associates in Sierra Leone died. Ella too would go on to give her life in the Lord's service in the troubled West African country in 1898.

A qualified teacher, Ella had felt a strong call to use her teaching skills in Africa and set off on her first missionary journey to Sierra Leone in 1891. She worked as a matron at a girls' school where she won the affection and respect of the pupils, as well as using her teaching gifts in various ways at church and meeting people in their homes. After three years she returned home to the USA, and after completing Bible and evangelistic training, felt compelled to return to Sierra Leone. As her ship set sail in 1897, hostility against British rule was rising in Sierra Leone and would soon become a violent and bloody revolt. At first, the rebels slaughtered the British and Creole, but soon turned their attention to American missionaries, who had been left unharmed during earlier conflicts.

Seven months after they had left their homeland, Ella and four other members of her mission station in Rotufunk were captured and hacked to death. The mission buildings – the church, school, barracks and hospital – were torched. Two years later, however, the station was rebuilt and the work that Ella and her team had started went on to flourish with five new mission stations later established.

Lord Jesus, you suffered for me – what am I suffering for you?
Corrie Ten Boom (1892-1983)

You must be on your guard. You will be handed over to the local councils and flogged in the synagogues. On account of me you will stand before governors and kings as witnesses to them. Mark 13:9

Marcellus (c. 178)
Stood Firm

Marcellus was a clergyman imprisoned for his faith during the persecution under the Roman emperor Marcus Aurelius. He managed to escape to Chalon-sur-Saone, in present-day France, where he found shelter.

From there he chose to travel north and on his journey, met a governor named Priscus who invited him for a meal. After arriving at the governor's table, Marcellus soon found himself in a compromising position, for Priscus was about to perform various pagan rites. He asked to be excused because he was a Christian, prompting the crowd that was present to call for his death. The governor forbade this, but had Marcellus brought before a court which ordered him to worship an image of the god Saturn. He refused, so was taken to the banks of the river Saone and buried up to his waist, where, after three days, he died.

To accept His kingdom and to enter it brings blessedness, because the best conceivable thing is that we should be in obedience to the will of God.
C H Dodd (1884-1973), *Parables of the Kingdom*

In the way of righteousness there is life; along that path is immortality.
Proverbs 12:28

Rómulo Sauñe (1992)
The Righteous Path

Quechua Indian Christians became targets of the violent opposition group, the Shining Path, in their fight against the Peruvian government.

The rebels wanted the Quechuas to back their cause but the Christians were opposed to their violent tactics.

Ròmulo, who was well-known for his ministry to the Quechua pastors, became a particular target because of his great influence among the tribe. In September 1992, while returning to the city of Ayacucho, Ròmulo and his companions were stopped at a roadblock set up by the Shining Path in the Andes of Peru. As soon as the truck stopped, the rebels opened fire and Ròmulo died from bullet wounds on the spot. His three nephews were killed alongside him.

Ròmulo's murder can also be seen as part of a campaign against the Sauñe family which started when Ròmulo's grandfather – one of the first Quechua converts – was savagely killed by the Shining Path when he defended his faith in front of them.

Lord God, the refuge and strength of your people in every hour of need; sustain all who suffer for their allegiance to the faith of Christ. Give them courage and patience to endure to the end; that by their example and witness they may win others to the service of him who suffered for all mankind, our Saviour Jesus Christ.
Contemporary Parish Prayers (adapted from *Worship Now*)

September 6

Sing joyfully to the LORD, you righteous; it is fitting for the upright to praise him. Psalm 33:1

Theodore of Amasea (c.306)
Proclaimed and Praised

Theodore is believed to have been born in the East, possibly Syria or Armenia. According to tradition, he enlisted in the Roman army and was sent to Pontus (in modern-day Turkey). After an edict was issued against Christians, Theodore was brought before the court at Amasea and asked to sacrifice to the gods. He denounced them and boldly proclaimed Jesus Christ as Lord. Gregory of Nyssa records that Theodore said:

I do not know the gods because they are false, whereas you err by honouring and addressing them... But as for me, Christ is God, the Only Begotten Son of God. Therefore on behalf of the true religion and by confessing him, let him who inflicts wounds go ahead and cut; let him who strikes thrash; let him who burns lead to the flame, and let him who is grieved by my words cut out my tongue.

The judges mocked Theodore but released him to give him time to reconsider his position. During this time, the temple of the goddess Cybele was torched, and it was reported to the magistrates that Theodore was responsible. He was brought back before the court and again refused to recant his faith in Christ. While being tortured, Theodore sang praises to God from Psalm 33. After much suffering he was finally killed by being burned at the stake.

> *Jesus, Thy blood and righteousness*
> *My beauty are, my glorious dress;*
> *'Midst flaming worlds, in these arrayed,*
> *With joy shall I lift up my head.*
> *Bold shall I stand in Thy great day;*
> *For who aught to my charge shall lay?*
> *Fully absolved through these I am -*
> *From sin and fear, from guilt and shame.*
> Count Nikolaus Ludwig von Zinzendorf (1700–1760)

September 7

Do not withhold your mercy from me, LORD; may your love and faithfulness always protect me. Psalm 40:11

Chrysostomos (1922)
"Treat him as he deserves!"

When Kemalist forces overran the ancient Christian city of Smyrna (now Izmir in Turkey) in 1922, Metropolitan Chrysostomos feared for the safety of the Greek Orthodox population. He was unconvinced by leaflets issued by the invading troops, which said, "Mustafa Kemal has given strict orders to the soldiers to harm no one. Those who disobey these orders will be punished by death. Let the people be assured of safety."

Chrysostomos' grave misgivings led him, on 7 September 1922, to write to the Greek Premier urging him to intervene on behalf of the Christian population. He warned that they were "descending into a Hell from which no power will be able to raise them up and save them … destined as we are … for sacrifice and martyrdom…"

Two days after writing this letter, Chrysostomos went to see the Turkish commander of the occupation forces, General Noureddin. When he extended his hand, the General spat, declaring he would not touch his filthy hand. He then told Chrysostomos that he had been sentenced to death, and ordered him out of his sight. As Chrysostomos walked out of the building, the General appeared on the balcony and shouted to a waiting angry mob, "Treat him as he deserves!" They dragged him to a barber's shop, tore out his beard, gouged out his eyes with knives, and cut off his ears, nose and hands. All this occurred while French marines stood by watching.

O Father, my hope
O Son, my refuge
O Holy Spirit, my protection,
Holy Trinity, glory to thee.
St Ioannikios, for the service of Compline, Eastern Orthodox Church

---

September 8

But he knows the way that I take; when he has tested me, I will come forth as gold. Job 23:10

Alexander Menn (1990)
Preached on Martyrdom

The day after Alexander, a priest in the Soviet Union, gave a lecture on Christian martyrs, he too was killed – undoubtedly because of his outstanding Christian witness.

Born to Jewish parents in 1935, he converted to Christianity when he grew up and followed his calling into the priesthood. His life was marked by joyfulness, the love of Christ and, what his friends called, an unusual gift of discernment. As a preacher and author he was very popular and many people were converted through his ministry. Alexander's bold Christian witness brought him to the attention of the Communist authorities. In the 1980s they tried to get him to denounce his ministry, but he refused.

Following his lecture on the night of 8 September about the uniqueness of those who had given their lives for Christ, Alexander was fatally struck on the head with an axe as he walked in a wood. It is likely the killers were linked to the KGB or the neo-fascist group Pamyat, which was believed to have been stirred up to take action against Alexander by the KGB. No one was ever brought to justice for the murder.

Time is given us to use in view of eternity.
Henry Allan Ironside (1876-1951)

September 9

Who shall separate us from the love of Christ? Shall trouble or hardship or persecution or famine or nakedness or danger or sword? As it is written: "For your sake we face death all day long; we are considered as sheep to be slaughtered". No, in all these things we are more than conquerors through him who loved us. Romans 8:35-37

Aslam Masih (2011)
Injustice and Illness

Aslam Masih, a young Christian man, was falsely accused of blasphemy by two Islamists in Pakistan. The pair registered a case against him under section 295-B of the Pakistan Penal Code, which carries a sentence of life imprisonment for desecration of the Quran. Despite there being no witnesses, Aslam was arrested in February 2010, the police having been pressured by the two accusers.

Aslam's mental as well as his physical health deteriorated while he was in prison. He and others accused of blasphemy were kept in solitary confinement without access to a toilet, water or electricity. Aslam was also denied basic products such as soap, toothpaste and clean clothes. He had lost contact with his family, who did not visit him during his time in prison.

Aslam became very unwell, suffering from various diseases including tuberculosis and dengue fever, and failed to receive proper medical care in the jail hospital. The prison authorities initially refused to allow Aslam to go to an outside hospital for proper treatment for security reasons. He was eventually admitted to hospital in Lahore, but it was too late and he died on 9 September 2011, aged 30. A post-mortem found the cause of death to be dengue fever, which can be treated in Pakistan.

A number of Christians have lost their lives as either a direct or indirect result of Pakistan's blasphemy laws, which are often used against them. Some, like Aslam, have died in prison while others are killed by Muslim vigilantes.

Receive every inward and outward trouble, every disappointment, pain, uneasiness, temptation, darkness, and desolation, with both thy hands, as a true opportunity and blessed occasion of dying to self, and entering into a fuller fellowship with the self-denying, suffering Saviour. Look at no inward or outward trouble in any other view; reject every other thought about it; and then every kind of trial and distress will become the blessed day of thy prosperity. That state is best, which exerciseth the highest faith in, and the fullest resignation to God.
William Law (1686-1761)

September 10

Jesus said, "If you hold to my teaching, you are really my disciples. Then you will know the truth, and the truth will set you free." John 8:31b-32

Bartholomew (c. 70)
"No Deceit"

Bartholomew was one of the twelve men chosen by Jesus as his apostles. They learnt from their master, "that he might send them out to preach and to have authority to drive out demons" (Mark 3:14b-15).

Bartholomew certainly fulfilled his calling, taking the Gospel to countries as far away as India where he translated the Gospel of Matthew into a local language.

Bartholomew and the man named Nathanael in John's Gospel are believed to be one and the same person. Nathanael is described by Jesus as "an Israelite in whom there is no deceit" (John 1:47b). In a conversation with Philip, Nathanael doubts that Jesus is the promised Saviour until he encounters "the Son of God… the King of Israel" for himself (John 1: 45-49).

In India, Bartholomew is said to have destroyed the images that were worshipped there. The king and queen, as well as many of the people, became Christians, which prompted the local religious leaders to complain to the king's older brother. On his orders, Bartholomew was flayed alive.

The valiant twelve, the chosen few,
on them the Spirit fell;
and faithful to the Lord they knew
they faced the host of hell.
They died beneath the brandished steel,
became the tyrant's prey,
yet did not flinch at their ordeal –
who follows them today?
Reginald Heber (1783-1826)

September 11

And the things you have heard me say in the presence of many witnesses entrust to reliable people who will also be qualified to teach others.
2 Timothy 2:2

Pothinus (177)
Pagan Uprising

Pothinus was the bishop of Lyon, a Roman province where a number of Christians lived in the second century. An elderly man by this time, he is said to have "listened to those who had seen the apostles".

In the summer of 177 the pagans in the city rose up against the Christians, and the authorities sanctioned the uprising by arresting Pothinus and other leading members of the Church. Pothinus, who was 90 years old when he was brought before the governor, stood firm in his faith. When asked by the governor who the Christian God was, he said, "If you had any understanding you would know."

Pothinus was beaten and died of his wounds two days later. Other Christians were tortured before being put to death in the public arena on the orders of the Emperor Marcus Aurelius.

Never, for fear of feeble man, restrain your witness.
C H Spurgeon (1834-92)

September 12

I am greatly encouraged; in all our troubles my joy knows no bounds.
2 Corinthians 7:4b

Susanna (295)
Refused Marriage

Susanna was the daughter of a priest in Rome. A relative of Emperor Diocletian, she refused his request to marry his son-in-law, Maximian, a persecutor of Christians. Her rebuttal angered the emperor, and his ire was further fuelled when she converted two of her uncles whom he had sent to persuade her to marry Maximian.

Diocletian then sent one of his court favourites, Julian, to resolve the issue. On Julian's orders the newly converted officials and their families were burnt to death at Cumae; Susanna was beaten, and she and her father were beheaded.

Lord Jesus,
You are my light
In the darkness
You are my warmth
In the cold
You are my happiness
In sorrow.

Praise be to the God and Father of our Lord Jesus Christ, the Father of compassion and the God of all comfort, who comforts us in all our troubles, so that we can comfort those in any trouble with the comfort we ourselves have received from God. For just as we share abundantly in the sufferings of Christ, so also our comfort abounds through Christ.
2 Corinthians 1:3-5

Antony Ixida (1632)
Captured while Caring

Antony, born in Japan in 1569, was educated by missionaries and became a Christian. He was ordained a priest and played an important role in bringing back those who had left the faith, as well as making new converts, following persecution in 1597. When further persecution broke out in 1614, Antony worked among the victims in the province of Arima until 1629.

Antony was captured while visiting a sick person in Nagasaki. He was brought before the governor and treated with some respect whilst he explained the Christian faith. The governor was moved by his words and wanted to release him, but did not have the authority to do so. Instead, Antony was sent to prison in Omura for two years. After this he was sent back to Nagasaki where he and others were tortured in an attempt to make them abandon their faith. They endured this ordeal for 33 days before being burnt to death in September 1632.

He who is filled with love is filled with God himself.
Augustine of Hippo (354-430)

Teach me knowledge and good judgment, for I trust your commands.
Psalm 119:66

Cyprian (c. 258)
Key Thinker

Cyprian was an early Christian theologian who played an important role in the history of the Western Church and the development of Christian thought in the third century, especially in Africa.

Born in Tunisia in around 200, Cyprian was a lawyer and teacher of public speaking for the greater part of his life, but his later years took a different direction after he became a Christian aged 46. Two years later he was made bishop of Carthage and when, in 249, Emperor Decius began persecuting Christians, Cyprian went into hiding. He was criticised for this move but it did enable him to stay with his church and look after them.

Persecution broke out again in 258 under Emperor Valerian and Cyprian was one of the first victims. He was examined by the proconsul and, because he stood firm in his faith and would not reveal any names of his priests, Cyprian was exiled. But then a new proconsul came into office and Cyprian was brought for trial in Carthage. Here, he refused to sacrifice to the Roman gods and was consequently given a death sentence.

On 14 September Cyprian was taken to the field of Sextus and blindfolded. He knelt in prayer and was then beheaded.

No subject of contemplation will tend more to humble the mind, than thoughts of God.
C H Spurgeon (1834-92)

For I bear your name, LORD God Almighty. Jeremiah 15:16b

Wedgewood Baptist Church (1999) Gunned Down

"This is an opportunity to tell the world about Kim's love of the Lord." These remarkable words were spoken at the funeral of 23-year-old Susan Kimberly Jones by her grieving mother. The graduate from Texas Christian University was one of seven people killed by a gunman who burst into Wedgewood Baptist Church in Texas, USA, on 15 September 1999. Around 150 teenagers and young people were attending a Christian concert at the time.

Larry Gene Ashbrook entered the church sanctuary, began to shout mocking remarks about God, threw a crude pipe-bomb, and opened fire on the congregation. The other six people who died were Sunday school teacher Shawn C Brown (23), Cassandra Griffin (14), Joseph D Ennis (14), Justin M Ray (17), Kristi Beckel (14) and seminary graduate Sydney R Browning (36). Seven others were wounded in the incident. After committing this massacre the gunman turned the gun on himself at the back of the church.

How sweet the name of Jesus sounds
In a believer's ear:
It soothes his sorrow, heals his wounds,
And drives away his fear.
John Newton (1725-1807)

And I, when I am lifted up from the earth, will draw all people to myself. John 12:32 (NRSV)

Ajay Topno (2007)
Village Tensions

Ajay was an Indian evangelist who worked with Trans World Radio in Jharkhand state, India. He would sometimes accompany a fellow evangelist to Sahoda village, where they would conduct worship services for a small number of Christian families. Tensions had risen between Christians and Hindus in the village following the "reconversion" of a Christian family to Hinduism by Hindu extremists.

On the evening of 16 September 2007, Ajay set off for Sahoda. When he didn't return home, his wife and friends tried to contact him but his mobile phone was switched off. They reported Ajay missing to the police but three days passed before a search was launched. Ajay's body was found in the jungle near the village; he had been shot dead. It is believed that Sahoda villagers, with help from Hindu extremist groups, killed Ajay and dumped his body. The Christian community felt that the killing was committed in a bid to restrict Christian activity and outreach in the area.

Thank you, living God, for your undying love, ever at work for us and the whole world, made known in every age; for its triumphant victory in the cross and resurrection of Jesus Christ, and for its continuing presence with us, to be proclaimed to the ends of the earth through your Holy Spirit.
Alan Gaunt (born 1935)

For what we preach is not ourselves, but Jesus Christ as Lord, and ourselves as your servants for Jesus' sake. 2 Corinthians 4:5

Gregorio Hapalla and Greg Bacabis (1992)
Airwaves for Christ

Gregorio, a Christian preacher from the Philippines, was shot dead alongside his Christian radio technician Greg while they were broadcasting in September 1992. They were killed by two unidentified gunmen in the southern city of Zamboanga, which is in a Muslim-majority part of the Philippines.

Islamic extremists were not happy with Gregorio's Gospel programmes being aired to the people in their own language; the radio station had received threatening phone calls, ordering them to "stop broadcasting your message in the Tausug language". But they were undeterred in getting the Christian message out across the airwaves and for this paid the ultimate price. An Islamist terrorist group called Abu Sayyaf claimed responsibility for the killings.

O God our heavenly father, who hast manifested thy love towards mankind in sending thine only Son into the world, that all might live through him: We pray thee to speed forth these good tidings of great joy to every nation, that the people who sit in darkness and in the shadow of death may see the great light, and may come, with us, to worship him whose name is called Wonderful, even our Lord and Saviour Jesus Christ.

Frank Colquhoun (1909-97), *Parish Prayers* (no. 49)

Don't you know that when you offer yourselves to someone as obedient slaves, you are slaves of the one you obey – whether you are slaves to sin, which leads to death, or to obedience, which leads to righteousness?
Romans 6:16

Geronimo (1569)
Slave to Christ

Geronimo was an Arab convert from Islam to Christianity in the 16th century when the Mediterranean coastline of Europe was troubled by raids by North African Muslims. Those who were captured often ended up at a slave market. This is what happened to Geronimo, who became the possession of Pasha Ali, a Calabrian renegade, at a slave market in Algiers in May 1569.

In order to survive, the slaves generally accepted the religion demanded by their captors. The Pasha tried hard to induce Geronimo to renounce Christianity and return to Islam but the slave stood firm in his Christian faith. On 18 September 1569, during the building of one of the Forts in Algiers, the Pasha sent for Geronimo and gave him the choice of either renouncing Christ or being put in one of the concrete blocks that were being made for the construction of the Fort. Geronimo would not deny Christ, so he was bound hand and foot and thrown alive into a mould in which a block of concrete was about to be made.

When the French removed the Fort in the 19th century, the skeleton of Geronimo was found and laid to rest in the Cathedral of Algiers.

O Jesus, I have promised
to serve you to the end –
be now and ever near me
my Master and my Friend:
I shall not fear the battle
if you are by my side
nor wander from the pathway
if you will be my guide.
J E Bode (1816-74)

Acknowledge and take to heart this day that the LORD is God in heaven above and on the earth below. There is no other. Deuteronomy 4:39

Procopius (c. 303)
"There is only one God"

Procopius was a godly and gifted man who was born in Jerusalem and lived at Scythopolis (Beit She'an in northern Israel). He cured those possessed with evil spirits and diligently studied the scriptures, translating Greek texts into Aramaic so that his countrymen could read God's word in their own language.

During the persecution of Christians under the Roman Emperor Diocletian, Procopius was brought, along with other believers, to Caesarea. Upon arrival, he was immediately brought before the governor and told to sacrifice to the gods. Procopius refused, declaring, "There is only one God, the Almighty". The governor said that if he would not acknowledge the gods, he should burn incense to the four emperors. At this, Procopius burst out laughing and replied with a line from Homer's Iliad, "It is not good to have lords many; Let One be Lord, One king." For this, which was considered treason, Procopius was beheaded.

O Lord Jesus Christ, Who art the Way, The Truth and the Life, we pray Thee suffer us not to stray from Thee Who art the Way, nor distrust Thee, Who are the Truth, nor to rest in any other thing than Thee, Who art the Life. Teach us by the Holy Spirit what to believe, what to do, and wherein to take our rest. We ask it for Thine own name's sake. Amen.
Erasmus (1466-1536)

Those who feared the LORD talked with each other, and the LORD listened and heard. A scroll of remembrance was written in his presence concerning those who feared the LORD and honoured his name.
Malachi 3:16

John Coleridge Patteson (1871)
Indigenous Ministry

When in 1861 John Coleridge Patteson became the first Anglican bishop of Melanesia – a large collection of islands in the South Pacific – he worked to establish an indigenous ministry, having learnt 23 of the languages and dialects. He also campaigned to bring an end to the virtual enslavement of Melanesian workers by British settlers from Australia and Fiji.

In September 1871 John was visiting Nakapu, one of the Santa Cruz Islands. Three of his companions, Joseph Atkin, an English priest, and two Melanesians, John Ngongono and Stephen Taroaniara, were wounded by arrows when they arrived on the island. A few hours later a canoe floated out from the shore containing John Coleridge Patteson's dead body.

It is likely that he was murdered by the islanders out of fear; a few months prior to his visit five islanders had been murdered by Anglo-Australian raiders. Atkin and Taroaniara died of tetanus only days later.

When the people of the island discovered that they had murdered a man who had sought their good and who had wanted to defend them against those who oppressed them, they sought reconciliation and went to John's successor to hear the Gospel. Today there is a Church in Melanesia that still remembers his martyrdom.

Almighty God, you called John Coleridge Patteson to be your witness in the islands of Melanesia and by his labours and suffering to raise up a people for your own possession. Pour out upon your Church in every land the Spirit of service and sacrifice, that the nations may acknowledge your sovereign law and all peoples may give you glory; through Jesus Christ our Lord, who is alive and reigns with you and the Holy Spirit, one God, now and for ever.
For All the Saints (New Zealand)

As the rain and the snow come down from heaven, and do not return to it without watering the earth and making it bud and flourish, so that it yields seed for the sower and bread for the eater, so is my word that goes out from my mouth: It will not return to me empty, but will accomplish what I desire and achieve the purpose for which I sent it.
Isaiah 55:10-11

Ancel Edwin Allen (1956)
Pilot Project

Hearing about the deaths of American missionaries Nate Saint, Jim Elliot, Roger Youderian, Ed McCully and Peter Fleming (see January 10) made Ancel, a trained pilot and mechanic, all the more determined to use his skills to take the Gospel to the unreached. Just nine months after these five were brutally killed by Auca Indians in Ecuador, Ancel too was martyred.

Having served in the United States Air Force as a radio technician during World War Two, Ancel had obtained his private pilot's licence while operating an airport. His upbringing had had a Christian influence but it was not until 1950 that he committed his life to Christ. In 1953 he entered a missionary technical course and during his final semester he met the director of a small mission called Air Mail From God that operated in Mexico. Ancel and his wife Naomi felt led to join this work.

The pair started work with zeal in mid-August 1956; Ancel flew the plane while Naomi dropped copies of John's Gospel into the villages below. Other Christian workers later followed up on the ground. This technique angered some of the villagers and on 21 September, gunmen in the village of San Bartono, Morelos, shot down the plane Ancel was flying and he was killed. Naomi was not on board on this occasion.

Mexican believers helped Naomi bury her 33-year-old husband the following day and she was greatly encouraged by those whose lives had been transformed by the Gospel. In Ancel's short service of just five weeks, they had distributed 55,000 copies of the Gospel.

He whose head is in heaven need not fear to put his feet into the grave.
Herman Hooker (1804-65)

*Blessed are those who are persecuted because of righteousness, for theirs is
the kingdom of heaven.* Matthew 5:10

Francis Namukubalo (2010)
Ambushed and Killed

When Francis' father, a Muslim sheikh, converted to Christianity
in 1998, the rest of the family soon became believers in Christ. They
were passionate to share their new faith around the strongly Muslim
part of Uganda where they lived, Bubyangu Sub County, Mbale District.
This was met with resistance from their Muslim neighbours and threats
against the family became commonplace. On 21 September 2010 Fran-
cis, a married father of three with another baby on the way, went to visit
his father. After spending the day with him, Francis set off on foot for
home – but never returned. He was lured into an ambush by two sup-
posed friends, then set upon and stabbed to death by a group of around
20 Muslims.

When Francis did not come home, his family were worried and a
search party was sent out to look for him. Francis' severely maimed body
was found in a river; he had been stabbed repeatedly in the ribs and left
hand, and his ears and tongue had been chopped off. It is a superstition
of the folk Islam practised in the region that by removing the tongue, the
victim's spirit cannot come back through another person to reveal the
facts surrounding his death. Influential Muslim leaders in the village are
believed to have been behind Francis' murder.

Till then I would Thy love proclaim
With every fleeting breath,
And may the music of Thy Name
Refresh my soul in death!
John Newton (1725-1807)

There is no fear in love. But perfect love drives out fear, because fear has to do with punishment. The one who fears is not made perfect in love.
1 John 4:18

'Ahmadey Osman Nur and Mansuur Mohammed (2008) Converts Killed

Converting from Islam to Christianity is a highly dangerous act in Somalia, where Muslim extremists are determined to kill apostates in accordance with all versions of sharia. Despite this, the truth and power of the Gospel are winning people for Christ in this strongly Islamic country.

Two such converts paid the ultimate price for following Jesus in September 2008. Ahmadey Osman Nur (22) was gunned down as he left a Muslim wedding after asking for a translation of the wedding service, which was held in Arabic – considered by Muslims to be the "language Allah hears." Not many Somalis speak Arabic and very few guests would have understood the service. The request offended the presiding sheikh, who knew of Nur's conversion to Christianity. He declared Nur to be guilty of apostasy and asked a guard to "silence" him. As Nur left the wedding, he was shot dead by an armed guard.

On 23 September, Mansuur Mohammed (25), a humanitarian aid worker, was beheaded by a group of Muslim extremists. They accused him of being an infidel and a spy for the occupying Ethiopian soldiers before cutting off his head in front of terrified villagers.

Lord, in the Garden of Gethsemane you shared with everyone who has ever been afraid. You conquered fear with love and returned saying, "Do not be afraid." In the light of your love death has lost its sting and so has fear. Lord, may your love be the key that releases me from fear.
Frank Topping (1909-1997), *The Words of Christ*

Therefore we do not lose heart. Though outwardly we are wasting away, yet inwardly we are being renewed day by day. 2 Corinthians 4:16

Betty Ann Olsen (1968)
Spiritual Strength

Betty Ann Olsen was the daughter of an American missionary couple in Africa who herself felt called to the mission field. She trained as a nurse and in 1964, aged 30, went to war-torn Vietnam to work in a leprosy hospital. This was a dangerous assignment; the mission was frequently harassed by the Viet Cong and three missionaries had already been abducted. But Betty was not afraid; she said:

Most of the people that I have told about going to Vietnam are greatly concerned, and I appreciate this; however, I am not concerned, and I am very much at peace. I know that I may never come back, but I know that I am in the centre of the Lord's will and Vietnam is the place for me.

In January 1968, six missionaries were killed when the mission compound was attacked by the Viet Cong for three days. Betty and Henry (Hank) Blood, a Bible translator, were taken captive while trying to save a wounded co-worker. Betty was chained to Hank and a fellow prisoner, Mike D Benge. For several months they were forced to march 12-14 hours a day through mountainous jungles to a succession of prison camps. They were malnourished and physically depleted, sick from dysentery and dengue fever, and suffered constantly from infections, leeches and ulcerated sores.

Mike was the only one of the three to survive the ordeal. He said that Betty was the most unselfish person he had ever known; she nursed Mike when he was sick and would give most of her meagre rations to the indigenous Christian prisoners. He said that her spiritual strength got him through but sadly, as the long treks took their toll, Betty became physically weaker by the day. The Viet Cong began to kick and drag Betty to keep her moving. She finally succumbed to death at the end of

September 1968. Mike paid this tribute to his fellow captive, "She never showed any bitterness or resentment. To the end, she loved the ones who mistreated her."

Our vision is so limited we can hardly imagine a love that does not show itself in protection from suffering... The love of God did not protect His own Son... He will not necessarily protect us – not from anything it takes to make us like His Son. A lot of hammering and chiselling and purifying by fire will have to go into the process.
Elisabeth Elliot (1926-2015)

September 25

"He will reign on David's throne and over his kingdom, establishing and upholding it with justice and righteousness from that time on and forever. The zeal of the Lord Almighty will accomplish this." Isaiah 9:7b

Christian Charity (2002)
Revenge Attack

On 25 September 2002, anti-government militants entered the offices of a Christian charity in Pakistan called the Institute for Peace and Justice. They proceeded to tie up all eight staff members and shot each one at point-blank range. Seven were killed on the spot but, miraculously, Robin Peranditta survived – albeit seriously injured.

The incident happened at a time when anti-American feelings were heightened by the Afghanistan war; the militants regarded Christians, who are seen as associated with the West, as targets for revenge.

The Institute worked on projects that gave Christians basic amenities, such as sewerage. It also spoke out against Pakistan's strictly enforced "blasphemy laws", which are often used against Christians. This too could have been a driving force behind the attack.

O Lord, let me not live to be useless!
Bishop Stratford (died 1707)

Those who suffer he delivers in their suffering; he speaks to them in their affliction. Job 36:15

Blandina (177)
Survived Torture

This young Christian slave girl was among the many Christians brought before the Roman governor of Gaul during an upsurge in persecution in the region around Vienne and Lyons in 177. Blandina displayed remarkable physical and spiritual strength as she endured a succession of horrendous tortures and while many of the others taken captive died in prison, she survived. But her ordeal was not over. She was thrown to wild animals in a special public exhibition before being hung on a stake and offered as food to the beasts that were let loose. When they would not touch her, Blandina was taken down and returned to jail. She was finally put to death on the last day of the public exhibition, having been brought in each day to watch the torturing of others and urged to swear by the idols, which she refused. Blandina was bound up in a net and thrown to a wild bull.

Those who had witnessed her treatment said that they had never seen a woman suffer so much for so long. Throughout her ordeal, she had been an inspiration to her fellow Christians, and the courage displayed by Blandina and her fellow martyrs inspired others to confess Christ, for which they also were put to death.

Almighty God, by whose grace and power thy holy martyrs triumphed over suffering and despised death; grant we beseech thee, that, enduring hardness and waxing valiant in fight, we may receive with them the crown of everlasting life; through Jesus Christ our Lord.
George Appleton (1902-93), *In His Name* (no. 151)

You were bought with a price; do not become slaves of human masters.
1 Corinthians 7:23 (NRSV)

Pastor Im (1951)
Defied Communists

When the Communists first took over South Korea they ordered pastors to include Marxist propaganda in their sermons. The Communists came to Pastor Im with the threat, "If you do not teach what we say you will die."

Pastor Im refused and was taken to prison, where he was held for two years. During this time he recited Bible verses he had memorised. When the UN troops arrived in September 1950, they did not believe Pastor Im's insistence that he was a Christian, and put him with the Communist prisoners. Pastor Im witnessed for Christ to his fellow inmates and saw many converted. The Americans finally realised Pastor Im was a Christian and allowed him to preach in prisons throughout South Korea, but he was never given his freedom. The inspiring evangelist died in prison in 1951.

O gracious and holy Father, give us wisdom to perceive thee, diligence to seek thee, patience to wait for thee, eyes to behold thee, a heart to meditate upon thee, and a life to proclaim thee; through the power of the Spirit of Jesus Christ our Lord.
Benedict (c. 480-550)

On this rock I will build my church, and the gates of Hades will not overcome it. Matthew 16:18b

Mohammad Bagher Yusefi (1996)
"Soul-Giver"

Mohammad converted to Christianity when he was 24 and became a greatly gifted member of the Iranian Church. He was an evangelist and song-writer, sometimes called "Ravanbakhsh" or "Soul-Giver". Mohammad also became a pastor and by the time of his death in September 1996, he was leading churches in Ghaemshahr, Gorgan and Sari.

On 28 September 1996, he left home at 6 am. In the evening of that same day the Iranian authorities told his family that he was dead, and that he had committed suicide. His body was found hanging from a tree in a forest near Sari, capital of Iran's Mazandaran Province.

Mohammad's family and Christian friends were, however, in no doubt that he had been murdered, particularly as the authorities would not give up the body. They had previously refused to hand over the bodies of other murdered Iranian Christians in order to hide the evidence that they had been mutilated, stabbed many times or decapitated. Mohammad was 34 when he died, leaving behind his wife Akhtar, daughter Ramsina (9) and son Stephen (7).

Iranian Christians, especially converts from Islam, face severe persecution under the country's strict Islamic regime. Nonetheless the Church is growing rapidly.

Upon this rock which you have confessed – upon myself, the Son of the living God – I will build my church. I will build you on myself, and not myself on you.
Augustine of Hippo (354-430)

Be gracious to me, O God, for people trample on me; all day long foes oppress me; my enemies trample on me all day long, for many fight against me. O Most High, when I am afraid, I put my trust in you. In God, whose word I praise, in God I trust; I am not afraid; what can flesh do to me? Psalm 56:1-4 (NRSV)

Tongin and Tongsin (1948)
Praying Brothers

As the Communists were advancing on Soonchun, Korea, where Tongin and Tongsin lived, the Christian brothers decided not to flee. They had already been expelled from school for refusing to bow down to Shinto shrines and they remained determined to stand firm, despite friends urging them to leave.

One September morning in 1948 the brothers rose early to pray together. They were set upon by a group of Communist students who started beating up Tongin, the elder boy. When Tongsin tried to help his brother, the students turned on him. Tongin would not deny his faith and the leader of the students, Ahn Chae Sun, prepared to shoot him. Tongsin again tried to put himself between Ahn and his brother, but was pulled away. Tongin was blindfolded then shot; Tongsin threw himself on his brother's body and was also shot.

The deaths were met with a truly remarkable act of grace by Tongin and Tongsin's father, Sohn Yangoon, who would also go on to be martyred for his faith (see 30 September).

Satan trembles when he sees the weakest saint upon his knees.
William Cowper (1731-1800)

For if you forgive others their trespasses, your heavenly Father will also forgive you; but if you do not forgive others, neither will your Father forgive your trespasses. Matthew 6:14-15 (NRSV)

Sohn Yangoon (1950)
Adopting a Killer

Even before the brutal murder of his sons Tongin and Tongsin (see September 29) in 1948, Yangoon's life had already been marked by much suffering for Christ. He was born in South Kyungsang Province, Korea, in 1902, and became an evangelist aged 23. In 1938 he came into conflict with the Japanese authorities over shrine worship. He was arrested in 1940 and imprisoned for ten months. For a long time the only way his family knew he was alive was when they were given soiled clothes in return for the clean ones they brought him. Yangoon was tried in November 1941 and convicted of violating the public peace, irreverence and giving aid to the enemy. He was sent to jail again and after his release endured another spell behind bars over the shrine issue.

Following the martyrdom of his sons, Yangoon learnt that their murderer, Ahn Chae Sun, had been arrested. He sent another pastor and his daughter to ask for Ahn Chae Sun's life and, remarkably, offered to adopt the assassin. The officer in charge was so impressed that he granted the request and Yangoon obtained permission from Ahn Chae Sun's parents to adopt the young man. Ahn Chae Sun was later enrolled in the Higher Bible Institute in Pusan. His parents, to whom Yangoon had also witnessed, then asked that one of Yangoon's daughters could live with them and teach them about Christ.

The murder of Yangoon's sons and his subsequent adoption of their killer made a profound impact in Korea and he was in great demand to speak at meetings. The Communists arrived in 1950 and Yangoon was urged to flee, but he was arrested and placed in a prison with many others. One night in late September he and 74 other prisoners were led out to a remote place and shot.

When Christ's hands were nailed to the cross, he also nailed your sins to the cross.
Bernard of Clairvaux (1090-1153)

October 1

On the day of prosperity be joyful, and on the day of adversity consider; God has made the one as well as the other, so that mortals may not find out anything that will come after them. Ecclesiastes 7:14 (NRSV)

Sonmin Grace Church (2000) Bomb Blast

On 1 October 2000, a stranger walked into Sonmin Grace Church in Dushanbe, the capital of Tajikistan, Central Asia, as the offering was being collected, and put down a bag. Within a few minutes the bag exploded; the power of the blast brought down the roof of the church, smashed windows and destroyed the pews. Ten people, aged between 21 and 60, were killed by the bomb and over 50 were injured.

The church had been formed in the 1990s by Korean missionaries. It was very active in evangelism and as a result had been threatened by the authorities with losing its state registration. The authorities also dealt harshly with the survivors of the explosion; twelve church leaders were arrested and questioned, not only about the bomb, but also about why they were believers in Christ and what plans they had to evangelise others. They were released a few days later, after several had undergone beatings. Two men were eventually arrested for the bombing.

When I draw this fleeting breath,
when my eyelids close in death,
when I soar through realms unknown,
bow before the judgment throne:
hide me then, my refuge be,
Rock of Ages, cleft for me.
A M Toplady (1740-78)

This man [Jesus], handed over to you according to the definite plan and foreknowledge of God, you crucified and killed by the hands of those outside the law. But God raised him up, having freed him from death, because it was impossible for him to be held in its power.
Acts 2:23-24 (NRSV)

Irfan Masih (2009)
Shot on Shift

In October 2009, Irfan Masih, a Christian security guard at a factory in Lahore, Pakistan, woke his Muslim colleague Ishfaq Niazi for the change of shift. This simple act would prove to be fatal. Ishfaq (31) is believed to have shot Irfan (20) because he was angry that a "Christian untouchable" had dared to touch his foot.

Sources say that the shooting followed a recent dispute between the two guards, when Ishfaq was enraged by Irfan's statement that the grave of Jesus Christ is empty and He is alive.

But lo! there breaks a yet more glorious day:
The saints triumphant rise in bright array;
The King of glory passes on His Way:
Alleluia! Alleluia!
W Walsham How (1823-1897)

O Blessed Lord, who didst promise thy disciples that through thy Easter victory their sorrow should be turned to joy, and their joy no man should take from them: Grant us, we pray thee, so to know thee in the power of thy resurrection, that we may be partakers of that joy which is unspeakable and full of glory; for thy holy name's sake.
Frank Colquhoun (1909-97), *Parish Prayers* (no. 329)

I am suffering... Yet this is no cause for shame, because I know whom I have believed, and am convinced that he is able to guard what I have entrusted to him until that day. 2 Timothy 1:12

Eritrean Christians (2010-11)
Imprisoned and Tortured

Many Eritrean Christians endure unimaginable suffering because they refuse to renounce their faith in Christ. Thousands are imprisoned without trial in horrendous conditions; many are held in metal shipping containers or underground prisons, enduring darkness and overcrowding, extreme temperatures and malnutrition, and sometimes torture and beatings. Those who fall ill may have medical treatment withheld unless they agree to renounce their faith. Some die in custody. The full extent of their suffering – and indeed the strength of their faith in the face of it – is known only to the Lord. But limited reports about some of these martyrs do occasionally escape from Eritrea.

Three such individuals were Teklesenbet Gebreab Kiflom (36), Mogos Hagos Kiflom (37) and Mehari Gebreneguse Asgedom (42). Teklesenbet's death was reported in October 2010; he died after being refused medical attention for malaria. Mogos, a husband and father, died as a result of torture after he refused to deny his faith. Then in August 2011, Mehari, who had been held in solitary confinement, died from both torture and complications related to diabetes.

Eternal God, help us always to remember the great unseen cloud of witnesses round about us. When in danger, give us their courage and when in difficulty, their perseverance; so that we too may be faithful until we rejoice with all the saints in your eternal kingdom, through Jesus Christ our Lord. Amen
William Hampson (*More Prayers for Today's Church*, no. 178)

Then we will no longer be infants, tossed back and forth by the waves, and blown here and there by every wind of teaching and by the cunning and craftiness of people in their deceitful scheming. Instead, speaking the truth in love, we will grow to become in every respect the mature body of him who is the head, that is, Christ. Ephesians 4:14-15

Zhou Dian Yu (2001)
Cult Victim

Eager to learn more about her faith and unaware of the danger, Chinese Christian Zhou Dian Yu attended a meeting of a group called Eastern Lightning in October 2001. But Eastern Lightning is a cult, founded in 1989 by Zhao Wei Shan, that has infiltrated many house churches in China and has around a million adherents. It teaches that Christ has come back a second time as a woman. A particular concern is that the group exercises control over its members through violence, drugs and a strict hierarchy. This means that Christians who may become involved can find it almost impossible to escape without risking harm to themselves or their families.

This is sadly what happened to Dian Yu. Upon returning from the meeting to her church she was alerted to the dangers of the cult and decided not to be part of it any more. She went to take back the books that they had given her but she did not return. Her body was found the following day; she had been poisoned by coal fumes.

Lord, I am blind and helpless, stupid and ignorant.
Cause me to hear, cause me to know, teach me to do, lead me.
Henry Martyn (1781-1812)

Where, O death, are your plagues? Where, O grave, is your destruction?
Hosea 13:14b

Aurelio Gomez Ramos and Gustavo Hernandez Perez (1995) Death Threats

Aurelio pastored a church with Gustavo as his assistant at a time of great threat to Christians in Mexico from the Zapatista Liberation Army (EZLN). This armed revolutionary organisation from Chiapas, a poverty stricken southern state of Mexico, went public in 1994 with the goal of overthrowing the Mexican government. Many local *caciques* (village leaders) issued death threats against evangelicals who refused to join the organisation.

On 5 October 1995, Aurelio and Gustavo were shot dead by five armed assailants in an incident that fitted the pattern of ongoing persecution of Christians in Mexico. In the previous year another church leader, Miguel Santiz, had been murdered in an attack along with his wife.

In addition to assassinations such as these, numerous evangelicals have been imprisoned under false allegations and, in 2003, a mob burned down the Wings of the Eagle Church in Los Pozos. These are but a handful of examples in a catalogue of persecution in Mexico's recent history.

When the day that [Mr Valiant-for-Truth] must go hence was come, many accompanied him to the river side, into which, as he went, he said, "Death, where is thy sting?" And as he went down deeper, he said, "Grave where is thy victory?" So he passed over and the trumpets sounded for him on the other side.
John Bunyan (1628-88), *The Pilgrim's Progress*

It is God who works in you to will and to act in order to fulfill his good purpose. Philippians 2:13

Rami Ayyad (2007)
Ever Smiling

"Rami was the most gentle member of the team, the ever-smiling one. He was the face of our Bible shop, always receiving visitors and serving them as Jesus would."

This warm tribute was paid to Rami by a colleague at Gaza Bible Society after the 30-year-old's kidnap and murder left the Christian community reeling. The father of two, whose wife Pauline was expecting the couple's third child at the time, was seized on 6 October 2007 after leaving the Bible Society's bookshop, which he ran. The next morning his body was discovered, showing knife and bullet wounds.

Rami's murder shocked the small Christian community in Gaza, which comprises around 3,000 people. The tragedy received much coverage in the local media, and the Christian community received many messages of condolence, prayer and support. Rami was the first known Christian martyr in Gaza in recent times.

There are four different kinds of martyrdom,
namely, innocence as in Abel;
uprightness, as in the prophets and John the Baptist;
love of the law, as in the Maccabees;
confession of faith, as in the apostles.

For all these various causes Christ the Lamb
is said to have been 'slain from the foundations of the world'.
The Dialogue of Caesarius

All the days ordained for me were written in your book before one of them came to be. Psalm 139:16b

Osman Sheik Ahmed (2005)
Significant Date

Osman was martyred on 7 October 2005, two years to the day after he made the decision to leave Islam and follow Christ. The evangelist and house church leader was shot and killed in the Somali capital Mogadishu. His congregation confirmed that Islamic extremists were behind the murder. The father of nine was a relief and development worker in southern Somalia.

Several other Somali Christians have been martyred in recent years. Since 1994, the persecution of Christians by extremists who want to institute an Islamic government in the country has accelerated. Because of the threat from warlords and extremists, the Somali Church, made up entirely of converts from Islam, has been driven underground. The country, which is almost 100 per cent Muslim, is statistically one of the least impacted by Christianity worldwide.

O Lord Jesus Christ, who by thy death didst take away the sting of death: Grant unto us thy servants so to follow in faith where thou hast led the way, that we may at length fall asleep peacefully in thee, and awake up after thy likeness; through thy mercy, who livest with the Father and the Holy Ghost, one God, world without end.
Parish Prayers (no. 868), from the American Prayer Book

Do not store up for yourselves treasures on earth, where moths and vermin destroy, and where thieves break in and steal. But store up for yourselves treasures in heaven, where moths and vermin do not destroy, and where thieves do not break in and steal. For where your treasure is, there your heart will be also. Matthew 6:19-21

Cosmas and Damian (c. 287) Skilled Servants

These twin brothers from Syria were skilled doctors who never took money for their services; they regarded their work as part of their Christian duty of caring for others. Cosmas and Damian were consequently held in high regard in Aegaen, Cilicia, where they lived.

The pair were among the many Christians arrested during the persecution under Roman Emperor Diocletian. They suffered various tortures before being martyred around 287. But the influence of the Christian lives they had lived endured, to the extent that "Cosmas" became synonymous with "disinterest in money" during the Middle Ages.

Set our hearts on fire with love of thee, O Christ Our God, that in that flame we may love thee with all our heart, with all our mind, with all our soul and with all our strength, and our neighbours as ourselves; so that, keeping thy commandments, we may glorify thee the giver of all good gifts.
Eastern Orthodox Prayer

The Lord is my light and my salvation – whom shall I fear? The Lord is the stronghold of my life – of whom shall I be afraid? Psalm 27:1

Maspero Martyrs (2011)
Besieged

"The army and police were waiting for us about 200 metres away from the Maspero TV building. They started firing at us before two army armoured vehicles came at great speed and drove into the crowds, going backwards and forwards, mowing people under their wheels."

This is how one of the organisers of a rally involving thousands of Egyptian Christians described the brutality they suffered as they protested near the state TV building in Cairo on 9 October 2011. The Christians came under attack by the security forces, Islamists and violent thugs; at least 26 people were killed and over 300 injured in the violence. They were shot at, beaten and dragged through the streets, and eyewitnesses reported seeing an armoured vehicle crush 15 people.

The Christians were protesting against the destruction of a church in Aswan province by Muslims on 30 September, as well as other injustices suffered by their community. The church attack was the latest in a long line of violent anti-Christian incidents in Egypt, which increased following the revolution in early 2011 as hard line Islamist groups grew in strength and influence.

A peaceful march by Christians to commemorate the Maspero martyrs – held on the 40-day anniversary, as is traditional in Egyptian culture – also came under attack. It is thought that Salafist Muslims were among those who hurled rocks, glass bottles and fire bombs at the Christians. Around 30 people were injured.

Lord of our life and God of our salvation.
Star of our night and Hope of every nation,
Hear and receive Thy Church's supplication,
Lord God Almighty.

See round Thine ark the hungry billows curling;

See how thy foes their banners are unfurling.
Lord, while their darts envenomed they are hurling,
Thou canst preserve us.

Lord, Thou canst help when earthly armor faileth;
Lord, Thou canst save when deadly sin assaileth;
Lord, o'er Thy Church nor death nor hell prevaileth;
Grant us Thy peace, Lord.
Matthaeus A. von Loewenstern (1594-1648)
Translated by Philip Pusey (1799-1855)

October 10

I consider that our present sufferings are not worth comparing with the glory that will be revealed in us. Romans 8:18

Ishak Christian (1996)
Killed at Prayer

On 10 October 1996, around 3,000 Muslims went on the rampage in East Java, Indonesia. They attacked the Assemblies of God Church in Situbondo where Pastor Ishak, his wife, daughter, niece and a church worker were burnt to death while praying.

It is not clear whether they were killed in revenge for a sentence that had been given to an Islamic preacher, accused of heresy, or because the Muslims were angry that Christians were using a hall in Situbondo for worship. The mob travelled through the city and neighbouring areas, torching 25 churches, two Christian schools and an orphanage.

If a man dies, he falls like a tree.
Wherever he falls, there he lies.
If he is not a believer, he goes to the fire-lake.

But on the other hand, a believer,
If death overtakes him,

Will not fall, rather will rise
That very moment, to God's house.
Quecha hymn by Jim Elliot (1927-1956) (see January 10)

I, the Lord, have called you in righteousness; I will take hold of your hand. I will keep you. Isaiah 42:6

Juan Coy (1957)
Revenge Killing

Juan, a 33-year-old farmer, was arrested along with a young preacher, Pedro Moreno, for holding private worship services near Saboya, Boyaco, Colombia. Juan was released after a day in prison, but Pedro was held for 14 days. Juan and his family – the only Christian family in the area – visited Pedro in prison and tried to secure his release. Despite plots to kill Pedro, he escaped to continue being a pastor.

Those who had tried to kill Pedro and failed then decided to take revenge on Juan. They went to his farm in October 1957 and waited until he had finished his work. When he appeared on the path, they shot him dead.

True virtue never appears so lovely, as when it is most oppressed; and the divine excellency of real Christianity, is never exhibited with such advantage, as when under the greatest trials: then it is that true faith appears much more precious than gold!
Jonathan Edwards (1703-58)

I will say of the Lord, "He is my refuge and my fortress, my God, in whom I trust"... You will not fear the terror of night, nor the arrow that flies by day. Psalm 91:2, 5

Indonesian Villagers (2003)
Islamist Rampage

A pregnant woman and a six-year-old girl were among the victims when Islamists went on the rampage, attacking five Christian villages in Central Sulawesi, Indonesia, on 10 and 12 October 2003. At least eleven Christians were shot dead or hacked to death with machetes, others were severely injured while many fled the violence to seek safety in the Christian town of Tentena. Some had only recently returned from Tentena to rebuild their homes after suffering terrible violence two years before. In one of the five villages, called Beteleme (meaning Bethlehem), children came with the attackers and set fire to 38 Christian houses and the church, while the adults shot and stabbed the villagers.

A few days later, police arrested 13 people suspected of being behind the two attacks while four others were shot and killed while resisting detention. The prompt response of the police was welcomed by the Christian community; the authorities had consistently turned a blind eye during previous attacks on Christians. But the police who made the arrests were Christians and, after protests by Muslims who were outraged that action had been taken against the militants, they were re-deployed to another area.

Christians around the world face difficult challenges. Do not be overcome by hopelessness or the troubles of life. Trust in the Lord and His unfailing mercy so that regardless of the circumstances you will, at all times, be heaven focused.

Forgetting what is behind and straining towards what is ahead. I press on toward the goal to win the prize for which God has called me heavenward in Christ Jesus. Philippians 3:13b-14

Crispin and Crispinian (3ʳᵈ century)
True Treasure

"Thy threats do not terrify us, for Christ is our life, and death is our gain. Thy rank and possessions are nought to us, for we have long before this sacrificed the like for the sake of Christ and rejoice in what we have done. If thou shouldst acknowledge and love Christ thou wouldst give not only all the treasures of this life, but even the glory of thy crown itself in order through the exercise of compassion to win eternal life."

These words are believed to have been spoken by brothers Crispin and Crispinian when they were brought before Maximianus, Roman co-emperor with Diocletian, who used a mixture of promises and threats in an attempt to turn them from their Christian faith.

The two were brothers of noble birth who had gone to Gaul as missionaries. The brothers spent their days preaching the Gospel and making converts, and their nights – in imitation of the apostle Paul – working with their hands, making shoes to support themselves. Their successful ministry was brought to the attention of Maximianus, who, after realising he could not persuade them to renounce their faith, handed them over to the governor Rictiovarus, a cruel persecutor of Christians.

Crispin and Crispinian were subjected to various tortures including being stretched on a rack and thrown into a river, each with a millstone round his neck, but miraculously survived them all. Despairing, Rictiovarus killed himself after which Maximianus ordered that the brothers be beheaded, which was duly done. They are believed to have died towards the end of the third century. They are remembered on this day, which was immortalised in Shakespeare's Henry V's famous speech on the morning of Agincourt.

I will place no value on anything I have or possess unless it is in relationship to the kingdom of God.
David Livingstone (1813-73)

I have been crucified with Christ and I no longer live, but Christ lives in me. Galatians 2:20a

Vipin Mandloli (2007)
Transformed Life

When Vipin Mandloli (27) from India converted from Hinduism to Christianity, his life was transformed. From alcohol abuse and a failed marriage he became a very devout Christian, supporting churches and evangelists in Jhabua District, Madhya Pradesh state. But his conversion and changed life angered the local Hindu priests. On 14 October 2007, Mandloli, a shepherd, left his home for a nearby mountain to graze his sheep; the site was near a new Hindu temple. He was shot dead in an attack suspected to have been carried out by three Hindu priests.

With gladness will I now sing;
My heart delights in God,
Who showed me such forbearance
That I from death was saved
Which never hath an end.
I praise Thee, Christ in heaven
Who all my sorrow changed.
Felix Manz (c. 1498-1526)

I meditate on your precepts and consider your ways. I delight in your decrees; I will not neglect your word. Psalm 119:15-16

Tarore (1836)
Gospel Necklace

The Word of God was very precious to this young Maori chief's daughter, who became a Christian while being educated at a mission school. She was given a copy of the Gospel of Luke, which she tied around her neck with a string. At this time very few people had a copy of any portion of the Bible. When she was travelling to a new mission school in October 1836, another tribe came and attacked her party and Tarore was killed. At her funeral her father preached forgiveness and against revenge.

Tarore's killer, Uita, had looked at the Gospel of Luke that she carried but did not know what it was or what to do with it. The book then passed to a slave named Ripahau who read it to Uita. This led to the eventual reconciliation of Uita and Tarore's father.

Ripahau took some pages of the Gospel and moved on, coming into contact with a warrior called Tamihana and his cousin Matene, to whom he also read the Gospel. In time they both became Christians, as did Ripahau. Tarore's Gospel finally went with Tamihana and Matene when they travelled to the South Island to preach Christ.

Tarore is honoured in New Zealand as one of the nation's first martyrs.

Gracious and loving God,
we thank you for Tarore,
whose death brought not vengeance but reconciliation;
create in us, your whanau [family],
a gospel love and a truth so deep,
that we too may live together in love with all your children,
in the unity of the Holy Spirit;
through Jesus Christ our Redeemer.
For All the Saints (New Zealand)

October 16

I am not ashamed of the gospel, because it is the power of God for the salvation of everyone who believes. Romans 1:16

Ayman Nabil Labib (2011)
"Martyr of the Cross"

Like many Egyptian Christians, Ayman, a 17-year-old schoolboy, had a cross tattooed on his wrist. He was in class at his school in Mallawi,

Minya province, on 16 October when his Muslim teacher began insulting and harassing the teenager, and told him to cover up the Christian symbol. Ayman refused and instead boldly displayed a cross necklace that he was wearing under his clothes. The teacher reportedly turned to the other students and said, "What are we going to do with him?"

A group of around 15 students set upon Ayman, who fled to the toilets in an attempt to escape the beating. But the assault continued and he was murdered at the scene. His body was reported to have shown signs of strangulation and having received a heavy blow to the head with a sharp object.

After the teenager's funeral over 5,000 Christians marched through the streets of Mallawi, denouncing the murder of Ayman whom they described as a "Martyr of the Cross".

The Cross of Christ is the primal, the supreme, the central, the universal, the eternal symbol of Christianity. Christ's messengers are messengers of the Cross and all it signifies, or they are not His messengers at all. "Christ Crucified" is the good news which Paul says he delivered "first of all".
Samuel Zwemer (1867-1952)

October 17

What good will it be for someone to gain the whole world, yet forfeit their soul? Matthew 16:26a

Ignatius of Antioch (c. 107)
"I am the Wheat of God"

As Ignatius, the second bishop of Antioch in Syria, was being transported to Rome to die in the arena, he wrote to the Christians of that city, urging them not to do anything that would deliver him from his impending martyrdom: "I am writing to all the Churches and I enjoin all, that I am dying willingly for God's sake, if only you do not prevent it. I beg you, do not do me an untimely kindness. Allow me to be eaten by the beasts, which are my way of reaching to God. I am God's wheat, and I am to be ground by the teeth of wild beasts, so that I may become the pure bread of Christ."

Ignatius, who was referred to as "Theophoros" meaning "bearer of God" or "borne of God", was sentenced to death under the emperor Trajan in around 107. The emperor had decreed that Christians should worship the pagan gods and those who refused were to be killed. Undaunted by facing Trajan himself, Ignatius courageously and eloquently defended the Christian faith before being sent to Rome to die.

Ignatius was an exemplary Christian leader, who prayed fervently for his flock and exhorted them to stand firm in the face of persecution. On his journey from Syria to Rome, several churches sent delegations to meet him and they encouraged each other in the hope of the Gospel. He also wrote letters, which have survived, to five of the congregations that had greeted him, as well as one to the Church in Rome and one to Polycarp, Bishop of Smyrna. They stress the importance of maintaining Christian unity and sound doctrine, and they present martyrdom as a great privilege that should be keenly grasped. Ignatius wrote that he himself was "eager to die for the sake of Christ." He was killed by wild beasts in the Colosseum.

All the pleasures of the world, and all the kingdoms of this earth, shall profit me nothing. It is better for me to die in behalf of Jesus Christ, than to reign over all the ends of the earth. 'For what shall a man be profited, if he gain the whole world, but lose his own soul?' Him I seek, who died for us: Him I desire, who rose again for our sake. This is the gain which is laid up for me. Pardon me, brethren: do not hinder me from living, do not wish to keep me in a state of death; and while I desire to belong to God, do not ye give me over to the world. Suffer me to obtain pure light: when I have gone thither, I shall indeed be a man of God.
Ignatius of Antioch (c. 107), letter to the Romans

He will wipe every tear from their eyes. There will be no more death or mourning or crying or pain, for the old order of things has passed away.
Revelation 21:4

Ezzat Habib (2005)
Car "Accident"

One evening in October, Pastor Ezzat, his son Ibram and a friend were hit by a taxi that seemed to drive deliberately at them as they crossed a street in Cairo's Matereya district. Ezzat was rushed to hospital and immediately operated on, but his life could not be saved; he died later that day of internal bleeding and a broken skull. His son and friend survived, but with severe leg injuries.

Many Egyptian Christians have been threatened by the security police that they could be killed in staged car accidents if they do not cooperate with their demands. Pastor Ezzat's death was apparently one such killing. His house church, Beit-El (House of God), in Giza had been constantly threatened by neighbours and the security police for two years before the incident. Further evidence that this was no innocent accident was the false paper Ibram was forced to sign upon reaching hospital, which reported the incident very differently from how it had actually happened.

Despite their loss and the harassment they continued to face, Pastor Ezzat's family continued to run the church that he had founded.

Lord,
teach me to accept
that when wickedness nailed goodness to the cross,
it was evil that received the mortal blow;
that in gentleness and love is strength that never fails;
that it is the proud who fall
and the meek who inherit the earth.
Frank Topping (1909-1997)

We cannot help speaking about what we have seen and heard. Acts 4:20

Jerzy Popieluszko (1984)
Atheist Authorities

Many people came to listen to Polish priest Jerzy's powerful sermons which demonstrated that his aim was "to include God in the difficult and painful problems" of their country at a time of Communist rule. His sermons were, unsurprisingly, very unpopular with the atheist authorities and he was accused of political activity and inciting people to violence.

Several attempts were made to silence Jerzy; he was followed, he was not allowed a passport to travel outside Poland and his car was smeared with paint. But it was not until a December night in 1982 when a brick with a detonator was thrown into the room next to his bedroom that Jerzy realised the danger he was in. The authorities stepped up the pressure, threatening him with legal action. An investigation was made into his alleged "abuse of freedom of conscience and religion"; between January and June 1984 he was interrogated 13 times. Charges brought against him on 12 July 1984 were later suspended.

Aware that his life was under threat, Jerzy said, "Even if I am afraid, I cannot act otherwise. In fact I'd only be afraid if what I was doing was wrong ... and then we always live with the risk of death. If we must die, it is better to meet death while defending a worthwhile cause."

On 13 October an attempt was made on his life when a man stepped out into the road and tried to throw something at his car, but failed. Nearly a week later Jerzy was kidnapped by agents from the Ministry of Interior in Bydgoszcz, northern Poland, while he was driving back to Warsaw. He tried to escape but was beaten very severely. Finally on 19 October Jerzy was bound and thrown into a reservoir with sacks filled with stones tied to him. Between 300,000 and 350,000 people attended his funeral, highlighting the impact his life had made in Poland.

So when people suffer and are persecuted the Church also feels the pain. The mission of the Church is to be with the people and to share with their joys and sorrows... To serve God is to seek a way to human hearts. To serve

God is to speak about evil as a sickness which should be brought to light so that it can be cured. To serve God is to condemn evil in all its manifestations... All who cause pain and suffering to their brothers are fighting against what Christ died for on the Cross... Through Christ's death and resurrection the Cross – a symbol of disgrace – became a symbol of courage, virtue, help and brotherhood. In the sign of the Cross we embrace today all that is most beautiful and valuable in man. Through the Cross we go on to resurrection. There is no other way. And therefore the crosses of our country, our personal crosses and those of our families, must lead to victory, to resurrection, if we are united with Christ who conquered the Cross.
Extracts from sermons by Jerzy Popieluszko (1984)

October 20

This is indeed the will of my Father, that all who see the Son and believe in him may have eternal life; and I will raise them up on the last day.
John 6:40 (NRSV)

George Fathi (2009)
Revenge for Conversion

Church deacon George was known all over Alexandria, Egypt, for his Christian witness, and his evangelistic endeavours are believed to have led to his murder. In October 2009 he was killed by two Islamist brothers, Mohamed and Ahmed Abdel-Moneim, whose sister had been helped by George to convert to Christianity. It seems they were acting in retaliation for this perceived affront to their Muslim faith.

The brothers entered George's flat at midday, and strangled and electrocuted him until his intestines burst out. George's dead, disfigured body was found shortly afterwards by his father, who was sitting in a coffee house facing their flat and came to investigate when he saw smoke coming out. The offenders had started a fire and opened a butane cylinder to spark an explosion, but this was averted by George's father and neighbours.

When the Abdel-Moneim brothers were arrested, they claimed George had tried to sexually assault them and they had acted in self-defence. But the Fathi family's lawyer said the investigation found no evidence that George practised homosexuality. Mohamed's defence later pleaded insanity, a strategy often used by Muslims accused of killing Christians in Egypt. The authorities are usually only too willing to go along with this defence plea.

Our Father in heaven, deliver us, we pray thee, from all manner of evil, whether it touch our body or soul, our property or good name, and at last, when the hour of death shall come, grant us a blessed end and graciously take us from this vale of sorrow to thyself in heaven, through Jesus Christ, thy Son, our Lord. Amen.
Martin Luther (1483-1546)

October 21

Praise be to the God and Father of our Lord Jesus Christ, who has blessed us in the heavenly realms with every spiritual blessing in Christ. For he chose us in him before the creation of the world to be holy and blameless in his sight. Ephesians 1:3-4

Ayad Tarik (2006)
Christian Identity

On 21 October 2006, Iraqi teenager Ayad Tarik was added to the country's long list of Christian martyrs.

The 14-year-old was at his work place in Baqubah, north east of Baghdad, maintaining an electric generator when a group of Muslim insurgents entered the building and asked for his identity card. When they saw that it stated that he was a Christian, they asked him if he really was a "Christian sinner". Ayad answered that he was a Christian but not a sinner. The insurgents then called him a "dirty Christian sinner", and beheaded him, pulling his limbs and shouting "Allahu Akbar" ("god is great").

Lord, help us every hour
Thy cleansing grace to claim;

In life to glorify Thy power,
In death to praise Thy Name.
Emma Leslie Toke (1812-1878)

Blessed art thou, O Lord God Almighty, the Ancient of Days, who has set thy Son Jesus Christ our Lord upon the glorious throne of thy kingdom, exalted far above all peoples, all places, all times, eternally; that he who hath worn out flesh, and borne our manhood into the holy of holies, should henceforth pour down heavenly gifts upon his brethren, and be both our righteous judge and most merciful intercessor; to whom with thee, O Father, and thee, O Holy Spirit, one God, be ascribed all might, majesty, dominion, and praise, now and for ever.
Parish Prayers (no. 360), from *After the Third Collect*

October 22

Serve the LORD with fear and celebrate his rule with trembling.
Psalm 2:11

Philip of Heraclea (c. 304)
Public Declaration

During the persecution under Roman Emperor Diocletian, Philip's church was closed by the authorities so he started holding meetings in the open air, publicly declaring that God dwells within human hearts and not within walls.

The aged Philip was bishop of the Roman province of Thrace. The governor, Bassus, then ordered him to hand over the church's vessels and books. Philip gave him the vessels but would not allow the Scriptures to be confiscated, so to get the books Bassus had Philip and his deacon, Hermes, beaten. The pair were then asked to sacrifice to the pagan gods, but they refused. They were imprisoned for seven months and on three occasions were brought before Bassus' successor Justin; on one visit Philip was beaten for again refusing to sacrifice to the gods.

Both men were eventually sentenced to death by fire. Philip was beaten so badly beforehand that he had to be carried to the pyre. Hermes sent a message to his son saying: "Tell him to pay back whatever I owe, and to work hard for his living as I have done, and to behave well to everybody." As the flames took hold, they gave thanks and praise to God until they were suffocated by the smoke.

Almighty God, by whose grace and power thy holy martyrs
triumphed over suffering and death;
Inspire us, we pray thee, with the same faith,
that, enduring affliction and waxing valiant in fight,
we with them may secure
the crown of everlasting life;
through Jesus Christ our Lord.
In His Name (no. 151)

October 23

Arrogant foes are attacking me; ruthless people are trying to kill me — *people without regard for God. Surely God is my help; the Lord is the one* *who sustains me.* Psalm 54:3-4

Mary Elizabeth Baker (1964)
Practised what she Preached

Psalm 54 was a source of great comfort and courage to Mary, a missionary in the Belgian Congo (now called Democratic Republic of the Congo), when she was captured by Simba rebels in late October 1964. She had been working in the village of Bopepe doing Bible teaching and evangelism for almost 20 years and had become a much-loved member of the community.

Mary became a Christian at the age of 25 and felt called to serve the Lord as a missionary. After completing her training in America, she went to the Congo in 1946, aged 32. When the Simba revolt erupted in mid-1964, the local pastor warned Mary and her co-worker Margaret Hayes, a nurse from England, that danger loomed. Margaret left for a much-needed break from the work, but Mary was unperturbed by being alone. One afternoon a carload of eight Simba men arrived at Mary's house and forced her out on the veranda. They held a gun to her head and asked if she wanted to die, to which she calmly responded that she wasn't afraid and was quite ready for death. Her serene courage impressed the Simbas, who left after taking valuables from her house. The villagers who witnessed the incident commented, "Truly she practises what she preaches." Margaret returned and the pair remained under the watchful eye of the Simbas who continued to harass them.

Towards the end of October, the rebels started rounding up foreigners; Mary and Margaret were marched 15 miles to the town of Banalia where they were held with other missionaries. Over the next three weeks, the rebels became increasingly hostile toward their captives and Mary prepared herself for death. Margaret was released because her medical skills were needed in Bopepe. After an international force of paratroopers descended on Stanleyville (now Kisangani) to free hundreds of expatriate hostages, the Simbas sought revenge on any remaining captives. Mary, along with her fellow Christian prisoners in Banalia, was killed. Days before her death, in a letter to friends in Stanleyville, she wrote, "with me, it was settled long ago, 'by life or by death' and there it rests! My special Psalm has been 54: read it!"

O God, our loving Father, we pray thee to keep us ever close to thyself, that we may find in thy love our strength and our peace.
William Temple (1881-1944)

October 24

I sought the LORD, and he answered me; he delivered me from all my fears. Those who look to him are radiant: their faces are never covered with shame. Psalm 34:4-5

Florence Constance Glover (1900)
"A blessed experience"

Florence was the last martyr of the Boxer Rebellion in China which claimed the lives of thousands of Chinese Christians as well as around 230 foreign Christians. As the Boxers rampaged through the country, many missionaries were forced to flee, usually on foot, covering long distances to escape being captured by those who wanted to kill them.

Florence and her husband, who were stationed at Lu'an, decided to move with their two young children after coming under attack by Boxer rioters who threw stones and caused a disturbance outside their premises. Heavily pregnant at the time, Florence undertook an arduous trek that lasted 40 days. Along the way they faced many ordeals including being stoned, robbed, surrounded by armed rebels and stripped of their clothing; they narrowly escaped death on several occasions. On 18 August, four days after their safe arrival at Han-Kow, an exhausted Florence gave birth to a baby girl called Faith. Sadly the new-born died just over a week later.

Barely recovered from the birth, Florence and her husband headed for Shanghai, but it was not long before she took a turn for the worse. She died on 25 October; the China Inland Mission in London received a cable to say that she had gone to be with Christ.

The sufferings are almost forgotten. All is deep praise to God, for the experience has been so blessed – the experience of His power to cover and keep in perfect peace, only seeing glory when face to face with death – the experience of His tender carrying and enabling love when brought nigh unto death on the road. All has been a blessed experience of Him.
Florence Glover, shortly before her death

October 25

Indeed, we felt we had received the sentence of death. But this happened that we might not rely on ourselves but on God, who raises the dead. He has delivered us from such a deadly peril, and he will deliver us again. On him we have set our hope that he will continue to deliver us.
2 Corinthians 1:9-10

Kang Enyoung (1950)
Communist Brutality

The Reverend Kang Enyoung was one of the first Christians to die under the Communist regime in the Democratic People's Republic of Korea (North Korea), which was created in 1948. He denounced the anti-Christian policy proclaimed by North Korea and was put to death in prison on 25 October 1950. The situation for Christians in the country systematically deteriorated.

North Korea remains the Stalinist-style state that it has been since its inception and is one of the world's most repressive regimes; citizens are denied political, religious and intellectual freedom. Everyone must adhere to the official ideology of "Juche" (self-reliance), which has almost the status of a religion. Christianity is particularly feared by the authorities and Christians are under constant threat of imprisonment, torture or execution if their faith is discovered.

Despite their unimaginable sufferings, Christians in North Korea continue to share the Gospel and the churches continue to grow. There are thought to be at least 400,000 believers, who mostly gather in small "underground" churches.

Eternal God, we thank you for the Church in North Korea. Bless these Christians as they seek to share your Son with their fellow citizens. Fill them with power and zeal as they struggle under persecution. We pray also for the many hungry and poor of that country. Give them this day their daily bread. Lord, may you open the eyes of its rulers, bring them to a higher understanding and free the country of oppression and injustice. We ask these things in the name of your precious Son, Jesus Christ.

October 26

At the name of Jesus every knee should bow, in heaven and on earth and under the earth, and every tongue acknowledge that Jesus Christ is Lord, to the glory of God the Father. Philippians 2:10-11

Joasaphat (1536)
Evangelist to Muslims

Joasaphat was a monk who believed that to die a martyr's death was a glorious thing. He lived in the Islamic Ottoman Empire in the 16th century. With the permission of his superior in the monastery he decided to go to the local *qadi* (Muslim judge) and witness for Christ. There, in front of the Muslim authorities, he preached the Christian faith.

This incensed those present, and Joasaphat was seized and beaten severely. He was asked if he would renounce Christianity, which he refused to do. As a result he was condemned to death, and he was beheaded on 26 October 1536.

Lord,
you taught your first disciples
that they were the salt of the earth,
told them not to hide their light
under bushels,
but to show that light,
not only in words,
but in their lives;
touch my tongue
with the salt of courage,
light my eyes
with the lamp of truth,
so that when righteousness
is persecuted,
I might, at whatever cost,
bear witness to the love
that opens the gates
of the kingdom of heaven.
Frank Topping (1909-1997)

October 27

I want you to know, beloved, that what has happened to me has actually helped to spread the gospel, so that it has become known throughout the whole imperial guard and to everyone else that my imprisonment is for Christ; and most of the brothers and sisters, having been made confident in the Lord by my imprisonment, dare to speak the word with greater boldness and without fear. Philippians 1:12-14 (NRSV)

James Hannington (1885)
Last Words

The last words of James, the first Anglican bishop of Eastern Equatorial Africa, were: "Go, tell Mwanga I have purchased the road to Uganda with my blood."

James, who had been sent from London to East Africa as a missionary bishop in 1884, was apprehended at the orders of Mwanga, king of Buganda (a region within Uganda) and an active persecutor of Christians, as he travelled towards Uganda. After a week of brutal captivity he was murdered along with many other Christians, who had also been detained, in late October 1885.

Almighty God and Creator. You are the Father of all people on the earth. Guide, I pray, all the nations and their leaders in the ways of justice and peace. Protect us from the evils of injustice, prejudice, exploitation, conflict and war. Help us to put away mistrust, bitterness and hatred... Lead us to find peace, respect and freedom. Unite us in the making and sharing of tools of peace against ignorance, poverty, disease and oppression. Grant that we may grow in harmony and friendship as brothers and sisters created in your image to your honour and praise. Amen.
Orthodox Prayer

October 28

The LORD has become my fortress, and my God the rock in whom I take refuge. Psalm 94:22

Bahawalpur Believers (2001) Church Shooting

On 28 October 2001, the Protestant congregation of St Dominic's Church in Bahawalpur, Punjab, Pakistan, gathered at 8 am for worship. As the pastor was finishing the service, three masked men quietly slipped into the church. Two stood guard while the third went and shot the pastor. He then proceeded to open fire on the congregation with his Kalashnikov rifle, killing 15 worshippers.

The attack was believed to be the work of militant extremists – one of the many examples of how the small Christian minority of Pakistan has been targeted in recent decades. An estimated 5,000 people – including both Christians and Muslims – attended the funeral for the victims.

Dear Name, the Rock on which I build,
My Shield and Hiding Place,
My never failing treasury, filled
With boundless stores of grace!
John Newton (1725-1807)

These are they who have come out of the great tribulation; they have washed their robes and made them white in the blood of the Lamb.
Revelation 7:14b

Theresia, Ida and Alfina (2005)
Teenagers Targeted

Three girls were making their way to their Christian school in Central Sulawesi, Indonesia, at 7 am on 29 October 2005 when they were savagely murdered by Islamic militants.

Christians Theresia Murangke (14), Ida Lambuaga (15) and Alfina Yarni Sambue (15), with their companion Noviana Malewa (14), were attacked in a cocoa plantation a mile from the village of Sayo, near Poso city. They were set upon by a group of men who slashed them with machetes. Half an hour later three decapitated bodies were discovered and, later that morning, one head was found outside a church eight miles from the scene of the attack. The other two heads were found near a police station five miles from Poso. Noviana was able to escape with her life, though she received a severe machete wound to her face.

On 3 December 2007 three Islamic militants were sentenced to up to 19 years in prison for the murders – a lenient sentence compared to the death penalty given to three Christians in a separate case who were convicted of violence on flimsy evidence.

The heartbreaking incident was not the only brutal anti-Christian attack in Central Sulawesi in 2005; at least 20 people, 19 of whom were Christians, lost their lives when two bombs were detonated in a market place in the mainly Christian town of Tentena on 28 May.

These have endured through sufferings great
and come to realms of light,
and through the blood of Christ the Lamb
their robes are pure and white.
Isaac Watts (1674-1748) and W Cameron (1751-1811)

October 30

It is the Lord your God you must follow, and him you must revere. Keep
his commands and obey him; serve him and hold fast to him.
Deuteronomy 13:4

Marcellus (298)
"I serve Jesus Christ"

Marcellus was a centurion in the Roman army during the reign of
Emperor Diocletian. On 21 July 298, as feasts and sacrifices were taking
place in the city of Tingis to celebrate the emperor's birthday, Marcellus
took a dramatic and costly stand for his Christian faith. He threw down
his soldier's belt and weapons, declaring:

> I serve Jesus Christ the eternal king. From now on I stop serving
> your emperors, and I refuse to worship your wooden and stone
> gods, which are deaf and dumb idols. If these are the terms of
> service, making men offer sacrifice to gods and emperors ... I
> renounce the standards, and refuse to serve.

Marcellus was reported to the legion's commander, Anastasius For-
tunatus, who ordered that the centurion be thrown in prison. Marcellus
was brought before Fortunatus and questioned about what he had done.
He confirmed that he had publicly declared his Christian faith and given
up his Roman allegiance. Fortunatus reported the matter to the highest
authorities and handed him over to Aurelius Agricolan, Deputy for the
Prefects of the Guard.

On 30 October, Marcellus was brought to court at Tigris, where he
again confirmed what he had said, to Agricolan's incredulity. Marcellus
was sentenced to death by the sword and, as he was being led out to be

executed, proclaimed, "May God bless you! For a martyr should leave this world in this way."

Eternal God, in whose perfect kingdom no sword is drawn but the sword of righteousness, and no strength known but the strength of love: we pray thee so mightily to shed and spread abroad thy Spirit, that all peoples and ranks may be gathered under one banner, of the Prince of Peace; as children of one God and Father of all; to whom be dominion and glory now and for ever.
The Churchpeople's Prayer Book (1935)

October 31

Be strong and courageous… the LORD himself goes before you and will be with you. Deuteronomy 31:7b, 8a

Baghdad Church Siege (2010)
"The True Heroes of Iraq"

"I am a martyr for Jesus," declared church minister Taher Saadallah Boutros (32) as he was killed trying to defend his congregation when armed militants took the church hostage on 31 October 2010.

Gunmen burst into the church in central Baghdad, where around 100 people were taking part in an evening service. Taking worshippers as hostages, the attackers, from Al-Qaeda front group the Islamic State of Iraq, demanded the release of Al-Qaeda prisoners as well as Muslim women they falsely claimed the Egyptian Church was holding captive. Negotiations failed, and more than 50 people – mostly worshippers – were killed as security forces stormed the building in an effort to free the hostages.

Among the dead were a second minister, Wassim Sabih (23), who tried to hide some of the worshippers in another room, and a young wife pregnant with her first child, Raghada al-Wafi. At the funeral, mourners and witnesses said both Taher and Wassim had pleaded with the hostage-takers to kill them but not harm the congregation. One mourner, Firas Chill (30), said, "These are the true heroes of Iraq, not the politicians or soldiers, but these two men who followed the teaching of Christ and sacrificed themselves while trying to persuade the killers to spare the lives of the worshippers."

Taher appeared to be prepared for his impending martyrdom, having considered the story of one of the Church's most well-known martyrs just days before his own: he was photographed teaching a session in the church where a line on the board behind him read, "Dietrich Bonheoffer: a witness and a martyr in Nazi jails."

The church siege was among the deadliest recorded attacks against Iraq's Christians, who endured repeated violence following the US-led invasion of 2003.

God, give me strength to run this race,
God, give me power to do the right,
And courage lasting through the fight;
God, give me strength to see your face,
And heart to stand till evil cease,
And at the last, O God, your peace.

November 1

When I called, you answered me; you greatly emboldened me.
Psalm 138:3

Lee Youghee (c. 1945)
Bold Preacher

Lee Youghee moved with his family from Korea, where he had been a church elder, to Japanese-controlled Manchuria, feeling that he needed to stand more openly and firmly against the shrine worship being imposed on Christians in Manchuria. He started to preach against this practice. After some time, the principal of a school in the area threatened the Christians, including Youghee, but he seemed impervious to whatever threats were made against him. On one occasion he was warned not to return to a certain village, but he and a missionary friend ignored the threats and boldly went into that village – without being harmed.

In time he felt he should return to Korea. He was not allowed to preach in the churches there so he held meetings in people's homes. One day the police surrounded the place where Youghee was staging such a gathering. A policeman entered, ordering him to come out. Many of the other Christians escaped, but Youghee was arrested and put in prison where he later died.

Ye have enemies; for who can live on this earth without them? Take heed to yourselves: love them. In no way can thy enemy hurt thee by his violence, as thou dost hurt thyself if thou love him not.
Augustine of Hippo (354-430)

November 2

Precious in the sight of the Lord is the death of his faithful servants.
Psalm 116:15

Arthur Tylee, Marian Tylee, Mildred Kratz and three Brazilians (1930) Tribal Missionaries

"I have nothing to do with how long I shall live. I am in the will of God. If He sees fit to let me live to complete the language and to present the Lord Jesus and His power to save, I shall be happy. If not, His will be done. Do you not know ... that a grave often speaks louder than life?"

This was Arthur's faith-filled response to concerns that the Amerindians he was trying to reach in Brazil would kill him. He felt called to take the Gospel to the Nhambiquara tribe, deep in the heart of the Amazon jungle, after leaving law school to complete missionary training. He made two arduous forays into the jungle with another missionary, but on both occasions was forced to turn back.

Arthur married Ethel Canary in 1925, and a week after their wedding the couple set out to establish a mission station in Nhambiquara territory. They suffered hardship, severe illness and near starvation during a year spent befriending the tribe. The couple returned in 1928 with their baby Marian and nurse Mildred Kratz, with whom they had studied, to continue the work.

In 1930, an influential tribal leader died following an outbreak of flu and the missionaries, who had tended him and other patients, were blamed for the death. For months the Nhambiquara stayed away from the mission station but they returned – to the missionaries' delight – on 2 November offering to help build a road. The next day, however, they launched an assault on the small team. Arthur was knocked unconscious then shot dead with arrows; Mildred was killed by an arrow to her chest. Ethel, who was pregnant with her second child, was struck on the back of the head and left for dead but incredibly she – and her unborn baby – survived. However little Marian was killed by an arrow, and three of their Brazilian co-workers were also slain.

It is not far to go
for you are near,
It is not far to go
for you are here
And not by travelling, Lord,
men come to you,
but by the way of love,
and we love you.
Amy Carmichael (1867-1951)

November 3

Preach the word; be prepared in season and out of season.
2 Timothy 4:2

Tak Myong-Hwan (1994)
Condemned Cults

North Korea has become known for its persecution of Christians, but it is unusual to read of a Christian dying because of their faith in South Korea. This is exactly what happened to Tak Myong-Hwan, a theologian from Seoul. Before his murder he had received numerous death threats for his outspoken views on cults, and he had even survived attempts to kill him. South Korea has hundreds of sects, such as the Unification movement founded by Sun Myung Moon in 1954, and Myong-Hwan was very concerned about such movements that hold unorthodox beliefs and engage in strange practices.

In early 1994 he was found beaten to death outside his apartment. A member of an unorthodox sect was reported to have confessed to the murder.

Almighty and everlasting God, who hast put thine own eternity into our hearts, and desires which the world cannot satisfy: Lift our eyes, we pray thee, above the narrow horizons of this present world, that we may behold the things eternal in the heavens, wherein is laid up for us an inheritance that fadeth not away; through Jesus Christ our Lord.
Parish Prayers (no. 535), from *The Daily Service*

November 4

Very truly I tell you, you will weep and mourn while the world rejoices. You will grieve, but your grief will turn to joy. John 16:20

Alexandrian Christians (249)
Mass Persecution

During a terrible persecution of Christians in Alexandria, which started in 249 on the order of a pagan priest, an elderly lady, Apollonia, was threatened by the crowd who wanted to burn her alive after she confessed Christ. A fire was prepared and Apollonia was tied up. Because she begged to be released, the onlookers had the impression that she would recant, so she was untied. But to their amazement she threw herself into the flames and to her death.

Many Christians were attacked and murdered by the mob, who broke into their homes and stole their property. Only three of their names are known including Apollonia described above. Metrus, an old and revered Christian, refused to worship the pagan gods so was beaten with clubs and stoned to death. A Christian woman named Quinta was taken to the temple but also refused to worship their idols. After being dragged over sharp stones, she too was stoned to death.

You are the Lord of fire
Present in the fiery furnace,
Present in the heat of life,
Present in situations of horror and despair,

Present in the prisons that incarcerate men for their beliefs.
Shadrach, Meshach and Abednego were lucky ones,
Lord. They came out unscathed
Not all are so lucky,
Not all understand the tyrannies of life and remain unharmed,
You are with men in their suffering, in their aloneness and ignominy
    and death.
Be with them.
Be with them through us who are your limbs.
Give us a glimmering of hope in hopeless situations;
For where there is no hope there is nothing.
Rex Chapman

November 5

You have been raised with Christ, set your hearts on things above, where
Christ is, seated at the right hand of God. Colossians 3:1

Nikolai Vasilyevich Odintsov (1939)
Homeward Bound

Nikolai, a Baptist preacher who was well known for his teaching in
many parts of the Soviet Union, was arrested on 5 November 1933. This
followed the arrest of his closest assistant as well as the forced closure
of the Baptist Bible School and the local and federal Baptist Unions, of
which Nikolai was chairman.

The preacher served a three-year sentence in Yaroslavl prison and was
then exiled to Makovskoye, eastern Siberia. In 1937 his wife visited him
and reported that though Nikolai was physically weak he was spiritually
strong. He sent greetings to the other believers and often told her, "I want
to go home" (i.e. to heaven). Some believers witnessed his worn-out and
exhausted body being tormented by vicious dogs, who would be set on
the weakest prisoners who fell behind the others. He was sentenced to
death by the Military Collegium of the Supreme Court of the USSR on
7 March 1939 and shot the same day.

Some of his writings from the prison remain: "My body is tired and
weak, my work for the Lord here in the camps is unbearably hard and the
repressions I suffer often hold me for long periods on my bare plank bed,

which represents my bed of ease... I have grown weak in body, but not in spirit. Jesus, the Lord, upholds me..." He knew that he would die without seeing his loved ones again and wrote, "As for the return to my family, I will wait for my and our family there, in heaven."

What will happen next? The Lord knows! May eternal glory be to Him! Rejoice, dear brothers and sisters, just as I rejoice – your brother, who will not forget you all until the end of his days. And may the name of our God and His Son, our Lord Jesus Christ, be blessed and glorified! Hallelujah! Amen!
Nikolai Vasilyevich Odintsov (1870-1939), last lines of his letter from prison

---

November 6

One thing I ask from the LORD, this only do I seek: that I may dwell in the house of the LORD all the days of my life, to gaze on the beauty of the LORD and to seek him in his temple. Psalm 27:4

Edmund Gikonyo (c. 1953)
Forgave Killers

The Kenyan school in which Edmund taught lost all its pupils when their parents took the Mau Mau oath and no longer wanted their children to attend a Christian establishment. He and another Christian teacher, Apolo Kamau Kamau, continued to go to the empty school simply to enjoy having fellowship together. Edmund, who had become a Christian in 1949, testified, "Jesus has saved me. I have not taken the Mau Mau oath and never will."

False rumours started to spread that Edmund and Apolo were travelling to Nairobi to make reports against the Mau Mau. The pair received a letter from the government warning them that they were in a high risk area and advising them to move. They planned to head for Weithaga but before they left, the Mau Mau came to Edmund's house. When he saw their guns he said, "I have forgiven you for what you are going to do now."

As they shot him, he called out, "Lord, receive my spirit!" and died.

O Thou who hast prepared a place for my soul, prepare my soul for that place. Prepare it with holiness; prepare it with desire; and even while it sojourneth upon earth, let it dwell in heaven with thee, beholding the beauty of thy countenance and the glory of thy saints now and for evermore.
Joseph Hall (1574-1656)

"No one can serve two masters. Either you will hate the one and love the other, or you will be devoted to the one and despise the other."
Matthew 6:24a

Evangelist Kim (1943)
Water Pressure

Thousands of Manchurians were led to Christ by missionaries in the early 1900s, and many churches had been established when Japan took control of the region following the 1931 invasion. The Japanese occupiers required reverence and submission to their emperor. Christians could not accept this, and many died when Japanese troops attacked Christian villages. It was also a requirement that small shrines be set up in church buildings.

Kim was a Presbyterian minister who preached that no-one can serve two masters: the emperor and Christ. He was arrested, tortured and released seven times. On the eighth occasion he was given the "water cure": he was stretched out on a bench with his head hanging back, whilst water was poured down his nostrils. When he was almost suffocated, Kim consented to sign a paper indicating his approval of Shinto shrine worship. He was then set free, but he was so filled with remorse that he wrote to the police station stating that he did not agree with shrine worship. As a result he was arrested, put in prison again and placed in a tiny cell. Eventually the police thought he was going to die so they contacted a friend to collect him. Kim recovered his strength and continued preaching. He was sent to prison one final time, where he died in 1943.

The trials that afflict you,
the sorrows you endure:
what are they but the testing
that makes your calling sure?
John Mason Neale (1818-1866)

If we are distressed, it is for your comfort and salvation; if we are comforted, it is for your comfort, which produces in you patient endurance of the same sufferings we suffer. 2 Corinthians 1:6

Cecilia (3ʳᵈ century)
Botched Beheading

Cecilia was a devout young Christian woman from a reputable family in Rome, who was given in marriage to a pagan man named Valerian. When she explained her faith in Christ to him, he too became a believer and was baptised. His brother Tibertius was also converted. The brothers were arrested by the Roman authorities after it was discovered that they had been burying the bodies of the Christian martyrs killed in the city. They were both executed.

Cecilia was also arrested after her preaching of the Gospel led to the conversion of 400 people. When she refused to perform any pagan sacrifices, she was sentenced to death by suffocation. But Cecilia survived this attempt to end her life, so a soldier was sent to behead her. Cecilia's death was prolonged by her executioner's failure to complete the task. She lived for three days after the botched beheading during which time she prayed and encouraged the Christians who visited her.

Merciful God, grant us feeble people endurance in adversity. May wicked roots of envy and malice not grow in us. Pull out the wicked root of covetousness from us… Grant us love towards friends and enemies, that we may follow in your ways, our Father, and the example of your only-begotten Son, Jesus Christ.
Miles Coverdale (1488-1568)

But because of his great love for us, God, who is rich in mercy, made us alive with Christ even when we were dead in transgressions – it is by grace you have been saved. Ephesians 2:4

Matthew (c. 60)
The Evangelist

The calling of Matthew is a wonderful example of Jesus' love and grace towards those deemed beyond the pale by society. Matthew was a tax collector – a greatly despised profession in New Testament times – who was chosen by Jesus to be one of his apostles, much to the consternation of the Pharisees who considered Jesus' association with "sinners" to be scandalous:

> As Jesus went on from there, he saw a man named Matthew sitting at the tax collector's booth. "Follow me," he told him, and Matthew got up and followed him. While Jesus was having dinner at Matthew's house, many tax collectors and sinners came and ate with him and his disciples. When the Pharisees saw this, they asked his disciples, "Why does your teacher eat with tax collectors and sinners?" On hearing this, Jesus said, "It is not the healthy who need a doctor, but the sick. But go and learn what this means: 'I desire mercy, not sacrifice.' For I have not come to call the righteous, but sinners." (Matthew 9:9-13)

After Jesus' ascension Matthew, who is referred to by the name Levi in the Gospels of Mark and Luke, preached in Judea for nine years, taking the Gospel to fellow Jews. The Gospel of Matthew, which is traditionally ascribed to him, is considered to have been written with a predominantly Jewish audience in mind.

Matthew is also reported to have preached in Persia, Parthia and Ethiopia; his wide-reaching evangelism led to him becoming known as "the Evangelist". Matthew is believed to have been martyred in Ethiopia, where he was killed with a halberd in the city of Nadabah around 60.

O Lord, grant all who contend for the faith, never to injure it by clamour and impatience; but, speaking thy precious truth in love, so to present it that it may be loved, and that men may see in it thy goodness and beauty.
William Bright (1824-1901)

November 10

Wide is the gate and broad is the road that lead to destruction, and many enter through it. But small is the gate and narrow the road that lead to life, and only a few find it. Matthew 7:13b-14

Hemanta Das (2007)
Hindu Convert

Before he converted to Christianity, Hemanta, from Assam in India, was a member of a Hindu extremist group called Rashtriya Swayamsevak Sangh (RSS). After his conversion he became very active in evangelism, which angered the radical Hindu groups who often carried out violent attacks against Christians.

Hemanta was threatened on several occasions that there would be dire consequences if he tried to convert people to Christianity, but he was undeterred. On 28 June 2007 he was beaten so severely in Guwahati, Assam, that he died of his injuries three days later in hospital. The attack was believed to have been the work of Hindu extremists. Hemanta was hailed as the first Assamese martyr by the Council of Baptist Churches in North East India.

Send out your light and your truth, that I may live always near to you, my God. Let me feel your love, that I may be as it were already in heaven, that I may do my work as the angels do theirs; and let me be ready for every work, ready to go out or go in, to stay or depart, just as you direct. Lord, let me have no will of my own, or consider my true happiness as depending in the smallest degree on anything that happens to me outwardly, but as consisting totally in conformity to your will.
Henry Martyn (1781-1812)

Remember the word that I said to you, "Servants are not greater than their master." If they persecuted me, they will persecute you.
John 15:20 (NRSV)

Mina (c. 303)
Prayer and Austerity

Mina (also called Menas) is regarded in Egypt as one of the great heroes of the Christian faith. The earliest depictions of Mina show him with two camels, suggesting that he may have been a camel driver. However, according to popular tradition he was an Egyptian soldier in the Roman army who served in Phrygia, Asia Minor (modern-day Turkey).

During the persecution under Diocletian, Mina went to the mountains where he led a life of prayer and austerity. Then at the games in Cotywus he publicly announced his Christianity, which led to his arrest. Mina was brought before the ruler of Phrygia, beaten, tortured, and finally beheaded. His body was returned to Egypt for burial at a place near Alexandria in around 303 that was later named Abu Mina after this martyr.

O Christ, the King of glory, who didst enter the holy city in meekness to be made perfect through the suffering of death: Give us grace, we beseech thee, in all our life here to take up our cross daily and follow thee, that hereafter we may rejoice with thee in thy heavenly kingdom; who livest and reignest with the Father and the Holy Spirit, God, world without end.
Church of South India

I am the good shepherd. The good shepherd lays down his life for the sheep. John 10:11

Nerses (373)
Banished Bishop

As a young man Nerses was a soldier in Caesarea, Cappadocia (modern day Turkey). Following the death of his wife he then became an official at the court of King Arshak of Armenia. In about 363 Nerses became bishop of the Armenian Church and attempted to spread Christianity among the people. The king however opposed this and banished him from Armenia.

When Nerses heard that Arshak had died, he returned to his former position. But the succeeding king, Pap, was a greater tyrant than Arshak and some of his contemporaries believed he was possessed by the devil. Pap invited Nerses to a dinner, at which he poisoned him.

O God of all power, you called from death the great pastor of the sheep, our Lord Jesus: comfort and defend the flock which He has redeemed through the blood of the everlasting covenant. Increase the number of true preachers; enlighten the hearts of the ignorant; relieve the pain of the afflicted, especially of those who suffer for the testimony of the truth; by the power of our Lord Jesus Christ.
John Knox (c. 1515-72)

Do not let your hearts be troubled. You believe in God; believe also in me. My Father's house has many rooms; if that were not so, would I have told you that I am going there to prepare a place for you? And if I go and prepare a place for you, I will come back and take you to be with me that you also may be where I am. John 14:1-3

Ghorban Tori (2005)
House Church Crackdown

A Turkmen convert from Islam to Christianity, Ghorban Tori, was the pastor of an independent house church in Gonbad-e-Kavus, Iran. He was kidnapped from his home in north-eastern Iran in November 2005 and stabbed to death. His body, soaked in blood, was thrown in front of his family home a few hours later. Ghorban left a wife and four children, aged 3 to 23.

The secret police arrived at his home within hours of his death, searching for Bibles and other Farsi-language Christian books. They also raided several other Christian homes within the same city. It was reported that Ghorban's death followed a meeting of Iran's provincial governors and President Ahmadinejad that discussed putting a stop to Iran's growing house church movement, "underground" churches comprising converts from Islam. Despite the government's brutal efforts to quash Christianity in the strictly Islamic Republic of Iran, many Muslims have turned to Christ.

Lord, you promised to prepare a place for us,
for me, in your father's house,
a promise underlined by the words,
'If it were not so, I would have told you'.
My Lord and my God, a heavenly reunion
outside the bounds of time is too great a vision
for my mind to encompass.
But I know that love cannot die,
truth cannot die – and you are perfect love and perfect truth.
Lord, with all my limitations,
I believe; help my unbelief.

Philip found Nathanael and told him, "We have found the one Moses wrote about in the Law, and about whom the prophets also wrote – Jesus of Nazareth, the son of Joseph." "Nazareth! Can anything good come from there?" Nathanael asked. "Come and see," said Philip. John 1:45-46

Philip (c. 52)
Early Follower

Philip, one of the twelve apostles, came from the Galilean city of Bethsaida and was a disciple of Jesus from early on, probably after following John the Baptist. Before Jesus performed one of his most well-known miracles – the feeding of the 5000 – he tested Philip with the question, "Where shall we buy bread for these people to eat?" The Gospel writer John tells us that Jesus "already had in mind what he was going to do" (John 6:5-6). Philip later asked Jesus to show the disciples the Father; Jesus' response was, "Anyone who has seen me has seen the Father." (John 14:8-9)

Philip passed on what he had learnt from his close contact with Jesus when he went to Asia to preach the Gospel. At Hierapolis in Phrygia he preached against the common practice of snake worship. This angered the pagan priests who sent him to prison; Philip was then scourged and crucified. This took place around 52.

Almighty God
you gave to your apostles Philip and James
grace and strength to bear witness to the truth.
Grant that we, mindful of their victory of faith,
may glorify in life and death the name of Jesus Christ,
who lives and reigns with you and the Holy Spirit,
one God, now and for ever.
For All the Saints (Canada)

Turn from evil and do good; seek peace and pursue it. The eyes of the Lord are on the righteous, and his ears are attentive to their cry; but the face of the Lord is against those who do evil, to blot out their name from the earth. Psalm 34:14-16

Joseph Mukasa (1885)
Protected Children

During the persecution of Ugandan Christians undertaken by King Mwanga in the late 19th century (see June 3), Joseph served as head of the king's page boys. He was a member of the royal family and a convert to Christianity. Being in control of the pages, Joseph was able to protect the youngsters from the lusts of the pagan king, who was attracted to them. This infuriated King Mwanga, who refused to have his orders to see the boys ignored. Under the influence of the prime minister, the king had Joseph arrested and on 15 November 1885 he was taken away to be killed. The reason for his martyrdom was twofold: his refusal to allow the king access to the page boys and his role as a leader of the young Christian community.

Ever loving God,
you made the blood of martyrs
the seed of your church in Uganda;
grant that, as you were steadfast in faith
and obedient unto death,
yielding a plentiful harvest,
so may we be encouraged by their example
to witness courageously to your gospel;
through Jesus Christ our Saviour.
For All the Saints (New Zealand)

For he guards the course of the just and protects the way of his faithful ones. Proverbs 2:8

Jameel Sawan (2011)
Minorities' Champion

Jameel was shot dead in Karachi on 16 November 2011 in a suspected Islamist attack. A leading figure in the Christian community in Karachi, Pakistan, he was also a champion of minority rights.

Jameel had a shop in the city but spent a lot of his time preaching, pastoring Christians and sharing the Gospel with Muslims. He was also a close aide to Saleem Khursheed Khokhar, chairman of the Standing Committee on Minorities Affairs in the Sindh Assembly and president of the All Pakistan Minorities Alliance in Sindh. Both men had received death threats from Muslim extremists because of their involvement in campaigning for minority rights and support for policies initiated by assassinated Minorities Minister Shahbaz Bhatti (see 2 March).

A two-minute silence, instigated by Mr Khokhar, was held at the Sindh Assembly for Jameel and three Hindu doctors who had been killed in Shikarpur a few days earlier. Jameel left a wife, two sons and three daughters.

Christians are a despised minority in Pakistan; they suffer widespread social and legal discrimination, as well as violence from Muslim extremists.

When I tread the verge of Jordan,
bid my anxious fears subside;
death of death and hell's destruction,
land me safe on Canaan's side.
Songs of praises, songs of praises,
I will ever give to thee.
William Williams (1717-91)

Be strong in the Lord and in his mighty power. Put on the full armour of God so that you can take your stand against the devil's schemes.
Ephesians 6:10-11

Victor of Marseilles (3rd century) Soldiered On

Victor, a soldier in the Roman army at Marseilles in the 3rd century, urged Christians to stand firm in their faith as the region prepared for a visit by the persecuting Emperor Maximian. As a result of this he was brought before the emperor and convicted of treachery.

Victor was dragged through the streets, put on the rack and imprisoned, but he still refused to worship pagan gods, saying, "I despise your deities, and confess Jesus Christ; inflict upon me what torments you please." Three prison guards with whom he had shared his faith converted to Christianity. But when this was discovered they were beheaded, while Victor was subjected to further torture. The soldier refused to offer incense to the god Jupiter, so he was crushed in a millstone and had his head cut from his body.

It is not armour as armour, but as armour of God, that makes the soul impregnable.
William Gurnall (1617-79)

Praise the LORD, my soul; all my inmost being, praise his holy name. Praise the LORD, my soul, and forget not all his benefits – who forgives all your sins and heals all your diseases, who redeems your life from the pit and crowns you with love and compassion. Psalm 103:1-4

Sabir John Bhatti and Family (1998) Praying for the Sick

Almost an entire family, including children and babies, was martyred in 1998 because of Sabir's Christian witness in his community. He was actively involved in praying for the sick in the city of Nowshera, in the Khyber Pakhtunkhwa Province of Pakistan. This seems to have angered Islamic extremists who most likely targeted Sabir and his family to dissuade other Christians from carrying out a similar ministry.

Nine Christians, eight of them members of Sabir's family, were murdered by a group of extremists. Most of them had their throats slit with knives. Those martyred were Sabir and his wife Ruth, daughter Shaheen, daughter-in-law Rosina, one-year-old grandson Mohsin, eight-year-old grandson Romi, ten-year-old granddaughter Sobia, a one-month-old grandson and fourteen-year-old family friend Ifzal.

And every tear is wiped away
By your dear Father's hands for ay;
Death hath no power to hurt you more,
Whose own is life's eternal store.
Who sow their seed, and sowing weep,
In everlasting joy shall reap,
What time they shine in heavenly day,
And every tear is wiped away.
The Venerable Bede (673-735)
Translated by John Mason Neale (1818-1866)

November 19

Do you not know that in a race all the runners run, but only one gets the prize? Run in such a way as to get the prize. Everyone who competes in the games goes into strict training. They do it to get a crown that will not last; but we do it to get a crown that will last forever.
1 Corinthians 9:24-25

Daniil Sysoev (2009)
A Martyr's Crown

After Russian church minister Daniil Sysoev (34) was murdered in his Moscow church on 19 November 2009, his wife Yulia said that he "expected the death some years prior to its happening; he always wished to receive a martyr's crown, and the Lord has given him this crown... He said that he would be killed."

Daniil was approached by a masked gunman who checked his name and then shot him in the head and chest. A choirmaster was also injured in the attack.

Daniil had been active in evangelistic outreach to Muslims, and many people think that this was the motive for his assassination. He had received threats via email that he would have his head cut off if he did not stop preaching to Muslims.

Grant, O Lord, that in thy wounds we may find our safety, in thy stripes our cure, in thy pain our peace, in thy cross our victory, in thy resurrection our triumph; and at the last, a crown of righteousness in the glories of thy eternal kingdom.
Parish Prayers (no. 198)

November 20

... instruments for special purposes, made holy, useful to the Master and prepared to do any good work. 2 Timothy 2:21

John Williams (1839)
Eaten at Erromanga

John Williams seemed to know that his voyage to the New Hebrides (now called Vanuatu) would be his last journey. For two decades he and his wife had served the Lord in the South Pacific, evangelising and building up the faith of the newly emerging Christian communities, teaching them to abandon not only their idols but also violent cultural practices such as infanticide. John was dearly loved by the local believers. His face showed his "simplicity of character, tranquillity of heart, and honesty of purpose".

On 20 November 1839, John Williams landed on the island of Erromanga. He was accompanied by a colleague, James Harris, and Vice Consul Cunningham. The inhabitants gave them a friendly welcome and exchanged gifts with them. The three separated. Suddenly James Harris came racing back towards the stony beach, followed by islanders yelling and carrying clubs and spears. Cunningham ran for the boat, but John Williams waited, apparently trying to identify the type of yelling – was it a war-cry or not? Then he too started to run, heading straight for the sea. He tripped and fell in the water, two islanders were on him immediately with their clubs, and more soon arrived, who thrust arrows into his body. James Harris died in the nearby river. The islanders ate the two bodies.

As news of the martyrdoms spread through the Pacific there was great mourning for John Williams. The Christians in Tahiti "cannot sleep at night for thinking of him," wrote the British consul.

The violence of the Erromangans perhaps reflected their previous experience of white men. Recent visitors had stolen their yams and pigs, cut their precious sandalwood, introduced a disease from which numerous islanders died, and killed many others.

> ... in the work of my Lord and Saviour I desire to live and to die. My highest ambition, dear father, is to be faithful to my work, faithful to souls, and faithful to Christ; in a word to be abundantly and extensively useful.
> John Williams, in a letter to his father, 1823

November 21

> Whenever you stand praying, forgive, if you have anything against anyone; so that your Father in heaven may also forgive you your trespasses. Mark 11:25 (NRSV)

Bonnie Penner Witherall (2002)
"I forgive them"

On the morning of 21 November 2002, American nurse Bonnie (31) answered a knock at the door of the medical clinic where she had worked for eight years. It was based at an evangelical mission in Sidon, Lebanon, and the clinic was part of the Unity Centre that also housed a chapel for worship services.

On opening the door, Bonnie was confronted by a lone gunman who shot her in the head three times. She was killed instantly. Her only "wrong" appears to have been speaking of Jesus to Muslim children when she and her colleagues dispensed food to them and ran Sunday School meetings.

Bonnie's husband, Gary, said at her funeral, "Whoever did this crime, I forgive them ... because God has forgiven me."

> To be a Christian means to forgive the inexcusable because God has forgiven the inexcusable in you.
> C S Lewis (1898-1963), The Weight of Glory

Very truly, I tell you, unless a grain of wheat falls into the earth and dies, it remains just a single grain; but if it dies, it bears much fruit. Those who love their life lose it, and those who hate their life in this world will keep it for eternal life. John 12:24-25 (NRSV)

Bashir Ahmad Tantray (2006)
Threatened Evangelist

"He is a martyr for the faith and we can only pray that his blood may be a seed for evangelisation." These were the words of the president of the Global Council of Indian Christians after Bashir became the first Christian convert to be killed for his faith in the northern state of Jammu and Kashmir.

Bashir (50), who had converted from Islam around ten years before his death, was shot dead in broad daylight on 21 November 2006 by two Muslim extremists, while he was chatting to friends in the village where he lived. The assassins fled the scene by motorbike.

Following his conversion, Bashir, a husband and father of four, had been active in evangelism and had received death threats. Violence against Christians in Jammu and Kashmir State had been on the rise around the time of Bashir's death; two Christian schools had been targeted with bombs by Islamic militants.

Suffering saints are living seed.
C H Spurgeon (1834-92)

And God raised us up with Christ and seated us with him in the heavenly realms in Christ Jesus. Ephesians 2:6

Miguel Pro (1927)
"Long live Christ the King!"

The Mexican Revolution that began in 1910 created great instability in the country and caused massive tensions between the Church and President Calles, who strictly enforced new anti-clergy laws and persecuted Christians. After spending some time abroad, Miguel returned to Mexico as a church leader, in defiance of the ban on church ministry. He was arrested along with his brothers Humberto and Roberto on the false accusation of attempting to blow up former president Álvaro Obregón. This was used to condemn Miguel and Humberto to death without a trial, but the real reason for their arrest was the fact that they were church leaders and were thus considered enemies of the regime.

President Calles sought to disgrace Miguel by inviting members of the press and photographers to capture the execution. But the plan seriously backfired when Miguel faced the firing squad on 23 November 1927 with grace and fortitude. He said: "May God have mercy on you. May God bless you. Lord, you know that I am innocent. With all my heart I forgive my enemies."

His last words were the defiant cry of the rebels who resisted the president's anti-clergy laws, "Long live Christ the King!" The photographs of Miguel's execution were printed and distributed around the world, and he was hailed as a martyr.

Persecution against the Church continued for years, and tens of thousands of Christians lost their lives. But their resolve to remain faithful to the end was strengthened by Miguel's example.

Your dear Son has taught us that life is eternal and life cannot die, so death is only an horizon and an horizon is only the limit of our sight. Open our eyes to see more clearly and draw us close to you... You have told us that you are preparing a place for us; prepare us also for that happy place, that where you are we may also be always, O dear Lord, of life and death.
William Penn (1644-1718)

The wicked earn no real gain, but those who sow righteousness get a true reward. Proverbs 11:18 (NRSV)

Hector MacMillan (1964)
Long-Serving Missionary

Canadian Hector was serving as a missionary in the Belgian Congo (now the Democratic Republic of the Congo) when a young woman called Iona arrived to join in the work after graduating from Bible school. The pair married, had six sons, and spent 23 years there.

In August 1964 the Simba Rebellion was sweeping through the Congo and finally reached the mission station, known as Kilometre Eight, where Hector, Iona and their family lived. The rebels kept the MacMillans and the other missionaries there under house arrest.

On the morning of 24 November the rebels suddenly burst into their home and ordered everyone outside. They separated the two men of the group from the women and children. The latter were herded back into the house, only to be showered with bullets by a young rebel. Amazingly no one was killed, although two of Hector's sons were hit. As Iona listened to what was going on outside, she heard raised voices and then more gunfire. When the rebels fled, they emerged from their home to find Hector's body. He had been shot dead. Soon after the incident the family was evacuated in trucks, leaving Hector's body behind in the place where he had faithfully served God.

Teach us, gracious Lord, to begin our deeds with reverence, to go on with obedience, and to finish them in love; and then to wait patiently in hope, and with cheerful confidence to look up to you, whose promises are faithful and rewards infinite; through Jesus Christ.
George Hicks (1642-1715)

If you do not stand firm in your faith, you will not stand at all.
Isaiah 7:9b

Arab Christians of Najran (523)
Stood Firm

In the sixth century, when the Christian kingdom of Abyssinia (Ethiopia) controlled the southern Arabian peninsula (Himyar and Yemen), a Himyarite Jew called Yusuf As'ar staged an armed revolt against Abyssinian rule. He attacked the Christian city of Najran in Arabia; the besieged citizens knew they could not last for long and eventually surrendered to Yusuf As'ar.

In command of his Jewish and Arab soldiers, he entered the city and set about massacring the inhabitants, killing around 2,000 people. In the following week many hundreds more were killed when they refused to renounce Christ. On 25 November 523 Yusuf As'ar slaughtered around 340 followers of Arethas, the leader of the Najran Christians, and further massacres took place when Christians refused to give up their faith. Eventually the Abyssinian king regained control, bringing the bloodshed to an end.

Be our strength in hours of weakness,
in our wanderings be our guide;
through endeavour, failure, danger,
Father, be there at our side.
Love M Willis (1824-1908)

Whatever you do, work at it with all your heart, as working for the Lord, not for human masters, since you know that you will receive an inheritance from the Lord as a reward. It is the Lord Christ you are serving. Colossians 3:23-24

Vitus (303)
Faithful Servant

Vitus was the only son of a Sicilian senator and gained a reputation for winning people for Christ. This attracted the attention of the administrator of Sicily, who had Vitus brought in and tried without success to undermine his faith.

Vitus escaped to Rome with his tutor and his servant. There he is said to have freed Emperor Diocletian's son from an evil spirit, but the cure was attributed to sorcery when Vitus refused to sacrifice to the gods. The trio were arrested and ill-treated but survived the various tortures they endured. They were released when a storm destroyed some pagan temples, but they were later arrested again and martyred at Luciana.

Let us keep our eyes steadily upon the goal... For when we hear the shout from the skies, all else will fade into utter nothingness. For the Lord shall descend – from heaven with a shout. Even so, come, Lord Jesus.
Robert Jaffray (martyred on Celebes island, Indonesia, 1945)

Do you think I came to bring peace on earth? No, I tell you, but division. From now on there will be five in one family divided against each other… They will be divided, father against son and son against father, mother against daughter and daughter against mother, mother-in-law against daughter-in-law and daughter-in-law against mother-in-law.
Luke 12:51-52a, 53

Gerges Israel (1995)
Family Split

Gerges was a Sudanese Christian who was reportedly killed by his own son, Vector, in late November 1995. Vector had previously converted to Islam, which had split family loyalties, and it seems that Gerges' active commitment to his Christian faith angered his son, for which the whole family paid a heavy price. Gerges had tried to prevent Vector from converting his sisters to Islam and also helped a relative to escape from Sudan after he had been denied an exit visa. The relative had been penalised in this way because Gerges was employing a Muslim who had converted to Christianity.

Sudan was torn apart by decades of civil war, with the largely Muslim and Arab North fighting to Arabise and impose sharia on the mainly non-Muslim, African South, where millions were killed or displaced by the violence. The Israel family was divided and destroyed by a microcosm of this conflict.

Dear Lord,
this body, this blood, this bread, this wine,
this love's tryst with you is the living heart of faith.
From this communion comes love and hope.
From this communion comes forgiveness and peace.
From this communion comes healing and strength.
From this communion comes life that never ends.
Lord, may I live in communion with you now and always.
Frank Topping (1909-1997), *The Words of Christ*

Oh, the depth of the riches of the wisdom and knowledge of God! How unsearchable his judgments, and his paths beyond tracing out! "Who has known the mind of the Lord? Or who has been his counsellor?" "Who has ever given to God, that God should repay them?" For from him and through him and for him are all things. To him be the glory forever! Amen. Romans 11:33-36

Sunday Aransi (2001)
Churches Mobbed

Nigerian Christian Sunday Aransi was murdered and at least ten churches were vandalised when Muslim youths rioted in Osogbo, Osun State, Nigeria on 28 November 2001. A mob of around a thousand angry youths flooded the streets of Osogbo after a Muslim preacher reportedly called on them, in a sermon given at midnight, to attack churches. Church leaders were forced to flee with their families as violent youths began breaking into one church building. Vehicles owned by Christians were also damaged. Two days after Sunday's death, four churches were vandalised when a mob took to the streets in a similar incident in Ilorin, Kwara State.

The attacks in Osogbo and Ilorin were most likely triggered by opposition to Christian festival and mission events that were due to take place in the two states in the following month.

O God, who never forsakest those that hope in thee; grant that we may ever keep that hope which thou hast given us by thy Word as an anchor of our souls, to preserve us sure and steadfast, unshaken and secure in all the storms of life; through Jesus Christ our Lord.
The Priest's Prayer Book (1864)

Be joyful in hope, patient in affliction, faithful in prayer. Romans 12:12

Ruslam and Arifin (2003)
Praying for Peace

On the evening of Saturday 29 November 2003 two Christians, Ruslam and Arifin, were murdered at a church service in Tabamawo, Central Sulawesi, Indonesia, where the worshippers were praying for peace just as Islamic militants descended on the building.

The militants fired their guns through the door and into the congregation as the service was closing. Ruslam and Arifin, both aged around 30 years old, were gunned down in front of their young families. Three other Christians were taken to hospital after the attack, suffering from gunshot injuries.

A few days after this incident, gunmen shot at the house of a Christian chief in the neighbouring Christian village of Tiwaa. Christian communities in parts of Indonesia frequently come under attack by Muslim militants.

Have mercy, O Lord, on all who have killed, robbed or destroyed Christians but go unpunished. Turn their hearts O Lord, and help them to repent. By the wounds of Christ, save them from the wounds of fruitless remorse. Give them instead that godly sorrow which leads to life. And may lives which have been slaves to evil become servants of love, through Jesus Christ our Lord. Amen.
Prayers for Today's Church (no. 91)

As he walked by the Sea of Galilee, he saw two brothers, Simon, who is called Peter, and Andrew his brother, casting a net into the lake—for they were fishermen. And he said to them, 'Follow me, and I will make you fish for people.' Immediately they left their nets and followed him.
Matthew 4:18-20 (NRSV)

Andrew (c. 60)
Fisher of People

Andrew was a Galilean fisherman, going about an ordinary day's work when Jesus called him to be an apostle. Without hesitating, Andrew and his brother Peter left behind the safety and familiarity of what they knew and embarked on an extraordinary journey following in Jesus' footsteps, ultimately to death.

Andrew is recorded as having preached the Gospel far and wide: in Scythia, Colchis, Greece, Epirus and Achaia. It is also reported that when he was crucified, he was tied to the cross rather than nailed. This was believed to have occurred at Patras in Achaia, on a cross in the shape of an X, called a saltire or decussate. An ancient writer wrote of the apostle's courage as he faced death and recorded his words:

O cross, most welcome and oft-looked for; with a willing mind, joyfully and desirously, I come to thee, being the scholar of Him who did hang on thee; because I have been always thy lover, and have longed to embrace thee!

Andrew hung on the cross for three days and continued to proclaim Christ, with the result that onlookers began to believe in Jesus and asked the governor that he should be taken down. The governor consented, but by the time Andrew was taken down, he had died.

No sacrifice can be too great to make for him who gave his life for me.
C T Studd (1860-1931)

Then Jesus came to them and said, "All authority in heaven and on earth has been given to me. Therefore go and make disciples of all nations, baptising them in the name of the Father and of the Son and of the Holy Spirit, and teaching them to obey everything I have commanded you. And surely I am with you always, to the very end of the age."
Matthew 28:18-20

Ansanus (304)
The Baptiser

Ansanus was born in Rome and decided to follow Christ at the age of 12. As a young man he was accused as a Christian to the Roman authorities by his own father, but for some time he managed to evade capture.

Ansanus became known by the title "the baptiser" because of his successful missionary activities in the Italian cities of Siena and Bagnorea.

During the persecution under Emperor Diocletian, Ansanus was eventually arrested and he was beheaded in 304 along with many other Christians. A church was later built upon the site of his execution.

Our Father in heaven, who spoke to Jeremiah, "Do not call yourself a child for you shall go to whatever people I send you," you have raised up many young witnesses to your name. We thank you for the courage of new generations of Christians and for the maturity of a young church. Grant that their zeal may warm the lukewarmness of our older Christianity and that we may all discern the power of the gospel to serve every generation; through Jesus Christ our Lord. Amen.
Prayers for Today's World (no. 101)

When they hurled their insults at him, he did not retaliate; when he suffered, he made no threats. Instead he entrusted himself to him who judges justly. 1 Peter 2:23

Joseph and Michael Hofer (1918)
Pacifists Penalised

In the summer of 1918, pacifist brothers Joseph, Michael and David Hofer, and their brother-in-law Jacob, were drafted into the US army. Because war went against their Christian beliefs, they objected, and were immediately arrested. The Hofers belonged to the Hutterites, a group of pacifist Christians that originated in 16th century Europe.

Following a court martial, they were sent to Alcatraz prison in San Francisco Bay where, for four months, they endured beatings and brutality before being transferred to Fort Leavenworth, Kansas. Here they suffered further, by being starved and chained for eight hours a day to the bars of their cells for two weeks. This harsh treatment took its toll and Joseph died at the end of November 1918. Soon after, on 2 December, Michael also died. David was immediately released in a desperate attempt by the authorities to prevent the brothers becoming martyrs in the public eye.

Jacob, who was not released until April 1919, wrote while in prison, "Why must only I continue to suffer? But then there is joy, too, so that I could weep for joy when I think that the Lord considers me worthy to suffer a little for his sake."

Let our mouth be filled with thy praise, O Lord, that we may sing of thy glory, for that thou hast counted us worthy to partake of thy holy, divine, immortal and life-giving mysteries: preserve thou us in thy holiness, that we may learn of thy righteousness all the day long. Alleluia, Alleluia, Alleluia.
Liturgy of John Chrysostom (c. 347-407) and Basil the Great (c. 330-79)

We remember before our God and Father your work produced by faith, your labour prompted by love, and your endurance inspired by hope in our Lord Jesus Christ. 1 Thessalonians 1:3

Hossein Soodmand (1990)
Faithful Pastor

"I am a follower of the great shepherd of the sheep, our Lord Jesus Christ, and I am ready to sacrifice my soul for my sheep. For me to escape from this persecution would cause the hearts of my flock to become cold and weak. And I never want to be a bad example for them. So I am ready to go to prison again and, if necessary, to give my life."

This was Hossein's response to the advice of an Iranian bishop that he should flee Iran, where his life was at risk as a convert from Islam to Christianity. He was the leader of a church that had been harassed and forced to close by the authorities, but Hossein continued to minister to the congregation, gathering them privately for teaching and encouragement.

In early 1990 Hossein was imprisoned, kept in solitary confinement and tortured. Churches campaigned for his release and after one month he was freed. It was at this point that Hossein was advised to leave Iran for his own safety, but he refused to abandon his flock.

Hossein was arrested again later in the year and given the choice either to renounce his Christian faith and the church he pastored, or else to be killed. He would not deny his faith so was hanged for apostasy under the sentence of a sharia court in Mashhad, Iran, on 3 December 1990. Hossein left a blind wife and four children. Cruelly, his wife was denied a last meeting with her husband before his death.

Hossein was actively involved in Christian ministry in Iran for 24 years before his martyrdom. His ministry included work for the Bible Society in Iran and also for the Christian Institute for the Blind, where he met his wife. Hossein was a fervent evangelist and became a church pastor, first in Isfahan and then in his home city of Mashhad. On several occasions he was told by Islamic mullahs to stop preaching Christ and return to Islam.

Lord, it belongs not to my care
Whether I die or live;
To love and serve Thee is my share,
And this Thy grace must give.

Christ leads me through no darker rooms
Than he went through before;
He that into God's kingdom comes
Must enter by this door.

My knowledge of that life is small,
The eye of faith is dim;
But 'tis enough that Christ knows all,
And I shall be with Him
Richard Baxter (1615-91)

December 4

By faith Moses ... chose to be mistreated along with the people of God
rather than to enjoy the fleeting pleasures of sin. He regarded disgrace for
the sake of Christ as of greater value than the treasures of Egypt, because
he was looking ahead to his reward. Hebrews 11:24a, 25-26

Japanese Christians (1623)
A Courageous Confession

On 4 December 1623, 50 Christians from Edo (now Tokyo) were taken to be burnt alive on slow fires. Among them were two ministers, who encouraged the others and proclaimed their faith to bystanders.

A Japanese nobleman was riding by and asked who the criminals were. When he was told they were Christians, he said that he also was a Christian and should be with them. His courage caused others to confess their faith in Christ and fall on their knees. The officers were afraid there would be a riot, so they hurried on the executions.

Among those who died were missionaries Jerome and Francis, and Simon Yempo, one of a number of Japanese Buddhist monks who had converted to Christianity.

Whatever sort of tribulation we suffer, we should always remember that its purpose is to make us spurn the present and reach out to the future.
John Calvin (1509-64)

December 5

If you love me, keep my commands. John 14:15

Crispina (304)
Obedient to Death

"I do observe an edict: that of my Lord Jesus Christ." This was the response of 4th century martyr Crispina when she was tried on the charge of not obeying the imperial edict to sacrifice to the gods for the welfare of the Emperor Diocletian. The proconsul Annius Anullinus tried to persuade her to change her mind and renounce her faith, but she refused.

Threats of death and shaming Crispina, a married mother of good position, by cutting off her hair failed to move her. So Anullinus, losing his patience, finally concluded, "We cannot put up with this impious Christian any longer."

The proceedings were read, and she died by the sword in the place of her birth, Numidia, North Africa, on 5 December 304. In his writing, Augustine of Hippo frequently praises Crispina as an obedient martyr who put God before other gods.

Eternal God, my sovereign Lord, I acknowledge all I am, all I have, is yours. Give me such a sense of your infinite goodness that I may return to you all possible love and obedience.
John Wesley (1703-91)

Let your light shine before others, so that they may see your good works and give glory to your Father in heaven. Matthew 5:16 (NRSV)

Evangeline Mataria (c. 1952)
Witness to the End

Evangeline, a Christian who lived on the north-east slope of Mount Kenya, was led to her death by her own brother, a member of the Mau Mau.

Following the death of her husband in 1949, Evangeline had taken over the care of his shop, which her brother wanted for himself. One day he said that he wanted to meet her to give her some profits from the shop, but it was a set-up, since he knew that members of the Mau Mau would be there to try to persuade her to take their oath.

When she was asked to swear their oath, Evangeline defiantly refused, "Never! The blood of Jesus has changed my life, and his blood can never be mixed with a goat's blood!" The Mau Mau were angered by this and pushed her out of the house, threatening to kill her. They tried to make her neighbour, Ezekiel Ntombogori, persuade her to take the oath, reminding her of her children. Evangeline, however, stood firm and entrusted her children to God's care.

Some of the Mau Mau then took her to the forest where she told them about Jesus' death on the cross and the offer of forgiveness. Her words touched two of them, who held back while the others led her to a grave, again threatening death if she did not take the oath. They tied her in a cloth and threw her to the ground. She called out to God to forgive them, at which point they strangled her and hurled her into the grave.

The two who had been moved by Evangeline's words also witnessed her victorious death; they deserted the Mau Mau and went to the British authorities to report the murder. Evangeline's neighbour Ezekiel also deserted and became a Christian. He and others confirmed to the police the names of Evangeline's killers, who were arrested, convicted and sentenced to death.

Heaven will pay for any loss we may suffer to gain it; but nothing can pay for the loss of heaven.
Richard Baxter (1615-91)

As servants of God we commend ourselves in every way; in great endurance; in troubles, hardships and distresses; in beatings, imprisonments and riots; in hard work, sleepless nights and hunger; in purity, understanding, patience and kindness; in the Holy Spirit and in sincere love.
2 Corinthians 6:4-6

Charles Garnier (1649)
Faithful Missionary

Charles was born in Paris in 1606, and in 1636 he went to Quebec to work among the native Americans as a missionary. He was stationed at a Huron tribal village, Saint-Jean, which was attacked by the Iroquois Indians, an association of several tribes, in 1649. Other missionaries fled but Charles stayed; at the time of his death, he was the only one left at the mission station.

On 7 December 1649 the enemy attacked as he was instructing his congregation on how to defend themselves and escape. Charles was shot down by musket fire but struggled to his feet and tried to reach a Huron who was dying. As he moved forward, an Iroquois killed him.

Charles' colleague wrote of him that "his very laugh spoke of goodness".

Lord, here I am, do with me as seems best in your own eyes; only give me, I beseech you, a penitent and patient spirit to expect you. Make my service acceptable to you while I live, and my soul ready for you when I die.
William Laud (1573-1645)

[Love] always protects, always trusts, always hopes, always perseveres. Love never fails. 1 Corinthians 13:7-8a

John and Betty Stam (1934)
Love for China

Two Chinese people gave their lives trying to save the Stams from death at the hands of the Communists.

The American missionary couple and their baby daughter Helen were captured by Communist soldiers in Tsingteh, Anhui Province, where the district magistrate had told them that there was no danger.

The soldiers left Tsingteh, taking the Stams with them. En route they considered killing the crying baby but an old farmer, one of the prisoners who had just been released to make room for the Stams, heard their conversation and protested. He was killed in her place. The Stams were then held in a house guarded by soldiers.

The next day, 8 December 1934, they were taken into the nearby town to be executed. On the way they stopped at the top of a hill where the town physician, Dr Wang, ran forward and asked the Communists to spare their lives. When it was discovered that he was a Christian, he was taken away to be killed. John began to plead for mercy for Dr Wang and at this moment one of the soldiers took his sword and killed John. Betty fell beside him and was also killed. Following their deaths, a Chinese evangelist called Lo arranged for the burial of the bodies and took care of their baby daughter. She was then taken to her grandparents, Dr and Mrs Charles E. Scott, who were in Shantung Province.

Betty had been brought up in China by her missionary parents and had felt God's call to go back during her time at Bible college in America. John also had a love for the people of China. They were married in Shanghai and the focus of their evangelistic work was in Tsingteh, Anhui Province, where they were captured.

"They have not died in vain. The blood of the martyrs is still the seed of the church. If we could hear our beloved children speak, we know from

their convictions that they would praise God because he counted them worthy to suffer for the sake of Christ."
Charles E. Scott, speaking of his daughter and son-in-law

Your word is a lamp for my feet, a light on my path... The wicked have set a snare for me, but I have not strayed from your precepts. Your statutes are my heritage forever; they are the joy of my heart. My heart is set on keeping your decrees to the very end. Psalm 119:105, 110-12

Kiroth's Brother (2008)
A Beloved Bible

During the brutal and sustained anti-Christian violence that broke out in Kandhamal, Orissa state, India, at Christmas 2007 (see December 24) and resumed in the latter part of 2008 (see August 25), Hindu extremists drove Christians out of at least 400 villages.

In December 2008 Christians in Bakingia village came under attack. As houses were set ablaze, the Christians fled to the jungle, but Kiroth and his brother decided to turn back to retrieve their beloved Bibles. Kiroth managed to rescue his badly burnt Bible and rejoin the other Christians hiding in the jungle, but his brother was caught by the attackers and hacked to pieces.

The Christians of Bakingia have struggled to rebuild their shattered community after the violence. They received compensation from the government and had started rebuilding the church that was destroyed by the extremists. But the work was brought to a standstill in October 2011 when over 400 radical Hindus descended upon the construction site; their leader claimed that the land belonged to their forefathers. The extremists chose the day of the Hindu festival of Dussehra, which signifies the victory of good over evil, to launch their assault on the church. They hoisted a saffron flag at the spot, an act that was interpreted by the Christians of Bakingia as an ominous threat.

God did not write a book and send it by messenger to be read at a distance by unaided minds. He spoke a Book and lives in His spoken words, constantly speaking His words and causing the power of them to persist across the years.
A W Tozer, *The Pursuit of God*

December 10

You shall have no other gods before me. You shall not make for yourself an image in the form of anything in heaven above or on the earth beneath or in the waters below. You shall not bow down to them or worship them; for I, the LORD your God, am a jealous God. Exodus 20:3-5a

Eulalia (304)
Teenage Martyr

Eulalia, one of Spain's most celebrated martyrs, was killed in Merida as a teenager in 304.

At the time of the Emperor Diocletian she was brought before a magistrate, Dacian, who tried to persuade her to give up her faith. She replied to his arguments very skilfully and spoke against the pagan gods. Dacian showed her torture instruments and said to her, "These you shall escape if you will touch a little salt and incense with the tip of your finger." But she trampled on the sacrificial cake and spat at the judge.

Greatly angered, he ordered her to be tortured and killed by burning. Following the torture, as she was burned, some fire caught her hair and surrounded her face and she was stifled by the fire and smoke.

Be Thou my Vision, O Lord of my heart;
Naught be all else to me, save that Thou art
Thou my best Thought, by day or by night,
Waking or sleeping, Thy presence my light.
Irish hymn c. 8th century
Translated by Mary E. Byrne (1880-1931)
Versed by Eleanor Hull (1860-1935)

*I remain confident of this: I will see the goodness of the LORD in the
land of the living. Wait for the LORD; be strong and take heart and
wait for the LORD.* Psalm 27:13-14

Indonesian Christians (2001)
Boat Attacks

Christians travelling by boat in Indonesia were targeted in two separate but very similar attacks in December 2001. At least ten were killed in the first incident on 11 December when the ferry *California* mysteriously exploded in a bay off Ambon Island. The ferry was transporting local Christians across the bay from Gudang Arang when the blast happened. Men on a passing speedboat were suspected of throwing a bomb into the vessel.

Then, on 19 December, gunmen opened fire from a speedboat on a vessel carrying eleven Christians who were on their way to a market. Nine of them were killed, one person escaped unharmed while the other was seriously injured. These attacks were believed to be the work of the Islamic extremist organisation Laskar Jihad.

*These have come out of the hardest oppression,
now they may stand in the presence of God,
serving their Lord day and night in His temple,
ransomed and cleaned by the Lamb's precious blood.*
Christopher Idle (born 1938)

I have become all things to all people, so that I might by any means save some. 1 Corinthians 9:22b (NRSV)

Antoine Aris van de Loosdrecht (1917)
Mission Minded

Dutch missionary Antoine is known for his work among the Toraja people of Celebes, Sulawesi, Indonesia. He became fluent in their tribal language, which endeared him to the Toraja people. His concern for them led Antoine to be critical of feudalism because of the way it exploited the ordinary people he lived among; this did not endear him to the feudal lords.

The feudal lords eventually rose up against the occupying Dutch authorities and Antoine was assassinated, ending a passionate Christian life that was devoted to Christ and the Torajas.

O God, who hast made of one blood all nations of men for to dwell on the face of the earth, and didst send thy blessed Son, Jesus Christ, to preach peace to them that are afar off, and to them that are nigh; grant that all the peoples of the world may feel after thee and find thee; hasten, O God, the fulfilment of thy promise to pour out thy spirit upon all flesh, through Jesus Christ our Lord.
George Cotton (1813-66)

Hark! the sound of holy voices
chanting at the crystal sea,
Alleluia, alleluia,
alleluia! Lord, to thee!
Multitude which none can number
like the stars in glory stands,
clothed in white apparel, holding
palms of victory in their hands.
Christopher Wordsworth (1807-85)

The peace of God, which transcends all understanding, will guard your hearts and your minds in Christ Jesus. Philippians 4:7

Bitrus Manjang (2002)
Peacemaker Killed

Three days before a thanksgiving service was due to take place in honour of the Reverend Bitrus Manjang, he was killed in an attack by Muslim extremists in the village of Rim, Plateau State, Nigeria, where he lived.

Ordained in 1969, Bitrus had taught for many years in the Church of Christ in Nigeria Bible School, becoming the vice president in 1992. Bitrus spent the final five years of his life working tirelessly for peace in the midst of sectarian fighting that was blighting the area. He housed Muslims who had been displaced by extremist violence, both in his own home and in the church in Rim. But his peace-making efforts did not save him and on 12 December 2002 he was shot dead outside his home along with his pregnant daughter-in-law, Victoria, and six-month-old grandson, Jessy. Bitrus' son Dan described him as "a man of peace who was loved by all".

As hundreds of Muslim extremists attacked Rim, these three were among 14 people who were killed with 20 more wounded; 70 houses were torched and many others were pulled down.

O Lord God, heavenly Father, who didst give up thine only-begotten Son into grief and sorrow, that we might have peace through him: grant us so surely to found our faith upon him alone that we may have peace in our souls. Quicken us with thy Word; grant already here on earth the peace which is a foretaste of the rest that remaineth for thy people. And while the cares and tumults of this life beset us round about, guide us in all our understandings by thy Holy Spirit, that we may abide in thy peace; through Jesus Christ our Lord.
Swedish Liturgy

The wicked are waiting to destroy me, but I will ponder your statutes.
Psalm 119:95

Peter of Alexandria (311)
Final Martyr

Peter was the last Christian to be put to death by the authorities in Alexandria during the final and most severe wave of persecution that took place under a succession of brutal Roman Emperors. As such he is referred to as the "Seal and Compliment of the Persecution" by the Coptic Church.

He was the bishop of Alexandria for 12 years, a role that he carried out in an exemplary manner. Church historian Eusebius described him as "an inspired Christian teacher ... a worthy example of a bishop, both for the goodness of his life and his knowledge of the Scriptures". Peter was arrested suddenly and unexpectedly in November 311, and then beheaded.

O God the Great and the Eternal, who formed man in incorruption, and death which entered into the world by the envy of the devil, you have destroyed, by the life-giving manifestation of your Only-Begotten Son, our Lord God and Saviour Jesus Christ. You have filled the earth with the heavenly peace, by which the hosts of angels glorify you saying, "Glory to God in the highest, peace on earth and good will toward men".
Coptic Liturgy

I will be glad and rejoice in your love, for you saw my affliction and knew the anguish of my soul. Psalm 31:7

Vietnamese Christians (2002) Worshippers Gassed

One December Sunday in 2002, over a hundred Christians in the Huoi Huong hamlet, Lai Chau Province, Vietnam, were gathered for worship. To their shock and amazement they were suddenly raided by the police and ordered to leave; they refused to do so, asserting their right to worship in freedom. The police responded by releasing gas into the congregation. Within moments most of the Christians were unconscious. Four small children died and three pregnant women lost their unborn babies. The entire congregation had to be taken to hospital.

This heartless attack is an example of the lengths to which the Vietnamese authorities will go in their efforts to eliminate Christianity in tribal areas. Other acts of intimidation have included killing pastors, closing churches and imprisoning church leaders.

Watch O Lord, with those who wake,
or watch, or weep tonight, and give your
angels charge over those who sleep.
Tend your sick ones, O Lord Christ.
Rest your weary ones.
Bless your dying ones.
Soothe your suffering ones.
Pity your afflicted ones.
Shield your joyous ones.
And for all your love's sake. Amen.
Augustine of Hippo (354-430)

He who began a good work in you will carry it on to completion until the day of Christ Jesus. Philippians 1:6

Rabindra Parichha, Saul Pradhan and Michael Nayak (2011) Indian Christian Leaders

On 16 December 2011, Rabindra Parichha became the third Indian Christian leader to be killed in Kandhamal district that year. The well-known Christian activist had formerly worked as a lay pastor, travelling to towns and villages in the area and discipling Christians in their faith. But at the time of his death he was working for a legal organisation that had formed in September 2008 to help victims of anti-Christian violence in Orissa state, the scene of widespread attacks by Hindu extremists that broke out in Kandhamal district at Christmas 2007 (see December 24).

A colleague described Rabindra as "a brave and fearless leader and a dynamic member of the team" who "provided support to many victims of communal violence." His murder, so close to Christmas, was interpreted by Sajan George, President of the Global Council of Indian Christians, as "a strategic move by extremists to create a climate of fear among Christians in Kandhamal." He said that it evoked memories of the "Black Christmas of 2007".

Two other Christian leaders had been killed in Kandhamal in 2011; in both cases, the authorities had tried to pass off the deaths as accidental, but it later transpired that the Christians had been murdered. Pastor Saul Pradhan was found dead on 11 January near a pond in the village of Pakal. Then on 26 July, Pastor Michael Nayak was killed in what appeared to be a road accident. Both men had been met by Hindus shortly before their deaths.

Come, let us join our friends above, who have obtained the prize,
And on the eagle wings of love to joys celestial rise.
Let saints on earth unite to sing with those to glory gone,
For all the servants of our King in earth and heaven are one.
Our spirits too shall quickly join, like theirs with glory crowned,

And shout to see our Captain's sign, to hear His trumpet sound.
O that we now might grasp our Guide! O that the word were given!
Come, Lord of Hosts, the waves divide, and land us all in Heaven.
Charles Wesley (1707–1788)

December 17

You have persevered and have endured hardships for my name, and have not grown weary. Revelation 2:3

Casper and Betsie Ten Boom (1944)
Place of Refuge

The Ten Boom family were dedicated Christians who used their home in Haarlem, Holland, to help anyone in need. During the Second World War it became a refuge for those hunted by the Nazis, notably Jews and members of the Dutch underground resistance movement. Casper Ten Boom and his daughters Betsie and Corrie risked their lives sheltering and caring for these fugitives; it is estimated that they helped to save 800 Jews.

In February 1944 the family was betrayed and the Nazi secret police, the Gestapo, raided their home; Casper, Betsie and Corrie were all arrested. The Gestapo were unable to find the four Jews and two members of the Dutch underground movement who were safely hidden behind a false wall in Corrie's bedroom. Nevertheless, the father and daughters were imprisoned. When Casper had been asked if he knew that he could die for helping the Jews, he replied, "It would be an honour to give my life for God's ancient people." That he did, dying after just 10 days in Scheveningen Prison at the age of 84.

In September 1944, Betsie and Corrie were transferred to the infamous Ravensbruck concentration camp near Berlin, Germany. They spent their time there sharing Jesus' love with their fellow prisoners, and many women became Christians because of their witness. On 16 December, Betsie died in Ravensbruck, aged 59.

Corrie survived and was released shortly afterwards. She realised her life was a gift and embarked on a world-wide preaching ministry; her book, *The Hiding Place*, which tells the family's remarkable story, became a best-seller. She preached forgiveness and reconciliation, saying, "There is no pit so deep that God's love is not deeper still" and, "God will give us the love to be able to forgive our enemies."

Come Thou long expected Jesus
Born to set Thy people free;
From our fears and sins release us,
Let us find our rest in thee.

Israel's strength and consolation,
Hope of all the earth Thou art;
Dear desire of every nation,
Joy of every longing heart.
Charles Wesley (1707-88)

December 18

He is the one we proclaim, admonishing and teaching everyone with all wisdom, so that we may present everyone fully mature in Christ. To this end I strenuously contend with all the energy Christ so powerfully works in me. Colossians 1:28-29

Saktinbai Usmanov (2005)
Threatened before Death

For many years Kyrgyzstan was a relatively free and safe place for Christians, at least in comparison with other countries in Central Asia. But in December 2005 Saktinbai, an indigenous Christian worker, was martyred for his faith in the village of Jety-Oguz.

Following his conversion from Islam to Christianity in 1990, Saktinbai had experienced harassment and threats from local Muslims. On one occasion, masked intruders burst into his home, held a knife to his throat and threatened to kill him if he did not return to the "faith of his ancestors".

Saktinbai lived on his own and was known for leading a small group of believers in the village. His body was found with numerous knife wounds and his head had been smashed in. At Saktinbai's funeral a huge anti-Christian crowd blocked the way as his body was taken to its burial place; a judge had to intervene to ensure the body was safely buried.

Grant us, O Lord, such boldness for thee, that we may set our faces as a flint and not be ashamed: but contending valiantly for the truth out of weakness we may be made strong and conquer in the fight; through Jesus Christ our Lord.
Wells Office Book

December 19

Not everyone who says to me, "Lord, Lord", will enter the kingdom of heaven, but only one who does the will of my Father in heaven. Matthew 7:21 (NRSV)

Volker (1132)
Pirate Raid

By the end of the 11th century, the Gospel had been taken to the whole area between Bohemia and the Baltic and 15 out of the 18 tribes had become Christian. The tribes, however, soon reverted to paganism and when in 1126 Albero, Bishop of Bremen, sent a missionary to the area there were no Christian buildings left. The missionary, whose name was Vicilien, built his first church in an area near a port that later became the city of Lübeck. He sent another minister, Lundmullus, to Siegeburg where he founded a monastery.

The missionaries were successful in making converts but their work was interrupted when pirates came to the area, attacking buildings and people. They especially targeted the Christians and many died. One of those killed was Volker, one of the monks in Siegeburg. He was described as "a brother of great simplicity" and was killed by the sword in 1132.

O God, who didst so love the world as to give Thine only-begotten Son, that whosoever believeth in Him should not perish, but have everlasting life: Look with compassion upon the [people] who know Thee not, and on the multitudes that are scattered as sheep having no shepherd; and so bestow upon us Thy grace, that we, with all thy believing people may be the messengers of Thy gospel, seek them that are lost, and restore them unto Thee; that they, being gathered out of all places whither they have wandered, may be strengthened, nurtured, protected and guided by the true Shepherd and Bishop of souls, Jesus Christ, Thy Son, unto Whom, with Thee and the Holy Ghost be honour and power, dominion and glory, world without end. Amen.

The Common Service book of the Lutheran Church, 1917

December 20

No one has power over the wind to restrain the wind, or power over the day of death. Ecclesiastes 8:8 (NRSV)

Alfonzo Lima (1996)
Prophesied Martyrdom

A couple of years after Alfonzo had begun his ministry as the pastor of a recently-formed church in Guatemala, he gathered his family around him and informed them that the Lord had told him that within three years he was going to be shot and killed, but would go to a place with a beautiful mansion. This prophecy was proved true as opposition to him and his church grew.

Alfonzo was already no stranger to persecution. Before he became the pastor of the church in 1992, he had been falsely accused by 15 local people who opposed the Christian witness of this new group of believers. They tried to get him imprisoned but the allegations were thrown out of court.

One night in December 1996, eleven men turned up outside his family home demanding that Alfonzo come out. When he refused, they proceeded to shoot at the building, at which point Alfonzo knew they were intent on killing him. Some days later seven men turned up at his house, broke in and dragged Alfonzo outside in front of his wife and children. After moments of panic his family escaped, but as Alfonzo walked away from the men, he was shot down. His family gathered around and heard him ask the Lord to forgive his murderers before he died.

If then we entreat the Lord that He would forgive us, we also ought to forgive; for we are before the eyes of our Lord and God, and we must all stand at the judgement-seat of Christ, and each man must give an account of himself.
Polycarp (martyred c. 155-56, see February 23)

December 21

Then Thomas (also known as Didymus) said to the rest of the disciples, "Let us also go, that we may die with him." John 11:16

Thomas (1st century)
"My Lord and my God"

Though Thomas came to be known as "doubting Thomas" because of his sceptical response to the news of Jesus' resurrection, at other times he displayed deep love and faith in the Lord. John records Thomas' understanding of what Jesus had come to do, and his willingness to share in His sufferings and to die. Thomas did indeed die for his Lord. And through Thomas, we learn about Jesus' compassion on those who doubt, as He graciously showed Thomas the evidence:

[Thomas] said to them, "Unless I see the nail marks in his hands and put my finger where the nails were, and put my hand into his side, I will not believe." A week later his disciples were in the house again, and Thomas was with them. Though the doors were locked, Jesus came and stood among them and said, "Peace be with you!" Then he said to Thomas, "Put your finger here; see my hands. Reach out your hand and put it into my side. Stop doubting and believe." (John 20:25b-27)

Thomas then worshipped the risen Lord. In the 6th century Gregory wrote, "By this doubting of Thomas we are more confirmed in our belief than by the faith of the other apostles."

According to tradition, it was Thomas who first took the Gospel to India, where he established seven churches in the south and converted over 13,000 people including two kings and seven village chiefs. He is believed to have been martyred near Mylapore, where Hindu priests killed him because he refused to worship the goddess Kali. The fruit of his evangelistic work in India has endured for two millennia.

Thomas said to him, "My Lord and my God!" Then Jesus told him, "Because you have seen me, you have believed; blessed are those who have not seen and yet have believed."
John 20:28-29

December 22

The Spirit and the bride say, "Come!" And let the one who hears say, "Come!" Let the one who is thirsty come; and let the one who wishes take the free gift of the water of life. Revelation 22:17

Eutychius (741)
Taken Captive

Roman nobleman Eutychius lived during the reign of Byzantine emperor Leo III, at the time when the empire was being attacked by invading Islamic forces. In this era the Christians suffered at the hands of both the emperor and the Muslims.

Eutychius was taken prisoner by the Muslim Arabs under the caliph and held in captivity for many months. Along with several other Christians he was put to death in Mesopotamia (modern Iraq) for refusing to renounce Christ in 741.

O come, O come, Immanuel
And ransom captive Israel,
That mourns in lonely exile here
Until the Son of God appear.
Rejoice, Rejoice! Immanuel
Shall come to thee, O Israel.

O come, Thou Day-Spring, come and cheer
Our spirits by Thine advent here;

Disperse the gloomy clouds of night,
And death's dark shadows put to flight.
Rejoice! Rejoice! Immanuel
Shall come to thee, O Israel.
Translated by John Mason Neale (1818-1866)

December 23

The apostles left the Sanhedrin, rejoicing because they had been counted worthy of suffering disgrace for the Name. Acts 5:41

Pak Eehum (1943)
"How am I worthy?"

Pak Eehum, a Chinese Christian, was among those who secretly met with Pastor Choo Ki-Chul (see April 13) in 1939 and promised to work for the abolition of shrine worship "to the end, even if it meant death". Eehum was harassed by the police but continued to preach against shrine worship. He was finally captured by the police in North China in 1940. When Eehum was tortured – bamboo splints were driven under his finger nails – he would cry, "Hallelujah to the Name of the Lord" and "How am I worthy?"

He was brought to trial on 3 February 1942 and sentenced to twelve years hard labour. Eehum's health suffered whilst serving this sentence in prison and he died some time in 1943 in the Mukden jail.

O Lord who hast promised a blessing for all who suffer for righteousness' sake: Grant to all our brethren persecuted for the truth that they may rejoice in being counted worthy to suffer dishonour for thy name.

Strengthen their faith and renew their love, that in their patience they may possess their souls and win their persecutors to penitence and new brotherhood in thee, for the sake of him who suffered shame and reproach and remained invincible in his love, even thy redeeming Son, Christ our Lord.

In His Name (no. 224)

The true light that gives light to everyone was coming into the world. He was in the world, and though the world was made through him, the world did not recognise him. John 1:9-10

Indonesian and Indian Christians (2000, 2007) Coordinated Attacks

While Christmas is a time of celebration for Christians in the West, for believers in other parts of the world it can signal danger and fear as their hostile neighbours step up persecution against them. This is exactly what happened on Christmas Eve 2000 when a series of around 20 coordinated blasts hit churches across cities in Indonesia; 19 Christians were killed and 120 were injured. Most of the bombs were planted in cars but some were sent as presents to church leaders. The terrorist group Jemaah Islamiyah, linked to al-Qaeda, carried out the attacks. Abu Bakar Baasyir, a leader of this group, was eventually tried and found guilty of involvement in the bombing campaign.

On 24 and 25 December 2007, Indian Christians were targeted by Hindu extremists, who launched a spate of violent but meticulously planned attacks in Kanhdamal District, Orissa State. Scores of churches were burnt to the ground, as well as hundreds of Christian homes. At least nine Christians were killed with many more injured as the attackers, who were armed with guns, knives, spears, home-made bombs and other weapons, rampaged through the area. They shouted slogans including: "Only Hindus to stay here – no Christians to stay here", "Christians must become Hindu or die" and "Kill Christians". The onslaught was followed by even more extensive violence and brutality between August and October 2008 (see August 25).

Heavenly Father, we pray that Your people throughout the world will be able to celebrate the birth of Your Son, our Saviour, in peace and freedom this Christmas. Protect them from those who would seek to harm them and give them hope for the year ahead. May their joy in Christ be a witness to all around them. Amen.

Suddenly a great company of the heavenly host appeared with the angel, praising God and saying, "Glory to God in the highest heaven, and on earth peace to those on whom his favour rests." Luke 2:13-14

Gideon Akaluka (1994)
Targeted by Extremists

In December 1994, a group of Muslims came to Gideon's home in Kano, Nigeria, and made the outrageous accusation that his family had desecrated the Quran by using a page from the book as toilet paper. They said that he should be punished with death for such an act, and appeared determined to see this was carried out.

Gideon, who was clearly being targeted because of his Christian faith, was taken into police detention and held in custody at Bompai prison. On 26 December a number of Muslims visited Gideon in prison and he was killed shortly afterwards. It is not clear whether or not the prison guards were complicit in Gideon's death but he was beheaded, and Muslim extremists then marched through the town triumphantly with his head on a pole. For a long time his family were not able to obtain the body for burial.

Yet with woes of sin and strife
The world has suffered long,
Beneath the angel-strain have rolled
Two thousand years of wrong;
And man, at war with man, hears not
The love-song which they bring:
O hush the noise, ye men of strife,
And hear the angels sing.
Edmund Hamilton Sears (1810–76)

While they were stoning him, Stephen prayed, "Lord Jesus, receive my spirit." Then he fell on his knees and cried out, "Lord, do not hold this sin against them." When he had said this, he fell asleep. Acts 7:59-60

Stephen (c. 35)
The First Martyr

Stephen is described in the book of Acts as "a man full of God's grace and power" who "performed great wonders and signs among the people" (Acts 6:8). His preaching of the Gospel brought him into conflict with Jews from his own Greek-speaking background. But those who argued with him "could not stand up against the wisdom the Spirit gave him as he spoke" (Acts 6:10). Consequently, they had him accused of blasphemy against Moses and God, had him brought before the Sanhedrin and produced false witnesses against him (Acts 6:11-14). Stephen gave a powerful speech (Acts 7), outlining the heritage of God's people rejecting His appointed leaders, and concluded fearlessly:

> You stiff-necked people! Your hearts and ears are still uncircumcised. You are just like your ancestors: You always resist the Holy Spirit! Was there ever a prophet your ancestors did not persecute? They even killed those who predicted the coming of the Righteous One. And now you have betrayed and murdered him – you who have received the law that was given through angels but have not obeyed it. (Acts 7:51-53)

This enraged the assembly, but Stephen was encouraged by an awesome vision of heaven opened and Jesus standing at the right hand of God. He was subsequently dragged out of the city and stoned. As they were killing him, Stephen, following the example of Christ, responded mercifully, praying that the Lord would not hold this sin against his murderers (Acts 7:54-60).

The martyr Stephen's eagle eye
could pierce beyond the grave;
he saw his master in the sky

and called on him to save.
By zealots he was stoned to death
and, as he knelt to pray,
he blessed them with his final breath –
who follows them today?
Reginald Heber (1783-1826)

Jesus, who was made lower than the angels for a little while, now
crowned with glory and honour because he suffered death, so that by the
grace of God he might taste death for everyone. Hebrews 2:9

Peter Yakovlevich Vins (1943)
Serving in Siberia

Peter was a minister of the Gospel in the 1930s in Siberia and eastern
Russia. He was first arrested in 1930 while he was involved in the assembly of the Russian Baptist Union in Moscow, and was sent to Svetlaya
Bay labour camp for three years. He was released in 1933 and went to live
in the town of Omsk. After working during the day, he would visit believers in the evening to teach and encourage them through Bible teaching,
despite Christian meetings being forbidden.

By 1936 there were 1,000 believers in Omsk. Peter was again arrested
and put on the fourth floor of Omsk prison where, for a while, his family
and friends could see him near a window until workmen came and covered over the windows. At some point Peter was taken to a closed camp
and forbidden contact with his family. He died on 27 December 1943,
aged 45.

He, the Wisdom, Word and Might,
God, and Son, and Light of Light,
Undiscovered by the sight
Of earthly monarch, or infernal spirit,
Incarnate was, that we might Heav'n inherit;
For He hath triumphed gloriously!
Cosmas the Melodist (died c. 760)

From that time on Jesus began to explain to his disciples that he must go to Jerusalem and suffer many things at the hands of the elders, the chief priests and the teachers of the law, and that he must be killed and on the third day be raised to life. Matthew 16:21

Innocent Children of Bethlehem (1ˢᵗ century) In Christ's Place

When told of Jesus' birth by the wise men, King Herod of Judea was filled with jealousy and fear because the King of the Jews had been born in his kingdom. He was then greatly angered by the wise men's failure to report the exact location of the young Messiah. He acted swiftly and ruthlessly in an attempt to protect his own position:

When Herod realised that he had been outwitted by the Magi, he was furious, and he gave orders to kill all the boys in Bethlehem and its vicinity who were two years old and under, in accordance with the time he had learned from the Magi. Then what was said through the prophet Jeremiah was fulfilled: "A voice is heard in Ramah, weeping and great mourning, Rachel weeping for her children and refusing to be comforted, because they are no more." (Matthew 2:16-18)

These deaths – considered martyrdoms because the little boys were the first people to die explicitly for Christ – are traditionally remembered on 28 December. God delivered Jesus from Herod's wrath by telling Joseph to take his family to Egypt. These children died in the place of Christ, just as He was to die in the place of them, and us, upon the cross.

O Christ, whose wondrous birth meaneth nothing unless we be born again, whose death and sacrifice nothing unless we die unto sin, whose resurrection nothing if thou be risen alone: raise and exalt us, O Saviour, both now to the estate of grace and hereafter to the state of glory; where with the Father and Holy Spirit thou livest and reignest, God forever and ever.
George Appleton (1902–93)

The LORD is a refuge for the oppressed, a stronghold in times of trouble.
Psalm 9:9

Wang Zhiming (1973)
Anti-Christian Revolution

Wang Zhiming was the pastor of a church in Wuding County in the Yunnan region of China during the Cultural Revolution of 1966-76, in which the authorities sought to eliminate religion from the country. Churches were closed, Bibles destroyed and Christians forced to meet in secret. Between 1969 and 1973 at least 21 Christian leaders in Wuding were detained; many of them were sent to camps, denounced or beaten. Zhiming was one of them; he was arrested, along with his wife and children, in May 1969 for criticizing the atheistic campaigns of the Red Guards. His wife was locked up for three years, two of his sons were detained for nine years and a third son reportedly committed suicide while in detention.

Zhiming was condemned to death and on 29 December 1973 he was publicly executed, aged 66, in front of a mass rally of around 10,000 people. The execution was intended to promote Chinese nationalism but led to riots among those who opposed such an act of cruelty.

In October 1980 Zhiming's name was "rehabilitated" by party officials and the following year a memorial to the martyr was erected in Wuding County. It is the only monument known to commemorate a Christian killed in the Cultural Revolution. At the bottom it reads, "As the Scripture says of the Saints, 'They will rest from their labours for their deeds follow them.'"

Take my life, and let it be
Consecrated, Lord, to thee;
Take my moments and my days,
Let them flow in ceaseless praise.

Take my love; my Lord I pour
At thy feet its treasure-store.

Take myself, and I will be
Ever, only, all for thee.
Frances R Havergal (1836-79)

You, Lord, are our Father. We are the clay, you are the potter; we are all the work of your hand. Isaiah 64:8

Charles de Foucauld (1916)
Caring Christian

In 1901, Charles, who was from Strasbourg, decided to set up a refuge in Algeria – a country he knew from serving there in the French army – where many people, including slaves, travellers, soldiers, the poor and sick, came to him. He worked there unassisted for some time before going to reach the Tuareg people, a proud and fierce tribe of the Ahaggar Mountains (also known as the Hoggar). He knew that a friend of his had been assassinated by them and he indicated in a letter that he expected the same might happen to him. Nevertheless, he set up a base at Tamanrasset, an isolated place up in the mountains. He received and helped many visitors, assisted only by Paul, a former slave whom Charles had helped to free.

In December 1916 a group of men from the Sanusiya Islamic Sufi order went to Tamanrasset. One evening, the Sanusiya attacked Charles in his home, took him outside and tied him up. A young boy guarded Charles whilst the men raided the house. Paul witnessed events that followed; he told how some movement that Charles made caused the boy guard to panic and shoot Charles in the head.

A Muslim friend who heard about his death wrote, "Charles ... has died not only for all of you, he has died for us, too. May God have mercy on him, and may we meet him in paradise". Some time afterwards the work that Charles had established was re-started by others.

My Father, I abandon myself to you. Do with me as you will. Whatever you may do with me I thank you. I am prepared for anything. I accept

everything, provided your will is fulfilled in me and in all creatures. I ask for nothing more, my God. I place my soul in your hands. I give it to you, my God, with all the love of my heart, because I love you. And for me it is a necessity of love, this gift of myself, this placing of myself in your hands without reserve in boundless confidence, because you are my Father.
Charles de Foucauld (martyred 1916)

December 31

Now to him who is able to do immeasurably more than all we ask or imagine, according to his power that is at work within us, to him be glory in the church and in Christ Jesus throughout all generations, for ever and ever! Amen. Ephesians 3:20-21

Nikolai Khmara (1963)
From Alcoholic to Martyr

Before he became a Christian at the age of 45, Nikolai, from Siberia, was well known in his community as an alcoholic who was often in trouble with the police. But after he converted, his life was turned around and he became an active witness for Christ.

Within six months he was arrested, along with three others, for religious activities and for not conforming to the Communist Statutes of the official All-Union Council. He was put on trial at the end of Christmas 1963 and sentenced to three years in prison. But two weeks later his body was returned to his wife; he had been severely tortured and had died as a result.

For us this is the end of all the stories... But for them it was only the beginning of the real story. All their life in this world ... had only been the cover and title page: now at last they were beginning Chapter One of the Great Story, which no one on earth had read, which goes on forever, and in which every chapter is better than the one before.
C S Lewis (1898-1963), *The Last Battle*

Select Bibliography

Akkara, Anto *Shining Faith in Kandhamal* (Bangalore, India, 2009).

Ambushed by Love: God's Triumph in Kenya's Terror compiled by Dorothy W Smoker (Fort Washington, PA, 1994).

Anderson, Gerald H (ed.) *Biographical Dictionary of Christian Missions* (New York, 1998).

Anglican Evangelical Group Movement *The Splendour of God: Prayers and Devotions for Private and Corporate Use* (London, 1948).

Appleton, George *In His Name: Prayers for the Church and the World* (London, 1956).
——— *Journey for a Soul* (Glasgow, 1974).

Arnold, Duane & Hudson, Robert *Beyond Belief: What the Martyrs Said to God* (Grand Rapids, MI, 2002).

Attwater, Donald & John, Catherine Rachel *The Penguin Dictionary of Saints* (3rd edition, London, 1995).

Banerjee, Brojendra Nath *Religious Conversions in India* (New Delhi, 1982).

Bergman, Susan (ed.) *A Cloud of Witnesses: 20th Century Martyrs* (London, 1998).

Blair, William & Hunt, Bruce *The Korean Pentecost and the Sufferings which Followed* (Edinburgh, 1977).

The Book of a Thousand Prayers compiled by Angela Ashwin (Grand Rapids, MI, 2002).

The Book of Saints compiled by The Benedictine Monks of St Augustine's Abbey, Ramsgate (London, 1921).

Booth, Ken (ed.) *For All the Saints* (Hastings, New Zealand, 1996).

Bridges, Erich & Rankin, Jerry *Lives Given, Not Taken* (Richmond, VA, 2005).

Briggs, G W & Dearmer, Percy (eds.) *The Daily Service* (revised edition, London, 1947).

Broomhall, Marshall (ed.) *Martyred Missionaries of the China Inland Mission* (London, 1901).

Brother Kenneth *Saints of the Twentieth Century* (revised edition, London, 1987).

Bunyan, John *The Pilgrim's Progress* (reprinted London, 2008).

Carter, T T *Treasury of Devotion* (reprinted Charleston, 2008).

Chandler, Andrew (ed.) *The Terrible Alternative: Christian Martyrdom in the Twentieth Century* (London, 1998).

Cho, Paul Yonggi *The Fourth Dimension* (New Jersey, 1979).

Christian History Institute at http://christianhistoryinstitute.org [accessed 27 April 2021]

Church of the Province of New Zealand *A New Zealand Prayer Book* (Glenfield, 1997).

The Churchpeople's Prayer Book (Monmouth, 1935), at http://justus.anglican.org/resources/bcp/Wales/Churchpeoples/index.html [accessed 27 April 2021]

Colquhoun, Frank (ed.) *Contemporary Parish Prayers* (London, 2005).
——— *Parish Prayers* (London, 1967), at https://newscriptorium.com/
parish-prayers/ [accessed 27 April 2021]
——— *Parish Prayers* (London, 1996).

Daily Prayer compiled by E Milner-White & G W Briggs (London, 1941).

Daily Strength for Daily Needs compiled by Mary Wilder Tileston (New York, 1928).

DC Talk & Voice of the Martyrs *Jesus Freaks* (Guildford, 2000).
——— *Jesus Freaks Vol II* (Minneapolis, 2002).

Dehqani-Tafti, H B *The Hard Awakening* (London, 1981).

A Dictionary of Saints compiled by Donald Attwater (London, 1938).

Diskin, Esther & Joyce, Marie "'It was just the highest calling": Beach's Korean community mourns Samaritans' brutal deaths in Russia', *The Virginian Pilot*, Friday March 31, 1995, at http://scholar.lib.vt.edu/VA-news/VA-Pilot/issues/1995/vp950331/03310534.htm [accessed 27 April 2021]

Elliot, Elizabeth *Shadow of the Almighty* (London, 1958).

Ellis, James J *John Williams of the South Sea Islands* (1889? reprinted Kilmarnock, 2014).

The Encyclopedia of Prayer and Praise compiled & edited by Mark Water (Alresford, 2004).

Farmer, David *The Oxford Dictionary of Saints* (5th edition, Oxford, 2003).

For All the Saints: Prayers and Readings for Saints' Days compiled by Stephen Reynolds (Toronto, 1994).

Foxe, John *Foxe's Christian Martyrs of the World* (reprinted Chicago, nd).

Freeman, J J & Johns, D *A Narrative of the Persecution of the Christians in Madagascar* (London, 1840).

Greene, Barbara & Gollancz, Victor *God of a Hundred Names* (London, 1962).

Hassiotis, Ioannis K 'The Armenian Genocide and the Greeks: Response and Records (1915-23)', in Richard G Hovannisian (ed.) *The Armenian Genocide: History, Politics, Ethics* (London, 1992), pp.129-151.

Hefley, James & Marti *By Their Blood: Christian Martyrs from the Twentieth Century and Beyond* (Grand Rapids, MI, 2004).

The Hodder Book of Christian Prayers compiled by Tony Castle (London, 1986).

Howse, Christopher (ed.) *Prayers for this Life* (London, 2005).

Jackson, Dave & Neta *The Complete Book of Christian Heroes* (Wheaton, IL, 2005).

Kévorkian, Raymond *The Armenian Genocide: A Complete History* (London, 2011).

Langridge, A K *Won by Blood: The Story of Erromanga the Martyr Isle* (London, 1922).

Lewis, C S *The Chronicles of Narnia* (reprinted London, 2002).
——— *God in the Dock* (reprinted London, 1998).
——— *A Grief Observed* (reprinted London, 1966).
——— *Mere Christianity* (reprinted London, 2011).
——— *The Problem of Pain* (reprinted London, 2002).
——— *The Weight of Glory* (reprinted Grand Rapids, MI, 2001).

The Lion Book of Famous Prayers compiled by Veronica Zundel (Tring, 1983).

Littledale, Richard Frederick & Vaux, James Edward (eds.) *The Priest's Prayer Book* (London, 1864).

Maier, Paul L *Eusebius: The Church History* (Michigan, 1999).

Marshall, Paul & Gilbert, Lela *Their Blood Cries Out* (Dallas, TX, 1997).

Milner-White, Eric (ed.) *After the Third Collect* (London, 1952).

Morgan, Robert J *On This Day* (Nashville, 1997).

The New Encyclopedia of Christian Martyrs compiled by Mark Water (Grand Rapids, MI, 2001).

The New Encyclopedia of Christian Quotations compiled by Mark Water (Alresford, 2000).

Newell, Marvin J *A Martyr's Grace* (Chicago, 2006).

Noble, Philip D *The Watkins Dictionary of Saints* (London, 2007).

Paul, Rajaiah D *They Kept the Faith* (Lucknow, 1968).

Peers, E Allison *Fool of Love: The Life of Ramon Lull* (London, 1946).

The Prayer Manual compiled by Frederick B Macnutt (4th edition, London, 1968).

Prayers for Use at the Alternative Services compiled by David Silk (London, 1980).

Praying with the Martyrs compiled by Duane Arnold (London, 1991).

Purcell, William *Martyrs of Our Time* (London, 1983).

Schaeffer, Francis A, Bukovsky, Vladimir & Hitchcock, James *Who is for Peace?* (Nashville, TN, 1983).

Seasons of Devotion: 365 Bible Meditations to Guide You Through the Year compiled by Phillip Law (London, 2005).

Shea, Nina *In the Lion's Den* (Nashville, TN, 1997).

Sikorska, Grazyna *A Martyr for the Truth: Jerzy Popieluszko* (London, 1985).

Singh, Jyotsna 'Indian Christians demand protection', *BBC News*, Monday 12 June 2000, at http://news.bbc.co.uk/1/hi/world/south_asia/788155.stm [accessed 27 April 2021]

Sookhdeo, Patrick *With the Eye of Faith* (Vienna, VA, 2020).

Streams in the Desert compiled by Mrs Charles E Cowman (reprinted Michigan, 1974).

Thompson, Phyllis *Minka and Margaret* (Sevenoaks, 1978).

Topping, Frank *The Words of Christ* (Guildford, 1983).

Tozer, A W *The Pursuit of God* (reprinted Milton Keynes, 2004).

Tucker, Angeline *He is in Heaven* (New York, 1965).

Tutu, Desmond *An African Prayer Book* (London, 1995).

United Lutheran Church *Common Service Book of the Lutheran Church* (Philadelphia, 1917).

Vaporis, Nomikos Michael *Witnesses for Christ: Orthodox Christian Neomartyrs of the Ottoman Period, 1437-1860* (Crestwood, NY, 2000).

Various Letters, Pamphlets and Reports of the Church Missionary Society and others working along the Borders of Afghanistan between 1850 to 1950.

Violence against Christians in the Year 2002 compiled by J G Orban de Lengyelfalva (s'-Hertogenbosch, 2003).

Violence against Christians in the Year 2003 compiled by J G Orban de Lengyelfalva (s'-Hertogenbosch, 2004).

Wells Office Book (Wells, 1929).

The Westminster Collection of Christian Prayers compiled by Dorothy M Stewart (Louisville, KY, 2002).

Williams, Dick (ed.) *More Prayers for Today's Church* (Eastbourne, 1991).
—— *Prayers for Today's Church* (Eastbourne, 1993).
—— *Prayers for Today's World* (Eastbourne, 1993).

Williams, William *Christianity among the New Zealanders* (Edinburgh, 1989).

The Wisdom of Saint Augustine compiled by David Winter (Oxford, 1997).

Zwemer, Samuel, *The Law of Apostasy in Islam* (London 1924).

Index of Martyrs

Abbodi, Yousif Adil 106
Abdi, Madobe 86-87
Abdon... 219
Acacius 101-02
"Adauctus" 250
Adurkwa, Ousman and Moussa 17
Agape 71-72
Agnes... 33
Ahmed, Osman Sheik 287
Ahmer, Naimat................................. 65
Aitolos, Kosmos 127-28
Akaluka, Gideon 365
Alam, Noor 40
Alban..182-83
Alexander 88
Alfina... 309
Ali, David Abdulwahab Mohamed ... 123
Alice (child)..................................... 173
Allen, Ancel Edwin 271
Alphege 28
Amador, Manuel............................... 201
Ananias.. 56
Anastasios... 44
Andrew 340
Andronicus 47
Angelo 136
Anjum, Javaid 144-45
Ann (Karen Christian) 166
Ansanus 341
Antipas 112
Antoninus....................................241-42
Apollonia................................... 52, 315
Apollonius 122-23
Aransi, Sunday 338
Arifin 339
Aron 196
Asgedom, Mehari Gebreneguse 283
Assadullah, Maulawi 181-82
Atkin, Joseph 270
Atwater, Lizzie 235
Aurea 25
Aydin, Necati................................... 120

Ayyad, Rami 286
Babar, Shamoun 107-08
Bacabis, Greg.................................... 267
Bagtasos, Severino 41
Baizar, Anwar 87-88
Baker, Mary Elizabeth.................303-04
Bakut, Musa and Alexander 147
Barbasymas... 26
Barnabas 171-72
Barsabas... 56
Barsabba'e, Simeon 117
Bartholomew 260-61
Beckel, Kristi 265
Bello, Clement Ozi............................ 151
Benjamin, Metropolitan 251
Berikjesu 99-100
Bessareb, Sergei 24-25
Bhatti, Sabir John 328-29
Bhatti, Shahbaz 73-74
Blandina 276
Blood, Henry (Hank) 274
Bobai, Aniyo.................................... 151
Bonhoeffer, Dietrich................7, 109-10
Boutros, Taher Saadallah 311-12
Brown, Shawn C. 265
Browning, Sydney R......................... 265
Buganda martyrs 164
Burton, Elizabeth 205
Butras, Rafah Toma Alkass................ 15
Bwede, Sunday Gyang.................126-27
Carleson, Nathaniel.......................... 190
Cecilia... 319
Chalmers, James 111
Chanel, Pierre.................................. 103
Chat, Manzoor Ahmad 210-11
Chickira, Paul.................................. 151
Chionia.......................................71-72
Chittilappilly, Job............................. 248
Choo Ki-Chul 114
Chou Wen-Mo.................................. 161
Christian, Ishak 290
Christina... 213

Christodoulos	217	Eulalia	350
Chrysostomos	257-58	Eulogius of Cordoba	82-83
Clarke, Mildred	68	Euplius	232
Claverie, Pierre	242-43	Eutychius	362
Columba	21	Evans, Philip, Sue and their 3 children	183-84
Concordia	95	Fathi, George	300-01
Concordius of Spoleto	23	Felicitas	129-30
Cosmas	288	Felicity	78
Coy, Juan	291	Felix	250
Crispin	293	Ferrel, Irene	36
Crispina	345	Fisher, Mary	183-84
Crispinian	293	Flavian	184
Cyprian	264	Fleming, Peter	22
Dabak, Nathan	126-27	Foucauld, Charles de	370
Dahan, Sabah Yacob	58	Francis (missionary to Japan)	344
Daniel, K.	154	Gachigi, Gadson and Rebeka	14
Daniels, Jonathan	237	Garnier, Charles	347
Das, Hemanta	321	George (d. 1515)	54
Davies, Winnie	157	George (d. 1437)	96
Daw Aye Nyein	166	George (d. 303)	124
Daw Pwa Sein	166	George (Egyptian convert)	4
Daw Sein Thit	166	George, Wissam	58
Dehqani-Tafti, Bahram	137	Geronimo	268
Demetrios	115	Geske, Tilman Ekkehart	120
Dennis of Paris	202	Gikonyo, Edmund	317
Desiderius	153	Girgis, Noshi	113
Dibaj, Mehdi	203	Gitau, Reuben	107
Diiriye, Ahmed "Goode"	244	Glover, Florence Constance	304-05
Dogari, Isma	119	Goehring, Harry	179-80
Donan	118	Gordon, George and Ellen	150
Edirisinghe, Neil	61	Gordon, James	150
Edward, Rabia	87-88	Green, Barbara	87-88
Ekka, Vijay	168	Griffin, Cassandra	265
Eldred, Annie	235	Gu Xianggao	128
Eleutherius	202	Gumesindus	25
Elias, Rayan Salem	58	Habib, Ezzat	298
Elizabeth, Grand Duchess	208-09	Habil	121
Elliot, Larry and Jean	85	Habta, Senait	51
Elliott, Jim	22	Hambroeck, Antonius	42
Emanuel, Daniel	107-08	Hameed (family)	221
Emmanuel, Rashid and Sajid	200	Hannington, James	307-08
Ennis, Joseph D.	265	Hanskamp, Minka	90-91
Epagathus. Vettius	35	Hapalla, Gregorio	267
Ethan, Esther	170	Harman, Muriel	157

Hassan, Shamimu Muteteri............... 191

Hazim and Amal............................... 163

Hdago, Mariam 131

Hedlund, Mina.................................. 190

Heine, Carl 167

Hewitt, John 27

Hilda (Karen Christian) 166

Hofer, Joseph and Michael 342

Hussein, Sayid Ali Sheik Luqman ....
193-94

Ia 224

Ida 309

Ignatius of Antioch 3, 296-97

Im, Pastor 277

Iqbal, Tahir 209-10

Irenaeus 187-88

Irene 71-72

Ishak, Pastor and family 290

Isma'il, Ziwar Muhammad 60

Israel, Gerges 337

Israel, Goda 210-11

Issa, Ashur Yacob............................. 132

Ixida, Antony.................................... 263

Jacob, Arkan Jehad 132

Jagerstätter, Franz 229

James the Just 43

James's family, Pastor (Nigeria).............. 6

Jerome (missionary to Japan)............. 344

Jiang Zongxiu 178-79

Joasaphat 306-07

John 186

John the Baptist................................ 249

John, Esther...................................45-46

Johnson, Paul and Priscilla 130

Jonah 99-100

Jones, Susan Kimberly 265

Julia of Carthage............................... 152

Justin Martyr 162

Kadah, Ishaya and Selina.............126-27

Kalphas, Ahmed................................ 134

Kanamuzeyi, Yona 38

Kang Enyoung................................305-06

Karim, Abdul................................146-47

Kattan, Akram.................................. 238

K'eh-t'ien-hsuen................................ 205

Ken, Paul Za.................................210-11

Kereopa 30

Khan, Mehr 80

Khan, Nasrullah................................ 223

Khan, Nazr Ullah 241

Khanam, Raheela.............................. 216

Khmara, Nikolai 371

Kiflom, Mogos Hagos 283

Kiflom, Teklesenbet Gebreab 283

Kilian.. 197

Kim.. 318

King, Annie 205

Kouame, Raphael Aka...................... 159

K'pa Lot 81

Kratz, Mildred.............................313-14

Kuksha.. 247

Kukumba, Mark 164

Kuzhikandum, George 168

Labib, Ayman Nabil 295-96

Lai Manping 100

Lawrence 230

Lee Youghee 312-13

Leggett, Chris 174-75

Leocritia 86

Leonides 75-76

Lima, Alfonso 360

Loosdrecht, Antoine Aris van de....... 352

Lopez, Moises Alean.......................... 71

Lucian of Antioch 39

Lucius... 184

Lull, Raymond................................... 48

Lundgren, Anton and Elsa 235

Luwum, Janani 59

Lynn, Roy, Joyce and Pamela........183-84

Ma Tin Shwe 166

MacMillan, Hector........................... 334

Maigari, David 151

Mandloli, Vipin................................ 294

Manihera 30

Manjang, Bitrus, daughter-in-law Victoria
and grandson Jessy....................... 353

Manuel 252

Marcellus (d. 178)............................. 255

Marcellus (d. 298)............................. 310
Mardy, Liplal 218
Marinus 74-75
Mark...108-09
Masemola, Manche 64
Masih, Ashish Prabash 174
Masih, Aslam 259-60
Masih, Bantu 175-76
Masih, Irfan (boy)............................. 104
Masih, Irfan (guard) 282
Masih, Irshad.................................... 97
Masih, Ishtiaq.................................. 140
Masih, Mukhtar 16
Masih, Samuel................................. 158
Masrul, Teuku...............................76-77
Massabki, Francis, Abdel-Mohti and
    Raphael.. 199
Mataria, Evangeline 346
Matthew.. 320
Maurus, Victor 139
Maximilian 92
Maximus......................................170-71
McCallum, John 141
McCann, Peter, Sandra and Joy....183-84
McChesney, Bill 157
McConnell, George, Isabella and Kenneth....
    205
McCully, Ed 22
McDonnall, David 85
McKee, Stewart.................................. 173
Mehr, Haik Hovespian 31
Menn, Alexander........................258-59
Metoka, Aiechoa, Mukhlos and Basem58
Metrus 315
Michelian, Tateos 191-92
Miki, Paul.. 46
Mina.. 322
Mitrophan (Chi-Sung)..................... 169
Mizeki, Bernard...........................177-78
Mohammed, Mansuur...................... 273
Moltke, Helmuth James Graf von 29
Montanus 184
Morgan, Margaret 90-91
Mosesa, Tula..................................72-73

Moussad, Magdi Ayad...................... 220
Mukasa, Joseph............................... 326
Munir, Fatukhi 58
Mup.. 246
Murmu, Ravi 133
Mutairi, Fatima al- 239
Naik, Kamalini and son 245-46
Namukubalo, Francis........................ 272
Nayak, Michael................................ 356
Nerses.. 323
Nestor.. 69
Nikolsky, Gregory............................ 187
Nodrad, Zia 93
Nur, Ahmadey Osman...................... 273
Odintsov, Nikolai Vasilyevich 316-17
Olsen, Betty Ann..........................274-75
Orjih, George 2, 198
Pak Eehum 363
Pak Kwanjoon.................................. 84
Pancras 143
Parichha, Rabindra 356
Patteson, John Coleridge 270
Paul (apostle)................................37-38
Paul (d. c.362).................................. 186
Peregrinus.. 148
Perez (family) 149
Perez, Gustavo Hernandez 285
Perpetua... 78
Peter (apostle)...................... 3-4, 188-89
Peter of Alexandria 354
Peterson, Ernst 190
Philip (apostle) 325
Philip of Heraclea........................302-03
Phocas the Gardener 212
Picken, Catherine 183-84
Pierre 214
Polycarp.. 66
Pontoh, Roy.................................... 32
Popieluszko, Jerzy 299
Pothinus 261-62
Pradhan, Saul.................................. 356
Pro, Miguel...................................... 333
Probus... 47
Procopius... 269

Puasa, Alexander 83
Quinta 315
Rafaralahy... 62
Rahho, Paulos Faraj.......................79-80
Raj, K. Isaac...................................... 154
Ramos, Aurelio Gomez 285
Rasalama 234
Ray, Justin M. 265
Rehman, Naveed ul-.......................... 227
Rifai, Jamil Ahmad al-...................... 138
Rodger, Jim....................................... 157
Romero, Oscar..............................94-95
Roy, Hridoy 125-26
Rugarama, Yusuf................................ 164
Ruiz, Emmanuel................................. 160
Ruslam... 339
Rusticus 202
Sabas the Goth 50
Sabih, Wassim 311-12
Sadd, Alfred....................................... 231
Sadoth 63
Saint, Nate... 22
Saleh, Safwat Zakher Saleh 155
Salib.. 5
Sanctus 165
Santiz, Miguel 285
Saune, Romulo 255-56
Sawan, Jameel.................................... 327
Schenck, Ella Mary 254
Scillitan martyrs................................ 177
Scott, Philip....................................... 253
Searell, Edith 190
Seko, Adamu 151
Semere, Magos Solomon 51
Sennen.. 219
Seruwanga, Noah................................ 164
Servusdei 25
Shmael, Ramsin.................................. 58
Simpson, William E 185
Sixtus... 226
Smith, John 49
Sohn Yangoon 280
Soodmand, Hossein........................... 343
Staines, Graham, Phillip and Timothy .. 34

Stam, John and Betty.......................... 348
Stamatios... 228
Stephen 366
Stevens, Jane...................................... 68
Sulaymaan, Sulaymaan Mahamed 244
Suleimanov, Artur.............................. 204
Susanna 262
Sysoev, Daniil 329-30
Taing, Chhirc 102
Tak Myong-Hwan........................314-15
Tantray, Bashir Ahmad...................... 332
Tapiedi, Lucian.............................211-12
Tarachus 47
Tarik, Ayad 301
Taroaniara, Stephen........................... 270
Tarore 294-95
Taylor, Cyril....................................... 157
Ten Boom, Casper and Betsie ..7, 357-58
Theodore of Amasea 256-57
Theresia... 309
Thomas (apostle)............................... 361
Thomas, Robert Jermain 236
Timothy 19
Tinulele, Susianty............................... 207
Toma, Zia 58
Tombiling, Helmy (Mrs) 207
Tongin 279
Tongsin.. 279
Topno, Ajay 266
Tori, Ghorban 324
Trophimus 56
Tylee, Arthur and Marian.............313-14
Ullah, Assad 227
Usmanov, Saktinbai 358-59
Valentine.. 57
Venard, Theophane 6
Victor 184
Victor of Marseilles 328
Vins, Peter Yakovlevich 367
Vitus.. 336
Voan, Minh Tinh................................ 102
Volker 359
Wafi, Raghada al-..........................311-12
Wallayat, Ali 141

Wang Zhiming 369
Wangechi, Mary 225
Watson, Karen 85
Whitchurch, Emily 190
White, Wendy 183-84
Williams, John 330
Wilson, William Millar, Dr and Mrs .. 68
Witherall, Bonnie Penner 331
Wormsley, Kristen 87-88
Xasan, Liibaan Ibraahim 91-92
Xuseen, Xaaji Maxamed 105
Yakubu, Sabo 198

Yan Weiping 144
Yelda, Samir 243
Yempo, Simon 344
Yi Ki-Poong 233
Young, John and Sarah 205
Youderian, Roger 22
Yuksel, Ugur 120
Yusefi, Mohammad Bagher 278
Zhang Xiuji 156
Zhizhilenko, Michael 195
Zhou Dian Yu 284

Index of Dates

This index contains the death dates for the Christians included in this book. Some of the dates are only approximate.

4 BC 368
30 249
35 366
50-100 361
52 325
60 .... 320, 340
61 171-72
62 43
64 .... 95, 188-89
66-67 56
67 37-38
68 108-09
70 260-61
92 112
97 19
107 .... 3, 296-97
155-56 66
165 162
177 .... 35, 165, 261-62, 276
178 .... 23, 255
180 177
185 122-23
2nd century 129-30
202 75-76

203 78
249 .... 52, 315
250 .... 170-71, 202
251 .... 69, 88
258 .... 226, 230, 264
259 184
261 148
262 74-75
269 57
283 288
295 .... 92, 262
298 310
3rd century 182-83, 293, 319, 328
303 .... 124, 139, 212, 219, 269, 322, 336
304 .... 47, 71-72, 143, 187-88, 232, 250, 302-03, 341, 345, 350
305 33
306 256-57
311 354
312 39
320 67
327 99-100
341 117
345 63

346 26
360 224
362 186
372 50
373 323
4th century 101-02, 213, 241-42
439 152
523 335
607 153
618 118
632 263
689 197
741 362
850-59 25
853 21
859 .... 82-83, 86
1012 28
1113 247
1132 359
1220 136
1315 48
1437 96
1515 54
1536 306-07
1569 268
1597 46
1623 344
1649 347
1655 44
1661 42
1680 228
1682 134
1777 217
1779 127-28
1801 161
1803 115
1824 49
1836 294-95
1837 234
1838 62
1839 330
1841 103
1846 30
1857 141

1860 .... 160, 199
1861 .... 6, 150
1866 236
1871 270
1872 150
1885 .... 307-08, 326
1885-87 164
1894-1923 194-95
1896 177-78
1898 254
1900 ... 68, 169, 173, 190, 205, 235, 304-05
1901 111
1906 146-47
1908 .... 223, 241
1909 116-17
1915 80
1916 370
1917 352
1918 .... 187, 208-09, 342
1918-19 89
1922 .... 251, 257-58
1927 333
1928 64
1930 313-14
1931 195
1932 185
1933 121
1934 348
1937 316-17
1942 .... 27, 166, 211-12, 231, 233, 253
1943 .... 229, 318, 363, 367
1944 .... 114, 167, 357-58
1945 .... 29, 84, 109-110, 312-13
1948 279
1950 .... 280, 305-06
1950-53 .... 1, 180-81
1951 277
1952 .... 130, 346
1953 .... 14, 225, 317
1954 .... 107, 131, 149
1956 .... 22, 271
1957 291
1959 214
1960 45-46

1963 371	1999-2001 142
1964 .... 36, 38, 303-04, 334	2000 .... 168, 174, 220, 281, 364
1965 237	2001 .... 53, 145-46, 151, 222, 284, 308,
1966 179-80	338, 351
1967 157	2002 .... 70, 83, 87, 192-93, 275, 331,
1968 274-75	353, 355
1970 215	2002-03 206
1973 369	2003 ... 60, 77, 125-26, 138, 170, 292, 339
1975 .... 90-91, 102	2004 .... 16, 24-25, 70, 85, 128, 144-45,
1977 59	158, 178-79, 181-82, 207, 227, 248
1978 183	2005 .... 97, 107-08, 154, 218, 238, 243,
1980 .... 94-95, 137	287, 298, 309, 324, 358-59
1983-2005 98	2006 .... 113, 301, 332
1984 299	2007 .... 51, 120, 163, 191, 210-11, 266,
1988 93	286, 294, 321, 364
1990 .... 258-59, 343	2007-08 .... 106, 245-46
1992 .... 65, 135, 147, 175-76, 209-10,	2008 .... 61, 72-73, 76-77, 79-80, 123,
255-56, 267	193-94, 239, 246, 273, 349
1993 100	2009 .... 2, 104, 140, 174-75, 198, 221,
1994 .... 31, 71, 91-92, 144, 191-92, 196,	282, 300-01, 329-30
203, 244, 314-15, 365	2010 .... 18, 51, 58, 81, 86-87, 126-27,
1995 .... 155, 201, 285, 337	133, 200, 204, 272, 311-12
1996 .... 41, 105, 156, 242-43, 278, 290,	2010-11 283
360	2011 .... 6, 13, 15, 73-74, 119, 132, 159,
1997 .... 20, 55, 216	259-60, 289, 295-96, 327, 356
1998 .... 40, 328-29	2011-12 17
1999 .... 32, 34, 252, 265	

Index of Places

The countries listed are the places where the Christians included in this book were martyred. For ease of reference, they appear according to their contemporary location, e.g. martyrdoms in Gaul are listed under France, and those in Asia Minor under Turkey.

Afghanistan 146-47, 181-82, 223, 227	Bulgaria 96
Albania 127-28	Burma 166
Algeria 48, 92, 242-43, 268, 345, 370	Cambodia 102
Armenia 67, 323	Canada 347
Bangladesh 125-26, 179-80, 218	China 68, 100, 121, 128, 144, 156, 169,
Brazil 313-14	173, 178-79, 185, 190, 205, 235, 284,

304-05, 318, 348, 363, 369
Colombia.............. 71, 149, 201, 252, 291
Cyprus 171-72
Democratic Republic of Congo ... 36, 157,
303-04, 334
Ecuador 22
Egypt. 4-5, 13, 18, 52, 55, 75-76, 108-09,
113, 135, 155, 220, 289, 295-96, 298,
300-01, 315, 322, 354
El Salvador 94-95
Eritrea 51, 283
Ethiopia.................................72-73, 320
Futuna Island.................................... 103
France...........35, 148, 152, 153, 165, 202,
255, 261-62, 276, 293, 328
Germany............7, 29, 109-110, 197, 229,
357-58, 359
Greece 44, 71-72, 115, 217, 224,
302-03, 340
Guatemala 360
Guyana 49
Holy Land... 43, 74-75, 88, 124, 206, 249,
269, 286, 366, 368
India 34, 133, 141, 145-46, 154,
168, 174, 210-11, 245-46, 248, 260-61,
266, 294, 321, 332, 349, 356, 361, 364
Indonesia 32, 53, 76-77,
83, 142, 192-93, 207, 253, 290, 292,
309, 339, 351, 352, 364
Iran 31, 63, 99-100, 117, 137,
191-92, 203, 278, 324, 343
Iraq 15, 26, 58, 60, 79-80, 85, 106, 132,
163, 238, 243, 301, 311-12, 362
Italy 3-4, 23,
33, 37-38, 56, 57, 95, 122-23, 129-30,
136, 139, 143, 162, 170-71, 186, 188-
89, 213, 219, 226, 230, 232, 250, 262,
296-97, 319, 336, 341
Ivory Coast....................................... 159
Japan...............................27, 46, 263, 344
Kenya........... 14, 107, 131, 225, 317, 346
Kiribati 231
Korea (exact location unknown) ...312-13
Kyrgyzstan.....................................358-59

Latvia.. 89
Lebanon 138, 160, 331
Libya...................................177, 184, 264
Madagascar................................. 62, 234
Marshall Islands 167
Mauritania...................................174-75
Mexico...............................271, 285, 333
Morocco 310
Netherlands 7, 357-58
New Zealand 30, 294-95
Nigeria...... 2, 6, 17, 70, 119, 126-27, 147,
151, 170, 198, 338, 353, 365
North Korea 84, 114, 236, 305-06
Pakistan 16, 40,
45-46, 65, 73-74, 80, 87, 93, 97, 104,
107-08, 140, 144-45, 158, 175-76,
200, 209-10, 216, 221, 241, 259-60,
275, 282, 308, 327, 328-29
Papua New Guinea....... 111, 211-12, 253
Peru 255-56
Philippines.....................41, 77, 222, 267
Poland... 299
Romania 50
Russia 187, 195, 204, 208-09, 247,
251, 258-59, 316-17, 329-30, 367, 371
Rwanda... 38
Saudi Arabia.............................. 239, 335
Senegal 214
Serbia.....................................54, 187-88
Sierra Leone 254
Solomon Islands 270
Somalia................86-87, 91-92, 105, 123,
193-94, 244, 273, 287
South Africa 64
South Korea 1, 9, 161, 180-81, 233, 277,
279, 280, 314-15
South Sudan 98, 215
Spain 21, 25, 82-83, 86, 350
Sri Lanka.. 61
Sudan.................................98, 196, 337
Syria 199, 241-42
Taiwan 42
Tajikistan 24-25, 281
Thailand 90-91, 130

Tunisia 78

Turkey 39, 47, 66, 69, 101-02, 112,
116-17, 120, 134, 194-95, 212, 228,
256-57, 257-58, 288, 306-07, 325

Uganda 20, 59, 164, 191, 272, 307-08, 326

UK 28, 118, 182-83

USA 237, 265, 342

Vanuatu 150, 330

Vietnam 6, 81, 246, 274-75, 355

Zimbabwe 177-78, 183

Index of Bible references

Genesis 50:20 98

Exodus 20:3-5a 350

Exodus 22:20 187

Leviticus 19:18 275

Deuteronomy 1:17b 132

Deuteronomy 4:39 269

Deuteronomy 6:5 229

Deuteronomy 8:3 232

Deuteronomy 10:12 112

Deuteronomy 13:4 310

Deuteronomy 31:7b, 8a 311

Deuteronomy 33:27a 203

Joshua 1:9b 71

Ruth 1:16 166

1 Samuel 12:16 144

2 Chronicles 14:11b 72

Job 19:25-26 83

Job 23:10 258

Job 36:15 276

Psalm 2:11 302

Psalm 4:1a 187

Psalm 4:8 190

Psalm 5:11 133

Psalm 9:9 369

Psalm 9:18 109

Psalm 10:16-18a 160

Psalm 11:7 145

Psalm 16:9-11 198

Psalm 18:2a 205

Psalm 18:5-6 214

Psalm 24:1 142

Psalm 27:1 .... 239, 289

Psalm 27:3 113

Psalm 27:4 317

Psalm 27:10 64

Psalm 27:13-14 351

Psalm 31:7 355

Psalm 33:1 256

Psalm 34:4-5 304

Psalm 34:14-16 326

Psalm 37:18 92

Psalm 37:39 81

Psalm 40:11 257

Psalm 42:2 15

Psalm 42:10-11 173

Psalm 45:6 56

Psalm 46:1-2 22

Psalm 54:3-4 303

Psalm 56:1-4 279

Psalm 56:10-11 62

Psalm 62:5-6 76

Psalm 69:7-8 239

Psalm 69:13-14 97

Psalm 73:3, 16-18 40

Psalm 79:11 51

Psalm 81:9-10 23

Psalm 90:10 170

Psalm 90:12 235

Psalm 91:2,5 292

Psalm 92:12 130

Psalm 94:22 308

Psalm 103:1-4 328

Psalm 116:1-4 253

Psalm 116:15 313

Psalm 116:16 152

Psalm 118:8-9 29

Psalm 119:11 25

Psalm 119:15-16................................. 294

Psalm 119:51 148

Psalm 119:66 264

Psalm 119:95 354

Psalm 119:105, 110-112 349

Psalm 119:161 153

Psalm 121:3-4..................................... 248

Psalm 130:1-2..................................... 116

Psalm 138:3 312

Psalm 139:7-10................................... 193

Psalm 139:16b 287

Proverbs 2:8 327

Proverbs 3:5-6 174

Proverbs 11:18 334

Proverbs 12:28 255

Proverbs 14:26a 119

Proverbs 15:33 247

Proverbs 20:24a 167

Proverbs 22:6...................................... 129

Proverbs 29:10 125

Proverbs 29:25 197

Proverbs 31:8-9 94

Ecclesiastes 7:14 281

Ecclesiastes 8:8 360

Ecclesiastes 8:12 215

Song of Solomon 8:6 95

Isaiah 7:9b 335

Isaiah 9:6b 42

Isaiah 9:7 194

Isaiah 35:9-10..................................... 222

Isaiah 41:10 184

Isaiah 42:6 291

Isaiah 51:11 90

Isaiah 53 45

Isaiah 53:4-5 187

Isaiah 55:8 135

Isaiah 55:10-11................................... 271

Isaiah 63:8 44

Isaiah 64:8 370

Jeremiah 1:7b-8 218

Jeremiah 15:16b.................................. 265

Jeremiah 31:3.. 57

Lamentations 3:22-24 221

Lamentations 3:32-33 144

Ezekiel 34:11-12 227

Daniel 3:17-18 213

Hosea 13:14b...................................... 285

Joel 2:13b.. 115

Malachi 2:6.. 202

Malachi 3:16.. 270

Malachi 3:17b, 18 47

Matthew 2:16-18................................. 368

Matthew 4:18-19................................. 188

Matthew 4:18-20................................. 340

Matthew 5:5 298

Matthew 5:10 272

Matthew 5:11 158

Matthew 5:12 251

Matthew 5:14 91

Matthew 5:16 346

Matthew 5:44-45a................................ 30

Matthew 6:14-15................................. 280

Matthew 6:19-21................................. 288

Matthew 6:24a 318

Matthew 7:13b-14............................... 321

Matthew 7:16-17................................. 195

Matthew 7:21 359

Matthew 8:15 95

Matthew 9:9-13 320

Matthew 10:7 210

Matthew 10:16-17............................... 161

Matthew 10:18-20............................... 101

Matthew 10:22 58

Matthew 10:28 .... 197, 224

Matthew 10:34-36............................... 123

Matthew 10:38-39............................... 196

Matthew 11:11 249

Matthew 11:15 93

Matthew 14:3-11................................. 249

Matthew 16:15-18............................... 189

Matthew 16:18b 278

Matthew 16:21 368

Matthew 16:24-25.........................1, 7, 8

Matthew 16:25 163

Matthew 16:26a 296

Matthew 18:20 128

Matthew 19:29 216

Matthew 24:14 207
Matthew 25:34b 74
Matthew 26:39a 17
Matthew 28:18-20.............................. 341
Mark 6:17-28 249
Mark 6:20b 249
Mark 8:34 69
Mark 10:29-30 45
Mark 10:38 4
Mark 11:25 331
Mark 13:9 255
Mark 13:10 252
Mark 14:50 3
Mark 14:51-52 108
Luke 1:66b 249
Luke 1:76-77 249
Luke 2:13-14 365
Luke 3:16a 249
Luke 6:27b-28 212
Luke 6:35 174
Luke 6:37b 141
Luke 9:22 219
Luke 10:20b 86
Luke 12:4-5 18
Luke 12:6-7 206
Luke 12:8 96
Luke 12:51-52a, 53 337
Luke 21:12-13 234
Luke 21:17-19 191
Luke 22:54-62 189
Luke 23:34a 120
Luke 24:48 9
John 1:5 107
John 1:9-10... 364
John 1:29b-34 250
John 1:45-46 325
John 1:45-49 261
John 1:47b 261
John 4:35 183
John 6:5-6... 325
John 6:40 300
John 7:17 103
John 8:31b-32 260
John 8:35-36 49

John 9:4 246
John 10:11 323
John 10:12-15 28
John 11:16 361
John 11:25 63
John 12:23-25 2
John 12:24-25 332
John 12:25-26 4
John 12:26 106
John 12:32 266
John 13:16 102
John 14:1-3 324
John 14:6 21
John 14:8-9 325
John 14:15 345
John 14:27 13
John 15:5 107
John 15:13 2
John 15:16b 185
John 15:20 322
John 15:21 55
John 16:20 315
John 16:33b 126
John 18:11 4
John 20:25b-27 361
John 20:28-29...................................... 362
John 21:18-19........................... 188, 189
Acts 2:23-24 282
Acts 4:20 299
Acts 4:29 146
Acts 4:36-37 171
Acts 5:41 363
Acts 6:8 366
Acts 6:10 366
Acts 6:11-14 366
Acts 7 366
Acts 7:51-53 366
Acts 7:54-60 366
Acts 7:59-60 366
Acts 10:34b-35 84
Acts 11:23-24 172
Acts 12:3 .... 109, 189
Acts 13:5b 172
Acts 13:44b... 172

Acts 13:49 172
Acts 15:7 189
Acts 15:12 171
Acts 15:37-39 109
Acts 17:24-25 122
Acts 20:24 150
Acts 23:11 9
Acts 26:14b-16 233
Romans 1:16 295
Romans 3:23-24 100
Romans 5:7-8 182
Romans 5:21 175
Romans 6:5 117
Romans 6:16 268
Romans 8:17 177
Romans 8:18 290
Romans 8:24b-25 105
Romans 8:31 104
Romans 8:35-37 259
Romans 8:38-39 245
Romans 11:33-36 338
Romans 12:1 82
Romans 12:12 339
Romans 12:14 46
Romans 12:17-19 136
Romans 14:4b 228
Romans 14:8 238
Romans 14:9 243
Romans 15:13 38
1 Corinthians 1:18 140
1 Corinthians 1:23 16
1 Corinthians 1:25 24
1 Corinthians 1:27-28 50
1 Corinthians 1:42-44a 118
1 Corinthians 2:1 9
1 Corinthians 3:11 220
1 Corinthians 4:3-5 200
1 Corinthians 7:23 277
1 Corinthians 9:22b 352
1 Corinthians 9:24-25 329
1 Corinthians 12:12, 26 250
1 Corinthians 13:7-8a 348
1 Corinthians 15:31 7
1 Corinthians 15:54-55 138

1 Corinthians 15:57 127
2 Corinthians 1:3-5 263
2 Corinthians 1:6 319
2 Corinthians 1:9-10 305
2 Corinthians 1:21 186
2 Corinthians 2:14 180
2 Corinthians 4:5 267
2 Corinthians 4:8-9 211
2 Corinthians 4:11 191
2 Corinthians 4:16 274
2 Corinthians 4:17 71
2 Corinthians 4:18 31
2 Corinthians 5:7 85
2 Corinthians 5:8 85
2 Corinthians 5:9 41
2 Corinthians 5:14 2
2 Corinthians 5:15 59
2 Corinthians 6:4-6 347
2 Corinthians 7:4b 262
2 Corinthians 10:3-4 131
2 Corinthians 10:5 162
2 Corinthians 11:23b-28 37
Galatians 1:10 236
Galatians 2:7 189
Galatians 2:20a 294
Galatians 3:26-28 78
Galatians 6:14 111
Ephesians 1:3-4 301
Ephesians 2:4 320
Ephesians 2:6 333
Ephesians 2:8-9 168
Ephesians 2:21-22 151
Ephesians 3:7 217
Ephesians 3:8 179
Ephesians 3:16-19 20
Ephesians 3:20-21 371
Ephesians 4:14-15 284
Ephesians 5:1-2 137
Ephesians 6:10-11 328
Ephesians 6:12 124
Ephesians 6:13 32
Philippians 1:6 356
Philippians 1:12-14 307
Philippians 1:20-21 37

Philippians 1:27-28 65
Philippians 1:29 54
Philippians 2:5 254
Philippians 2:7-8 208
Philippians 2:10-11 306
Philippians 2:13 286
Philippians 2:15b-16a 170
Philippians 2:17 139
Philippians 3:7-9a 26
Philippians 3:10 159
Philippians 3:13b-14 293
Philippians 3:18 89
Philippians 4:4 27
Philippians 4:7 353
Philippians 4:11b 75
Philippians 4:13 68
Colossians 1:6 121
Colossians 1:28-29 358
Colossians 3:1 316
Colossians 3:2 242
Colossians 3:13b 34
Colossians 3:23-24 336
Colossians 4:5 154
1 Thessalonians 1:3 343
1 Thessalonians 5:16-18 164
1 Timothy 1:18b-19 237
1 Timothy 4:10 77
1 Timothy 4:12 143
1 Timothy 4:12-13 19
1 Timothy 6:12 73
1 Timothy 6:18-19 230
1 Timothy 6:20 19
2 Timothy 1:7 19
2 Timothy 1:12 283
2 Timothy 2:2 261
2 Timothy 2:8b-10a 178
2 Timothy 2:11b-13 209
2 Timothy 2:21 330
2 Timothy 3:10-11 88
2 Timothy 3:12-13 156
2 Timothy 4:2 .... 19, 314
2 Timothy 4:6-8 48
2 Timothy 4:11 108
2 Timothy 4:18 201

Titus 1:15 33
Titus 2:7a, 8b 231
Titus 3:7 120
Hebrews 2:9 367
Hebrews 3:6 149
Hebrews 3:14 165
Hebrews 4:12 39
Hebrews 10:23 80
Hebrews 10:32b, 36 79
Hebrews 11:13, 16 70
Hebrews 11:24a, 25-26 344
Hebrews 11:36-38a 226
Hebrews 12:1 8
Hebrews 12:1-3 223
Hebrews 12:14 147
Hebrews 13:5b 86
James 1:2-4 43
James 1:12 114
James 2:18 177
James 4:14 60
1 Peter 1:3 157
1 Peter 1:6-7 52
1 Peter 1:8-9 225
1 Peter 2:13-15 134
1 Peter 2:19 169
1 Peter 2:20b-21 99
1 Peter 2:23 342
1 Peter 3:17 155
1 Peter 4:1-2 61
1 Peter 4:12-16 189
1 Peter 4:19 36
1 Peter 5:10-11 179
2 Peter 2:9 192
1 John 1:7b 44
1 John 3:16 67
1 John 3:21 241
1 John 4:8 35
1 John 4:18 273
1 John 5:4 204
1 John 5:11 181
1 John 5:12 244
Revelation 2:3 357
Revelation 2:8a, 10 66
Revelation 3:21 241

Revelation 6:9...9
Revelation 6:9-11 6
Revelation 7:9-10 87
Revelation 7:9-17 6
Revelation 7:14b.............................309
Revelation 13:10.............................199

Revelation 17:6.......................................9
Revelation 19:7-8a, 9b.........................14
Revelation 20:4.......................................9
Revelation 21:4.....................................53
Revelation 22:17.................................362

Index of Quotations

This index contains the authors of the quotations that finish each day's reading.

Abelard, Peter.....................................120
Adams, Sarah F...........................104-105
Afra of Augsburg.................................60
African Christian..............................184
After Prayers of 1585 213
After the Third Collect 133, 302
Alcuin...65-66
Alexander, Cecil Frances 159
Alfred the Great, King 29
Alternative Service Book, The 36, 207
American Prayer Book 287
Anabaptist Martyrs' Hymn 52
Apollonius 59-60
Appleton, George 276, 368
Aquinas, Thomas...............................165
Arcadius of Caesarea 102
Augustine of Hippo...... 19, 43, 81-82, 95, 123, 130, 236, 263, 278, 313, 355
Baker, Henry Williams.......................180
Baring-Gould, Sabine 16, 124-125, 164, 186
Basil the Great (liturgy).....................342
Baxter, Richard 344, 346
Bede, The Venerable....... 38-39, 196, 329
Benedict...277
Bennett, Sanford Fillmore.................181
Bernard of Clairvaux 219, 281
Bernard of Cluny..............................156
Bernard of Morlaix.........33, 76, 136, 163
Bode, J. E..268
Bonar, Horatius 44, 92-93, 166-167

Bonhoeffer, Dietrich..........................110
Book of Common Prayer 18, 118, 167
Book of Hours.....................................242
Booth, William...................................112
Boris of Kiev.......................................161
Brainerd, David 92, 243
Bray, Billy 178
Briggs, G. W.......................................200
Bright, William 153, 321
Broomhall, Marshall......................68-69
Bunyan, John 75, 179, 209, 285
Byrne, Mary E....................................350
Calvin, John...........................69, 144, 345
Cameron, W. 310
Capillas, Francis de............................103
Carmichael, Amy.............. 17-18, 72, 314
Caswell, Edward.................................219
Celtic Prayer...71
Chambers, Oswald 117
Chapman, Rex.............................315-316
Cherry, Edith Gilling 22-23
Chinese Christian (prayer) 235-236
Chinese Student's Prayer.....................49
Christudas (from Kandhamal)...........246
Chrysostom, John (liturgy)................342
Church of South India (prayer). 154, 322
Churchpeople's Prayer Book, The............311
Clarke, Carlisle..............................56-57
Clement of Alexandria 8, 113
Clement of Rome 115

Columba.. 194

Colquhoun, Frank 75, 202, 267, 282

Colson, Charles 49

Common Service Book of the Lutheran Church, The 96, 359-360

Compline, Eastern Orthodox Church 258

Contemporary Parish Prayers 256

Coptic Liturgy.................................... 354

Coptic Liturgy of St Basil 135

Cosmas the Melodist......................... 367

Cotton, George 352

Coverdale, Miles........................ 222, 319

Cowper, William 24, 227-228, 279

Cox, Frances Elizabeth........... 89-90, 245

Dabney, R. L.. 11

Daily Prayer 146

Daily Service, The 315

Dialogue of Caesarius, The................... 286

Dix, William C..................................... 70

Dodd, C. H. 255

Donne, John 57

Duffield, George 169

Eastern Church (prayer)..................... 136

Eastern Orthodox Prayer.......... 140, 288

Edwards, Jonathan...................... 145, 291

Elliot, Elisabeth................................. 275

Elliot, Jim 76, 149, 221, 290-291

Erasmus.. 269

Everest, C. W. 241

Farnham Hostel Manual 246-247

Fleet, Andrew..................................... 224

Flint, Annie Johnson .. 100-101, 121-122

For All the Saints (Canada)...... 46-47, 160, 253, 325

For All the Saints (New Zealand) 270, 295, 326

Foucauld, Charles de 370-371

Francis, Samuel.................................. 183

Frere, W. H... 177

Gadsby, W. 107

Gardiner, Allen.................................... 28

Gairdner, Temple............................... 229

Gaunt, Alan................................. 14, 266

Gaunt, Howard Charles Adie.... 112, 202

Glover, Florence 305

Gothic Missal....................................... 46

Graham, Billy 157, 170

Greek Orthodox Prayer..................... 128

Gurnall, William 328

Hall, Joseph 317

Hamilton, John.................................. 111

Hampson, William 130, 223, 283

Havergal, Frances R...................369-370

Heber, Reginald.. 139, 234, 261, 366-367

Henry, Matthew 138

Herbert, George 25-26

Hicks, George 334

Hill, Raymond...................................... 21

Hooker, Herman 271

Hosmer, F. L....................................... 176

How, W. Walsham 9-10, 77-78, 103-104, 282

Hsieh Ping-Hsin 129

Hughes, Selwyn................................... 15

Hull, Eleanor..................................... 350

Ibaim, Akanu..................................... 193

Idle, Christopher 351

Ignatius of Antioch 3, 27, 297

Imam, Nagla al-................................. 191

In His Name 235-236, 276, 303, 363

Ingemann, Bernhardt S. 16, 186

Ioannikios, St..................................... 258

Irenaeus of Lyon............................... 212

Ironside, Henry Allan............... 187, 259

Isaac of Syria 58, 132

Jaffray, Robert.................................... 336

Jewel, Bishop John............................ 100

Joannikios. *See* Ioannikios, St

Jonas of Beth-Iasa 83

Justin Martyr 162

Kao Chun-Ming 173

Kempis, Thomas à 64

Kierkegaard, Soren 148

King, Jr., Martin Luther 237

Kingsley, Charles 61

Knox, John.................................. 63, 323

Krishna, Paul 168

Langridge, A. K................................. 150

Laud, William 217, 347
Law, Philip 97
Law, William 260
Lewis, C. S. 39, 62, 95, 331, 371
Livingstone, David 293
Loewenstern, Matthaeus A. von.289-290
Lucian of Antioch 55
Luther, Martin.......... 16, 67, 83, 137, 301
Malay Christian Song 91
Manz, Felix....................................... 294
Maronite Shehimto 40-41
Martyn, Henry 284, 321
Matheson, George...........7-8, 54-55, 225
McCheyne, Robert Murray 216
Merriam, George Spring 51
Messenger, John A............................... 67
Milner-White, Eric 97, 200
Moody, Dwight L............................... 204
More Prayers for Today's Church... 130, 223, 283
Mother Teresa 175
Mozarabic Prayer............................... 26
Muller, George 47
Murray, Andrew 201
Mutairi, Fatima al- 239-240
Neale, John Mason 33, 38-39, 76, 120, 136, 163, 196, 220, 318, 329, 362-363
Nelson, Horatio....................38, 109, 172
Nemesian... 30
New Zealand Prayer Book.................... 151
Newman, John Henry 106
Newton, John 233, 265, 272, 309
Odintsov, Nikolai Vasilyevich 317
Origen of Alexandria............................ 3
Orthodox Prayer............................... 308
Papylus of Thyateira 197
Parish Prayers 20, 32, 33, 105, 118, 123, 133, 146, 153, 154, 163, 177, 184, 186, 214, 228-229, 267, 282, 287, 302, 315, 330
Pascal, Blaise...................................... 196
Patrick of Ireland.............................. 248
Penn, William.......................... 212, 333
Pierson, Arthur Tappan 50

Piper, John 85
Polycarp...................................... 66, 361
Popieluszko, Jerzy 299-300
Prayer 13, 42, 134, 195, 211, 215, 238, 252, 262, 306, 312, 324, 364
Prayer (14th century)......................... 131
Prayer for the Year 2000 99
Prayer from Ghana 197
Prayer from the Middle East.............. 79
Prayer of a Muslim Convert 86
Prayers for Today's Church 339
Prayers for Today's World 218, 341
Prayers of the Worldwide Church.......... 231
Primer of 1559.................................... 224
Priest's Prayer Book, The..................... 338
Puritan Prayers ("Sleep").................... 171
Pusey, Philip 289-290
Quecha Hymn.............................290-291
Quirinus of Siscia 81
Rauschenbusch, Walter 182
Richard of Chichester......................... 148
Ridley, Nicholas................................ 232
Rodigast, Samuel.............................. 199
Ryle, J. C.. 31
Sabas the Goth 87
Sapulete, Rony...............................53-54
Schaeffer, Francis...........................84-85
Schenk, Heinrich Theobald....89-90, 245
Schweitzer, Albert 155
Scott, Charles E..........................348-349
Searell, Edith..................................... 190
Sears, Edmund Hamilton.................. 365
Seraphim of Sarov 35
Simeon's Prayer................................. 117
Simon of Seleucia 188
Simpson, William............................. 185
Singh, Sadhu Sundar........................ 174
Smith, J. Danson 126
Sookhdeo, Patrick............................. 108
Spafford, Horatio Gates 243-244
Spurgeon, C. H............77, 262, 264, 332
St Mark's Church, Bedford (prayer) ..114
Staines, Gladys 34
Stratford, Bishop 275

Strauss, Lehman 141
Studd, C. T. 340
Swedish Liturgy 353
Syrian Orthodox Daily Office Book ...40-41
Syrian Orthodox Liturgy 88-89
Tauler, Johann 80
Taylor, Hudson 103
Taylor, Rachel Annand 2
Teerstegen, Gerhard 94
Temple, William 304
Ten Boom, Corrie 210, 254
Teresa of Avila 142
Tertullian 9, 203-204
Thelica of Abitine 143
Theodota of Philippopolis 152
Theodotus of Ancyra 127
Toke, Emma Leslie 301-302
Tolstoy, Leo 250
Toplady, A. M. 281
Topping, Frank ... 247, 273, 298, 307, 337
Tozer, A. W. 350
Treasury of Devotion 226

Turner, Kevin 25
Tutu, Archbishop Desmond 74
Uganda Martyrs' Hymn 164
Venard, Theophane 6, 124
Vicars, Captain Hedley 88
Wako, Gabriel Zubeir 99
Watchman Nee 119
Watson, William 3
Watts, Isaac 42, 73, 158, 198, 230, 310
Wells Office Book 359
Wesley, Charles .. 206, 252, 356-357, 358
Wesley, John 147, 345
Westcott, Bishop 192
Williams, John 331
Williams, William 327
Willis, Love M. 335
Winkworth, Catherine 199
Wordsworth, Christopher 352
Young, Sarah 205
Zinzendorf, Nikolaus Ludwig von 257
Zwemer, Samuel 296